T0283447

THE LOST QUEEN

THE
LOST
QUEEN

The Surprising Life of Catherine of Braganza—the
Forgotten Queen Who Bridged Two Worlds

SOPHIE SHORLAND

PEGASUS BOOKS
NEW YORK LONDON

THE LOST QUEEN

Pegasus Books, Ltd.
148 West 37th Street, 13th Floor
New York, NY 10018

Copyright © 2024 by Sophie Shorland

First Pegasus Books cloth edition October 2024

ISBN: 978-1-63936-726-9

10 9 8 7 6 5 4 3 2 1

Printed in the United States of America
Distributed by Simon & Schuster
www.pegasusbooks.com

For everyone living forgotten lives

Contents

Key Characters

Afonso VI – King of Portugal, Catherine's brother

Anne Stuart, Duchess of York – Catherine's sister-in-law, daughter of Edward Hyde

Anne Stuart – James II and Anne's daughter; later Queen Anne

Anthony Ashley Cooper, Earl of Shaftesbury – politician, prominent antagonist of Catherine and James II

Barbara Palmer, Countess of Castlemaine – Charles II's principal mistress in the first half of his reign

Charles II – King of England, Scotland and Ireland from 1660 to 1685

Edward Hyde, Earl of Clarendon – Lord Chancellor, Charles II's chief adviser

Frances Stuart, Duchess of Richmond – Catherine's close friend, distant connection of the royal family

Francisco de Melo e Torres, Marquês de Sande – Portuguese ambassador to England, Catherine's godfather

Henriette-Anne, Duchess of Orléans – Charles II's youngest sister; later sister-in-law to Louis XIV

Henry Hyde – politician, involved in a legal wrangle with Catherine; later 2nd Earl of Clarendon

James Crofts, Duke of Monmouth – Charles II's eldest illegitimate child

James Stuart, Duke of York – Charles II's brother and heir to the throne; later James II

João IV – King of Portugal, Catherine's father

Louise de Kérouaille, Duchess of Portsmouth – Charles II's principal mistress in the second half of his reign

Luisa de Guzmán – Queen of Portugal, Catherine's mother

Maria Sophia of Neuburg – Queen of Portugal, wife of Pedro II

Marie Françoise of Savoy – Queen of Portugal, wife of both Afonso VI and then Pedro II

Mary Beatrice of Modena – James Duke of York's second wife

Mary Stuart – James II and Anne's daughter; later Mary II, Queen of England, Scotland and Ireland

Pedro II – King of Portugal, Catherine's youngest brother

William of Orange – Mary Stuart's husband and cousin; later William III of England and William II of Scotland

The Lost Queen

Prologue

WHEN QUEEN CATHERINE of Braganza entered London for the first time in May 1662, knots of people formed in the city's twisting medieval streets, jostling to catch sight of their new queen. It was overwhelming and hot, and she stood stiffly, looking a little like a doll. She didn't speak a word of English, but nobody minded that. An effusion of terrible but joyous poetry followed in her wake, celebrating her recent marriage to Charles II, himself newly restored as king after the tumult of the Civil War and then Oliver Cromwell's Protectorate.

Catherine would be England's Restoration queen. Although the Restoration is frequently ignored in favour of its more famous relative, the Tudors, the period is generally associated with hedonism, flirtation, silks, heavy drinking and finally the human embodiment of all these things: the Merry Monarch Charles II himself. It has given us the poetry of John Wilmot, Earl of Rochester, whose favourite rhyming couplet involved 'arse' and 'tarse' (penis). It was a time of great scientific discovery, of invention and the relatively early days of colonialism. Following the killjoy Parliamentarian era and the Protectorate, Charles's reign has usually been associated with fun, at least onstage and screen.

The return of the Royalists unleashed female actors onstage for the first time, wearing scandalously tight breeches or hiking their skirts up to reveal a shocking amount of leg. Dancing and Christmas were allowed again. Of course, history is always more complicated than that. Opera actually flourished in Cromwell's reign. But we will leave the nuances of this debate for another book.

What concerns us is a shadowy figure at the edge of this hedonistic tale of the Restoration. She was present at a meeting with famous architect Christopher Wren after the Great Fire of London had destroyed the city. She was observing the sky just as Isaac Newton was trying to work out earth's place in the solar system and how exactly meteors worked. In one way or another she was present for every great event of Charles's reign. But in history she has remained a spectre in the background. Her story has effectively been lost.

For the last 350 years or so, the very few mentions of Catherine have placed her reputation at rock bottom. She has been characterised as an unintelligent, cheated-on wife who had very little impact on the world. As her entry in the *Oxford Dictionary of National Biography* casually states: 'Catherine had not been unwilling to fulfil her role as the British queen consort but circumstances conspired to make her success unlikely. Her "ordinary mind" and lack of beauty and sophistication disappointed her court, and while she came to love her husband, who for his part welcomed her non-interference in politics and praised her goodness, his mistresses were the bane of her life, and her childlessness the cause of great misery.'[1] Other accounts have gone further, branding her reign a failure thanks to her childlessness.

The definitive biography of her life, while much more sympathetic, has not helped matters. Written by Lillias Campbell Davidson and published in 1928, it has a distinctive early-twentieth-century feel in enumerating Catherine's virtues: 'Catherine lived in her husband's court as Lot lived in Sodom. She did justly, and loved mercy, and walked humbly with her God in the midst of a seething corruption and iniquity only equalled, perhaps, in the history of Imperial Rome. She loved righteousness and her fellows, and, above all, the one man who won her heart on the day of her marriage, and kept it till the grave shut over her. She was one of the purest women who ever shared the throne of England.'[2]

How boring! A hundred years later, purity and humility are not very fashionable virtues for a woman, and this version of Catherine seems like a rather embarrassing chapter in our current telling of history, one that is being rewritten to include strong women who forged their own paths. Campbell Davidson's description skates over Catherine's love of parties, fun and gambling. She smiled far too much. She dressed all her ladies in matching costumes, played with cross-dressing and scandalised the prudish by displaying her slim ankles.

I first became interested in Catherine of Braganza as a historical woman when visiting the National Portrait Gallery, its rows of kings and queens predictably grave and unsmiling. That is, until I reached the portraits of Charles II and Catherine. Not only is Charles half smirking back at the viewer, he is surrounded by portraits of women – his mistresses – shining in satin and gazing seductively out from their frames. I knew enough of history to know that other kings had had mistresses who had been powerful and influential, so why were they not pictured?

Why was Charles singled out and Catherine – by extension – obscured?

It is often forgotten that, while her husband had plenty of lovers, Catherine was still the queen. Throughout history, she has been compared unfavourably with her husband's mistresses, the real women who ran the show. In the last century, there have been at least four books written about the mistresses, with two in the last decade.[3] Catherine has also been blamed for Charles's sexual licentiousness, as though a man having an affair is somehow his wife's fault. Her Wikipedia entry tells us that 'Catherine's personal charms were not potent enough to wean Charles away from the society of his mistresses.'[4] If only she had been more beautiful, more charming, more clever and more worldly, perhaps he would not have strayed.

Compared with any constitutional monarch in the UK today, Catherine had unfathomable levels of power. She had immense spending capacity, alongside influence as a diplomat and patron of the arts. She was a taste-maker, popularising tea, for example, which was to become a feature of life that is still closely associated with English national identity. She commissioned art and music, turning English tastes towards the baroque, then a highly avant-garde new style yet to be fully adopted in England. Many an eighteenth-century church would probably be missing its curlicues or golden cherubs without her. If we think of the fun and the hedonism of the Restoration, it is impossible to remove Catherine's presence. The organiser of countless parties, theatricals and trips to one watering hole or another, she developed her own distinctive salon culture.

Catherine took her role as a diplomat very seriously, regularly corresponding with other heads of state, the King of France,

Louis XIV, responding to her missives in a sprawling, extravagant hand that reflects the man himself. Indeed, throughout Europe at the time, the art of diplomacy was often seen as a queen's primary function. Many of the diplomatic visits that took place during Charles's reign were conducted in Catherine's rooms, and it was a sign of favour if Charles asked a visitor to kiss the queen's hands. She was an active participant in these important diplomatic exchanges. In fact, her very arrival in England was a diplomatic act, hurling England into war with Spain.

Throughout her childhood and the first eight years of her reign in Britain, Portugal was fighting a fierce war with Spain for independence. Rather than – as historians tell us – Catherine and Charles II's marriage being immediately disliked by the English because of her Catholicism,[5] her arrival in England was heralded as a union of two oppressed powers. In the vein of 'the enemy of our enemy is our friend', Catherine's anti-Spanish associations vastly outweighed her Catholicism, one poet crying, 'Let Bonfires blaze, and Bels out loud Ring' at the coming of Queen Catherine.[6]

Furthermore, her dowry brought the first Indian possession into British hands, as well as the important port of Tangier. She is the woman after whom Queens in New York is named, and there remain several streets in London named after her. She found positions for her friends and supporters in both the English and Portuguese courts, and would later become regent of Portugal, ushering in a new era of Anglo-Lusitanian alliance that still exists today.

It is convenient – and suits our modern version of monogamy – to see the relationship between Catherine and her husband's mistresses as one based on rivalry. But the reality is far more complicated. Charles's mistresses were often friends of the queen, and they spent a great deal of time together. Barbara Palmer, Countess of Castlemaine, perhaps the most influential of the mistresses, copied Catherine in having her portrait painted as Catherine of Alexandria, the queen's namesake. It has been assumed that this was a deliberate insult to Catherine, showing off Barbara's superior charms in the same posture, but if we look more closely at the historical record, we see a whole spate of such pictures, mostly from Catherine's supporters and as a compliment to her. Could their relationship in fact have been one of both collaboration and competition, containing a range of complex human emotions?

Rather than portraying her as either pitiable or pure, a new and more complex picture of the real woman emerges. Catherine was plagued by fits of depression throughout her life. As a dedicated hypochondriac, she loved to self-medicate, but she was also great fun, laughing and talking too much and too enthusiastically. Visitors to court were shocked by this informal woman who showed too many teeth. She was mostly uninterested in English politics, but cared passionately about Portugal, doing everything she could to preserve its independence. She was not a great social reformer, but she advocated for more liberties for women, and left money in her will to free slaves.

This biography attempts to show Catherine neither as a saint nor a sinner, but rather as a woman of her time, living in an era of immense scientific, global and social change, who had a profound impact on the world around her. All the reasons why she has so far been largely forgotten by history – her wonky teeth, her fits of depression and the odd bout of social awkwardness – in fact make her a hugely relatable figure to us today, when we accept the imperfect and the difficult life.

I

*Assassination, Education
and an Accidental War*

THE SIGNAL WAS a pistol shot. As the sound rang out, a group of conspirators stormed Lisbon's Ribeira Palace, the seat of power and the home of the viceroy. It was an incredibly risky enterprise; the few conspirators were pitted against the might of the Hapsburgs, the most powerful dynasty Europe had ever seen. They demanded both an end to Spanish rule and a new king. The new king they called for was a shy man who had spent most of his life buried in the countryside and had no experience of politics. His name was João, Duke of Braganza.

João's daughter Catherine was two years old when the revolution began. She was not born Infanta (Princess) of Portugal, but into the risky business of would-be royalty and imminent civil war. Her childhood was one of plots, assassins and the whispered legend of a hidden king who would come forth to solve the nation's ills. While she may not have been born an infanta, however, she was a daughter of Portugal's wealthiest and most powerful aristocratic house. The Braganzas were responsible for around 80,000 vassals and owned over a third of

Portugal's land.[1] They were also royalty, with a significant claim to the throne.

To understand the Braganza claim, we need to travel a little in time and space. A visitor to northern Morocco in 1578 would have observed two armies camped on either side of the Loukkos River, at Alcácer Quibir: King Sebastian of Portugal with his ally the deposed Sultan Abu Abdallah Mohammed II on one side, facing the current Sultan of Morocco, Abd Al-Malik I, on the other. They were lining up to fight a battle that was only ever going to end one way. Sebastian had ignored warnings about taking an army to the heart of Morocco, and the Portuguese were doomed: his force of 24,000 troops faced Al-Malik's army of 50,000.[2] It was a slaughter. All three kings would die in the ensuing battle, known *in memoriam* as the Battle of the Three Kings.

Since no one had seen the young, impetuous King Sebastian die at Alcácer Quibir, and no clearly identifiable body was found, four fake Sebastians emerged in the years following the battle, all claiming to be the lost king and capitalising on the popular belief that he could not really be dead. In Portugal today, 'Sebastianism' still has mythological power: one of his titles is 'Sebastian the Asleep', and it is believed that, at a time of great national need, he will emerge from wherever he is sleeping to fight for his country once more.[3] At birth, his astrologer had predicted that Sebastian would have dark hair and would enjoy the company of women, concluding that the presence of Venus in the Eleventh House signified multiple sons.[4] The astrologer was wrong on all counts. Sebastian had light hair, no wife and no issue. After his death, only his cantankerous elderly uncle, the Cardinal Henrique, remained as the clear heir to the ruling Portuguese House of Aviz.

As a servant of the Church, Henrique could have no legitimate children, and the Pope refused to release him from his
vows of celibacy. The cardinal's death in 1580 inevitably led to a
succession crisis for the Portuguese crown, for which Sebastian
unfortunately stayed asleep. There were three contenders for
the throne, all grandchildren of Manuel I, Sebastian's great-
grandfather: the illegitimate António, Prior of Crato; King
Philip II of Spain; and finally Catarina, Duchess of Braganza.
With the resources of the world's greatest empire behind him,
Philip II emerged the winner and Portugal became part of the
Hapsburg Empire.

King Philip was descended from Manuel's daughter, while
the Duchess of Braganza was descended from his son, Duarte.
As Portuguese succession prioritised the male line, it was technically Catarina who had the greater claim to the throne. She
had an international reputation as 'a Couragious and very
Witty Princess, well skill'd in the *Greek* and *Latin* tongues, as
also in the Mathematicks and other curious Sciences, which she
carefully instructed her Children in'.[5] They were an educated,
cosmopolitan family, and as the wife of the wealthiest nobleman
in Portugal, Catarina would have been able to afford the very
best tutors for her children, including Catherine's grandfather,
Teodósio.

Teodósio was a page and favourite of the much-mythologised
King Sebastian, who took the ten-year-old with him on campaign
to Morocco. When the fighting at Alcácer Quibir began to
get dangerous, he sent the boy behind the lines. This was not
acceptable to Teodósio, who stole a horse and charged recklessly
into the heart of the ill-fated battle. He was taken prisoner, but
on hearing of his valour, the new Sultan of Morocco, Ahmad

al-Mansur, released him without ransom, a high compliment for the boy's incautious bravery.[6] Luckily for Philip II, Teodósio was uninterested in the throne of Portugal, and faithfully served the new king as he had Sebastian. He was rewarded with even more lands to add to the vast Braganza patrimony.

It was on these huge estates that Catherine was born, between eight and nine in the evening on 25 November 1640, St Catherine's Day. It was a fortuitous date in the Catholic calendar. St Catherine had been a princess and scholar, one of the three 'holy maids' who provided protection against sudden death, and whose voice was heard by Joan of Arc. Catherine would identify with her namesake throughout her life.

The third child of João and Luisa, she was baptised just over a fortnight after her birth in the opulent chapel of her family home, the Vila Viçosa. Its monolithic foundations had been laid by her ancestor Duke Jamie I, who wanted to live in something a little more modern than the draughty fourteenth-century castle that still stands today. Everything about the Vila Viçosa celebrated the wealth and power of the Braganza dynasty, from the huge square outside, designed to gather crowds and make the palace look even grander, to its tapestries, its lacquered cabinets imported from Asia, and its hundreds of intricately painted *azulejos* (tiles). For the first few years of her life, Catherine grew up in this vast structure, looking out over silver-green olive groves and the reddish bark of cork oak.

The family remained in countryside retirement rather than enjoying the bustle of Lisbon for two reasons. The first was that their claim to the throne of Portugal meant that they were a constant threat to Spanish rule merely by existing. The second was a character trait that helped João and his family survive many tumultuous years of politics and intrigue: the Duke of Braganza was a naturally cautious, retiring man. He was not particularly flamboyant and did not have a taste for power.[7] His greatest pleasures were music, reading and the life of the mind.

Music was a family tradition that Catherine too would inherit, along with the Braganzas' intense spiritual life. In his will, João's father, Teodósio, had written, 'I remind my son, the Duke, that the best thing I leave him in this house is my Chapel,' and instructed him to maintain the chaplains and musicians within as one of the chief cares of his life.[8] In a move relatable to teenagers and their frustrated parents everywhere, he forced João to continue with his music when as a boy he rebelled against lessons and wanted to give it up. Despite this flicker of early reluctance, music was to become one of the chief passions of João's life.[9] Some of his compositions are still played today; we may owe the tune of 'O Come, All Ye Faithful' to him. He was a virtuoso of polyphony, experimenting with six voices, and also wrote technically on the subject. Catherine's childhood was filled with excellent and experimental music, something that continued to fascinate her later in life. Like her father, she was interested in anyone, regardless of rank, who could create beautiful sounds, and never tired of her musicians.

When the English poet and musician Richard Flecknoe visited Lisbon in 1648, João 'no sooner understood of my arrival, but he sent for me to Court'. They had two or three hours 'tryal of my skill', and João apparently greatly exceeded Flecknoe, especially when it came to composing music. However, he was well pleased, and gave Flecknoe permission to see him as often as he liked. Returning the flattery, Flecknoe wrote some very bad poetry about Lisbon and its environs, stressing the marvellous surroundings and – to him – exotic fruits such as 'Silk animating *Mulberies*' and '*Pomegranads*'.[10] The rhymes get considerably worse towards the end of the poem, finishing with the dubious combination '*Hesperides*' and '*Alcinous'es*'. This inspired forcing of language led to considerable fame for Flecknoe, though not of the type he dreamed of, with the better-known and better-respected poet John Dryden calling him 'Through all the realms of Non-sense, absolute'.[11]

Besides music, João's other great love was hunting, and a French visitor attributed his unassailable good health to this form of physical exercise, riding out for long days on the trail of spotted fallow deer or long-toothed wild boar. João was of average height and slightly stocky, with brown hair neither light nor dark, and pale eyes.[12] Perhaps his most distinguishing feature was his dramatically curling brown moustache. He liked to dress all in black with gold buttons and braid; in the seventeenth century, wearing black was a sign of wealth as well as sobriety, since the garments had to be dyed multiple times for the colour to look anything other than a nondescript grey, and washing quickly faded the garment.[13]

Catherine's mother, Luisa de Guzmán, was artistic like her husband, but enjoyed painting over music, using a trowel to apply thick oil paints to canvas.[14] She was a gifted linguist, picking up languages easily, including Portuguese (she was Spanish), and her education was humanist, although highly focused on religion.[15] Her youthful 1632 portrait (when she was 20) shows an oval face with rosy cheeks, dramatic black eyebrows and an intense gaze. Like João, she seems to have favoured expensive and fashionable black, enlivened with delicate white lace and deep pink ribbons. Together they were a power couple. It had made sense for one of the richest families of Spain to marry *the* richest of Portugal. And the Guzmán fortunes were vast: when Luisa's grandfather inherited his lands, over 400 folio pages (the biggest size of paper then available) were needed to record all his properties.[16]

However, their marriage was by no means a foregone conclusion. João's father, Teodósio, was looking further afield for a bride, and had fixed on Maria Catarina Farnese, the daughter of the Duke of Parma.[17] Ambitious for his son and his dynasty, Teodósio required a lady with both dowry and international connections. He may also have been seeking to bolster the Braganza claim to the throne, since Maria Catarina was a cousin of sorts, descended from João's grandmother's elder sister. However, João was rejected by Maria Catarina and her family, and when his father died in 1630, he was still unmarried. He was now the grand old age of twenty-six, and the question of an heir to carry on the dynasty was becoming urgent.[18] Unsure of where to look, and aware of the importance of marriage, he wrote to close family friend Francisco de Melo, then resident at the Spanish court, asking him for advice.*

De Melo was loyal to his Spanish master, the Count-Duke Olivares. Effectively the prime minister for the entire Hapsburg Empire, Olivares was almost as large in stature as he was in personality. Ruthless, dynamic and willing to work himself to exhaustion, he was unafraid of unpleasant tasks. And he needed to be – the empire spanned continents, from New Spain in the Americas to the Philippines in Asia, and much of Europe.

---

* De Melo was a trustworthy pair of hands. The whole family would prove invaluable to the Braganza dynasty, and Francisco, Catherine's godfather, would be particularly important in her life and reign.

All papers requiring King Philip IV's signature went through Olivares first.[19] Spain's policy in Portugal was geared towards greater Iberian union, attempting to neutralise any threat of Portuguese independence. And thanks to his claim to the throne, João was one of the greatest symbols of that independence. His marriage was a delicate matter for Olivares. How could he turn this problem into an advantage for Spain? To promote unity, Olivares had long been trying to arrange Spanish–Portuguese matches. What better than for João to be similarly tied to Spain? He instructed de Melo to recommend one of Spain's wealthiest and best-connected maidens as a bride, Olivares' own relative Luisa de Guzmán, of the House of Medina Sidonia.

De Melo duly wrote to João that 'The Count-Duke informed me he would be pleased if Your Excellency would make this marriage to reunite the two largest houses in Spain' (referring to Portugal and Spain as one, and to a past match between the houses of Medina Sidonia and Braganza). United, de Melo argued, they could carry out the 'service and maintenance of Spain'.[20] Ironically for the future leader of an independence movement, these arguments found favour with João, and he agreed to the match. Luisa, it was assumed, would do what was good for Spain, and for the Guzmáns as a family. She would act as a diplomat and mediator, as countless other barely remembered women in history had done. Little did anyone know that she had been brought up to think of ambition as the greatest aristocratic virtue. She would prove to be the dynamic force behind her husband's political career, propelling the Braganza dynasty from dukes to kings.

For now, João had ticked off that most important of tasks for a feudal lord: securing the future of the dynasty. To celebrate his betrothal, he ordered two hundred torches to be lit, an extra-ordinary extravagance of fuel, while the whole village of Vila Viçosa was filled with shouts of approval and festivities.[21]

In the cool of the autumn of 1633, when Luisa had just turned twenty and João was twenty-nine, the couple were married by proxy on the Spanish side of the border, in the ancient city of Badajoz, its encircling walls and labyrinthine fortress seeming to rise from the rock. Luisa travelled to Portugal as a married woman, despite not yet having met her husband. It must have been an anxious time for her, but she was made of stern stuff. Apparently her ambitious father's parting words were: 'Go, daughter, very happy, for you are not going to be a duchess, but a queen.'[22] There were many such legends surrounding her. Another was that on the day of her baptism, a Moorish guest announced that the little girl would live one day to be a queen.[23] Although both prophecies are almost certainly later imaginings, they speak to the legend that Luisa was to become for Portugal. It was a symbolic moment for the whole Iberian peninsula as the dark-eyed young woman crossed the waters of the Río Caya into her new home and her new country.

João and Luisa finally met at a second marriage ceremony on 13 January 1632, at the fortress-like Our Lady of the Assumption Cathedral in the town of Elvas – this time on the Portuguese side of the border. Dusk was just beginning to fall, tinting the butter-yellow stones of the cathedral a deeper orange. Both bride and groom were determined to make a good first impression. João was dressed in an almond-coloured velvet overdress ornamented with gold braid, a gold choker, and a hat glittering with diamonds. Not to be outdone, Luisa wore an enormous diamond necklace and a green dress showcasing her family's wealth, partly through the great quantity of unnecessary material employed in the dress's sleeves; there were four of them, cut open to reveal a taffeta lining, embroidered with flowers of silver thread and decorated with yet more diamonds.[24]

The marriage seems to have been a happy one. Luisa adapted to her new life as though she had been born in Lisbon, and quickly learned Portuguese, as well as the customs of the country.[25] She had a persuasive tongue and 'an insinuating way' that 'drew all mens hearts . . . and had by her extraordinary Application and Carriage gained an absolute Ascendant over her Husband, who never undertook anything of moment without her Advice'.[26] Their peace was only disturbed when João's brother Duarte had an affair with one of Luisa's ladies-of-honour, shocking the religious and deeply conservative duchess. The irresponsible Duarte was sent away from the palace, only for João himself to embark on an affair with a travelling actress.[27] However, this was short-lived and more socially acceptable by the standards of the time, since it did not involve any of Luisa's ladies. Women were expected to accept their husband's dalliances, as long as it did not interfere in their domestic sphere. Essentially, it was more acceptable for an aristocratic man to have a discreet affair with a lower-status woman.

While overseeing the vast ducal interests and pursuing their artistic pleasures in the countryside – João at his music and Luisa at her easel – the young couple were firmly on track to secure the dynasty. This was not without its heartbreak, however. Like her mother before her, Luisa was plagued by miscarriages. But in 1634, she carried a baby to term. They called him Teodósio, after his grandfather, and in the spirit of goodwill invited the wayward Duarte back to the fold, making him Teodósio's godfather.[28] A girl they named Joana came close on her brother's heels in 1635, followed by Catherine in 1638. Two further children, Manuel and Ana, tragically died when they were hours old.

The main differences between João and Luisa seem to have been in ambition and decision-making. While Luisa knew what she wanted and was quick to side with one cause or another, João was more careful. This often served him well, as many problems find their own inevitable solution if left to time. Luisa was intelligent and decisive, well aware of the risks of the political game that the family would soon be playing, and the undercurrents of dissent circulating through Portugal. As Duchess of Braganza and claimant to the throne of Portugal, she famously announced, 'Better queen for one day, than duchess all my life.'[29]

2

A Play for the Throne

POPULAR DISSENT IN Portugal had been brewing against Spain for longer than João had been alive. Besides questions of national identity, much of the dispute revolved around money. During the early honeymoon days of Iberian union, a new river route to Spain had been proposed. Greater wealth and trade opportunities seemed to be on their way. The Portuguese also gained access to New Spain, a vast territory spanning from California and Florida to southern Mexico and the Philippines, and to the Spanish silver there, mostly mined in terrible conditions using coerced labour. However, as the Spanish economy stuttered, so too did Portugal's. The Hapsburgs were constantly fighting wars of one kind or another on multiple fronts. As fast as the silver was mined, it was spent again – on luxuries, foreign mercenaries and arms. No industry was fostered within Spain or Portugal. A vast influx of Central American silver led to an inflation crisis across Europe, since more money was being put into circulation without more goods being produced, leading to a price spiral.

The latest conflict was the bitterly destructive Thirty Years War, which raged through Europe from 1618 to 1648, decimating its population and resources. Spain was seriously in need of money, and Olivares looked to Portugal to raise it.

Used to relatively light taxation, the Portuguese protested at tax rises, coming as they did on top of a run of bad harvests. Farmers resented the Spanish for taking food from their mouths, and the provincial gentry resented them for taking their power. Traders were dissatisfied too: thanks to Spain's long-running conflict with the Netherlands, they could not bargain freely with the Dutch, a huge, very wealthy market and one of their most important trading partners. Portugal's position as an effect-ively Spanish nation made them fair game for Dutch and British incursions into their ships and territories in Brazil and Asia.[1] The country simmered with resentment.

In 1637, large-scale disturbances broke out in Évora, southern Portugal, and like a spark to tinder, riots ignited throughout the south. Increasingly, the protests were not just about money, but about the very idea of being ruled from Spain. Popular dissent swirled, with a sepia-tinted version of Portugal's glorious past revivified. People fantasised about how much better, how much richer Portugal would be if only they weren't under the Spanish yoke.[2] Influential was a semi-messianic text written by a lowly cobbler from Beira Alta, in the south. His mystical writings foresaw a new age for Portugal, after an *encoberto*, or hidden king, came forth to liberate his people. It was stirring stuff, imagining through metaphors like the pruning of vines how the country would be cleansed and remade. Other prophecies circulated seductively, telling of old hermits seeing a line of kings, or three-score years of chastisement for the Portuguese, followed by God's mercy. Spain had been ruling them for close to sixty years.[3]

And who was the *encoberto* likely to be? There were few claimants to the throne, other than our very own João. However, at this point, he was not very interested in claiming it. He was offered the crown by the rebels but turned it down. Did he not want it, or did he feel that it wasn't the right time?[4] French power-broker Cardinal Richelieu, forever wishing to get one over on Spain, even contemplated supporting illegitimate heirs to the throne, since João seemed so uninterested. Inside Portugal, other noblemen or even a republic were discussed.[5] But it was difficult to ignore João – the Braganzas were the biggest land-owning family in the country, and roughly a third of the vassals, or peasantry, owed allegiance to him as their feudal lord. He was needed if any rebellion was to be successful.[6]

Although the riots were eventually suppressed by Castilian troops, they were an important turning point, proving to any would-be revolutionary that Portuguese independence had almost universal popular support.

In an attempt to secure João's loyalty to Spain and prevent any attempt at independence, Olivares made him commander of Portugal's royal forces. João accepted in 1638, albeit with every appearance of reluctance, and began touring the country, looking suitably kingly and doing exactly the opposite of what Olivares intended. He was finally out of his countryside obscurity, wielding power and beginning to look like a viable king. The Portuguese leapt on the idea, believing that this man might be 'the incarnation of Hope'.[7] Rumours began to circulate that João was indeed the *encoberto*, as had been foretold.[8] It seems rather a stretch, since he was always quite plainly in sight as the likeliest heir to the throne, but it made an excellent piece of propaganda, and of such tales kings are made. A contemporary account records that he had become such a threat that Olivares attempted to kidnap him and smuggle him safely to Spain, first on a ship that was to pretend to need succour from a storm, and then by Spaniards stationed at various coastal forts. However, luck and João's large entourage foiled every attempt. The duke continued to gain in popularity as he made his tour of Portugal's defences.[9]

As tensions simmered in Portugal, long-held dissent in Catalonia finally boiled over. In the first week of May 1640, the ringing of church bells summoned armed, well-organised revolt against Castilian overlordship. The French, sensing blood in a financially weakened Spain, supported Catalonia. When the call went out for the Portuguese to join the Spanish army being gathered to put down the revolt, and also support beleaguered Spanish forces in Italy, word spread that this was a clever trap to crush Catalonian and Portuguese dissent simultaneously. It was feared that, while the Portuguese nobility were out of the country fighting, Spain would enact its 'cruel design', crushing Portugal without the organised resistance the nobles might have offered.[10] Something must be done to counteract any such dastardly scheme. But what?

Again the answer was independence, and again came the question: who would be the next ruler of Portugal? Still the obvious answer was João, but, despite his newly regal status, in June 1640 he again refused to accept the crown from a small group of conspirators.[11] He knew that he only had one chance: if he allowed himself to be crowned king of Portugal, or even publicly supported rebellion of any kind, it could mean death for himself, his family and the whole Braganza line. The Spanish could not allow them to live if they showed any sign of mutiny.

When asked by conspirators whether, if push came to shove and they founded a republic, he would support the republic or Spain, João replied that he had 'decided to never go against the common sentiment of the kingdom'.[12] This was promising.

The story goes that Luisa provided the final impetus. She told her prevaricating husband, 'if thou goest to Madrid thou runnest the hazard of losing thy head. If thou acceptest the throne thou runnest the same hazard. If thou must perish, better die nobly at home than basely abroad.'[13] However, even this was not enough to convince him. So she brought the family into it, saying to him on Catherine's second birthday, 'This day our friends are assembled to celebrate the anniversary of the birth of our little Catherine, and who knows but this new guest may have been sent to certify you that it is the will of Heaven to invest you with that crown of which you have long been unjustly deprived by Spain. For my part, I regard it as a happy presage that he comes on such a day.'[14]

As the final nail in the coffin of persuasion, she brought in their daughter for some emotional blackmail. Getting Catherine to kiss her father, she asked, 'How can you find it in your heart to refuse to confer on this child the rank of a king's daughter?'[15]

In October 1640, João told the rebel faction that he would accept the kingdom of Portugal. It might have been Luisa's reasoning that persuaded him: Portugal was boiling over, and, as the best candidate to be king, he must either go with the times or be executed by one great power or another.

The conspirators acted, converging on the Ribeira Palace separately, some by horse and some concealing their arms in litters normally used to carry nobles between merriments.[16] There was remarkably little bloodshed, the Castilian troops stationed in the capital surrendering when they saw the way the wind was blowing. The viceroy, Philip IV's cousin Margaret of Savoy, was left unharmed, fleeing to a convent, although her deeply unpopular secretary, Miguel de Vasconcelos, was hunted down.

Described as 'a man Composed of Pride, Cruelty and Covetousness, knowing no moderation but in excess', who 'gave birth to hatreds & enmities among the Great ones of the Realm', Vasconcelos had unfortunately become a scapegoat for all of Spain's crimes.[17] There are different versions of his death, but the most popular tells how the rebels found him cowering in a cupboard, trying to cover himself with a stack of papers.[18] His bloodied body was defenestrated, thrown to the crowd below, a visible sign that the regime had changed.[19] The mob 'ran like Madmen to express Living Sentiments of Revenge upon his dead and senseless Corps, vaunting who could invent the newest wayes of disgrace and scorn, till at length almost wearied with their inhumane sport, they left it in the Street so mangled, that it did not seem to have the least resemblance of a Man'.[20]

Bonfires were lit throughout Lisbon, the citizens cheering their new monarch and crying for joy as horsemen rode around the city calling out proclamations in the name of King John IV. As one disconsolate Spaniard put it, 'John IV was very happy, since his kingdom cost him no more than a bonfire, and Philip IV much otherwise, who had been stripped of so sure a crown only by acclamations and illuminations.'[21] It was seen as quite remarkable how fast, how comprehensive and how bloodless the revolution had been. But would it hold?

Spain categorically did not accept this handover of power. The two nations were now at war. Should the full weight of the Spanish juggernaut turn on Portugal, they were likely to be crushed. Luckily for them, Spain was tied up with rebellion in Catalonia, war with France and the Thirty Years War, which would rage across the continent for another eight years.

João was now King of Portugal. Luisa had reached the height of her ambition: she was finally queen. And Catherine had the new title – and the new status – of infanta.

The Braganza family quickly decamped to Lisbon, two-year-old Catherine in tow, alongside her elder siblings Teodósio, five, and Joana, six. She would have been too young to remember the move, although her brother and sister may have recounted it to her. Couriers were dispatched by sea to the far corners of the Portuguese Empire, from Brazil to Tangier to China, with news of the coup. It was widely accepted and even acclaimed throughout the territories, except where Hapsburg control and military might were at their strongest. Accordingly, Ceuta remained with Spain, but Tangier and all the other territories went with Portugal.

The Portuguese parliament, the Cortes, had the power to decide on the succession, and were called in 1641 to approve the choice of João as ruler. They did so with gusto.

His rule was helped hugely by the popular backing for the Braganza coup. State bureaucracy, magistrates and minor clergy were all strongly in favour, and during the long war for Portuguese independence, the *povo*, or people, continued to support João, whose piety appealed to their traditional attitudes. Without the *povo*, independence would most likely have failed, since they provided the foot soldiers, the food and the taxes with which war was waged. They also suffered as their fields and houses were burned, their cattle stolen and many of their number killed.[22]

The monarchs of Portugal had no crowning ceremony. Instead, they held a stately exchange of promises: the monarch swore to serve God and Portugal, while the people, through their representatives, swore loyalty to the monarch. Six years into his reign, in 1646, João introduced his own twist on the classic ceremony of acclamation, dedicating his kingdom to Mary, Our Lady of the Conception, and having her crowned as queen. This pious and humble relationship became an important feature of the Braganza monarchy: no monarch again wore a crown, and in images the crown sat on a nearby table.[23]

Luisa acted as the power behind the throne, having 'a goodly presence' and 'more of the Majestick in her' than her husband.[24] However, João did enjoy sitting in Portugal's high court, and gained a reputation as a just king. His title – handed down to history – is 'the Restorer', for his role in Portuguese independence.

Now that Catherine was an infanta, her life inevitably changed. Court life in Lisbon was old-fashioned and rather stuffy by contemporary European standards. In a portrait painted when she was around five years old, she stands stiffly, fan in one hand, grasping the back of a chair with the other. Dark-eyed, with delicately arched brows, she looks directly at the viewer, her stance that of a little adult. Her body is swathed in black velvet, sleeves cut open to show the fine linen beneath, and her shoulders are covered in a lace wrap. Her chubby cheeks are the only feature that mark her as a young child rather than a court lady. Portraits of her elder siblings are equally stiff, projecting an iconographic quality that emphasises their status rather than their distinct personalities.[25]

It was lucky the family was so rich, since the Braganzas had to bring their own furniture to Lisbon, as well as subsidise the war effort. The Ribeira Palace, on the shores of the sprawling Tagus – the river that was the source of Lisbon's wealth – was a vast edifice, added to under Philip's rule. Other than the lack of marble, it was very similar to the Vila Viçosa: a huge, symmetrical building, its many windows reflecting the sky and the river, fronted by an enormous square where festivities and ceremonies took place.

Though the palace itself was architecturally unexciting, the interiors of Lisbon drew the eye. As the Venetian ambassadors recorded: 'Lisbon doesn't possess any nobleman's or bourgeois palace that deserves attention; the buildings are merely very big without any worthy particularity, except for the way in which the Portuguese decorate them, so that they become truly magnificent, with the chambers lined in winter with satins, damasks, and with the finest tapestries.'[26]

Visitors also noted the city's cosmopolitan nature, with different cultures doing strange things like eating bananas. There were many slaves, alongside also free Moorish traders, Ethiopian Christians (Ethiopia and Portugal had a special relationship, the kings of Portugal petitioning for Ethiopian Christianity to be recognised by the Pope), and blonde English and Dutch traders, all mingling with native Portuguese and Moors still present after the Reconquista of the peninsula.[27]

Catherine lived a very sheltered life. It is perhaps a slight exaggeration, but when she arrived in England, one eyewitness claimed that 'she hath hardly been ten times out of the palace in her life', being 'bred hugely retired'.[28] We know little about her childhood, beyond the fact that her mother watched over her education carefully. It was a style of education that was, by Luisa's own admission, 'more useful than pleasant', with little time for frivolity and much time devoted to religion.[29] Catherine at least turned out more literate than her younger brothers, Afonso and Pedro, neither of whom had much time for writing – it's possible they could barely sign their names. This is an indictment rather than a triumph of Luisa's parenting style. In not allowing tutors and insisting on educating the children herself, she was taking helicopter parenting to a new level. It led the boys to rebel whenever they could, while Catherine coped by just going along with whatever was asked of her.

Since Castilian influence was still very strong in Portugal, and Luisa was Spanish, many of the texts Catherine studied and the 'high' culture she consumed would have been Castilian. However, the reading deemed appropriate for young women was mainly religious; satire and comedy might have bred loose morals.[30] Partly thanks to Luisa, Catherine spoke Spanish fluently. In her letters, she also displays at least a smattering of French and Italian, and she picked up English after a few years in the country, though she didn't learn any Germanic language until she was in her twenties. She and her mother had a very close relationship, Luisa keeping careful watch over all aspects of her upbringing.

In a letter written to Catherine soon after she left Lisbon in 1662, Luisa signed herself 'your mother who only idolises you'. Her expressions of love are constant, addressing her daughter as 'My Catalina', or 'My daughter and all my love', and declaring herself 'your mother who adores you'.[31] We do not have the letters from Catherine to her mother, most likely because of the earthquake-fire-tsunami combination that shattered Lisbon in

1755, but we do know that she loved her mother deeply. Of her younger brothers, Pedro, born in 1648, seems to have been her favourite, much preferred to the awkward Afonso, who had been born in 1643.

The great ceremonials that marked Catherine's childhood were saints' days and religious holidays like Corpus Christi, a spring festival celebrating the transubstantiation of Christ's body into bread and his blood into wine during the Mass. A wafer would be carried through the streets, showcasing Christ's sacrifice of his body for the world, and in Portugal this grew into one of the biggest processions in Europe, Lisbon's guilds competing with one another for the grandest procession and the most impressive figures of giants or dragons. Buildings and hastily erected platforms were garlanded with flowers and tapestries, while the smoke from fireworks filled the air.[32]

Another occasion for celebration and pageantry was the king's birthday, when his courtiers lined up to kiss his hands in a ceremony called the *beija-mão*. It was a formal statement of the relationship between king and courtier, confirming João as the source of power and patronage. The same ritual happened every year without fail, performed with punctuality and gusto. For an infanta of Portugal, the court was a predictable space, with nothing to shock or challenge her beyond the normal trials of growing up. Her father's affairs were discreet, with no mistresses flaunting their power at court. He only had one illegitimate child that we know of, and she was educated far from her half-siblings; they might not even have known about her. Their mother certainly did not believe in noticing such things.

However, even sheltered in the luxurious Ribeira Palace, the life of any member of the ruling family always held the potential for danger, and the future of the Braganza dynasty was far from assured. There was a reason João had wanted to remain in countryside retirement making music.

In August 1641, the first threat to the new regime was discovered. Rather awkwardly for the Braganzas' reputation for piety, the central conspirator was the pro-Castilian Archbishop of Braga, who had plotted to assassinate João, set fire to the Portuguese fleet and then storm Luisa's apartments, returning the country to Spanish rule. There are competing tales as to how the plot came to João's attention, the wildest being that the conspirators employed a Bohemian messenger to carry letters about the rebels' plans to Spain. One of João's spies met the Bohemian on the road and, immediately suspecting the poor man, got him drunk, stabbed him and stole the letters. It would have been an incredibly cold-blooded act, and the Bohemian must have been acting in a remarkably suspicious manner. More likely one of the plotters betrayed the affair.

Either way, such an escape, hot on the heels of his miraculously bloodless coup, could only boost João's reputation for being specially protected by God. A contemporary marvelled, 'if Heaven had not protected him, there had been but a short space betwixt the Birth and the Grave of his Sovereignty'.[33] When the plot was discovered, the noble conspirators were hanged. Dealing with ecclesiastical dissent was considerably more awkward; the clergy, being Catholic, were not directly answerable to João, but to the Pope in Rome, who was controlled by Europe's greatest political power, Spain. This was a tricky state of affairs for the Braganzas: they were not only deeply personally religious but ruling an intensely religious country. The difficult situation would be at the forefront of Catherine's mind for many years and – as pious as any good Braganza – she would try to solve it later in life.

However, as a child there was little she could do, and since Rome did not acknowledge Portugal as an independent country, no new bishops could be installed, causing its religious framework to totter on unsteady legs for many years as bishops died and could not be replaced.[34] Portugal was potentially the most religious country in Europe in the seventeenth century – or at least it had a strong claim to that title – with a contemporary merchant estimating that a third of the population was in some way employed by the Church.[35]

It is important, when thinking about her actions later on, to remember that Catherine grew up in a world in which it was entirely normal to have priests working in all areas of life, and where the Church was the dominant institution in the land. Carried in a litter around the crowded streets of Lisbon, she would inevitably have passed begging friars (there were around 5,000 of these) who asked for alms in a sing-song tone and would not accept leftover scraps of food. Little girls were often dressed as nuns, while young men took vows for holy orders, ready to become monks as soon as their elder brothers had married and fathered children. Even for those not inside a church, every evening was punctuated by moments of prayer. Whenever the church bells rang during the day at Mass times, everyone stopped what they were doing – even carriages, and plays halfway through their performance – and said an Ave Maria. At 9 p.m., the bells rang again and prayers were said for souls suffering the torments of purgatory.[36]

One assassination plot had been foiled, but as the bishops died off, the fabric of Portuguese religious life was called into question, impacting on the rule of João and Luisa. The next twenty-seven years – all of Catherine's childhood and well into adulthood – would remain precarious for the Braganzas. Spain may have been exhausted by constant war and split by internal and external dissent, but it remained Europe's greatest power, able to borrow huge sums from Italian and other European banks, and to levy vast armies of both Castilian soldiers and mercenaries. Portugal, in contrast, had not been in charge of its own finances or armies for the last sixty years. Many soldiers were abroad in Catalonia or the Netherlands, fighting Spain's wars, and border fortresses had long been neglected, since there had been no need to repair them. It was a conflict that was stacked heavily against Portugal. Gradually, they managed to put money into their border defences, but they could ill-afford offensives. Spanish incursions and raids targeted crops and cattle, weakening the economy and Portugal's ability to survive the war.

João set about trying to cultivate alliances. But what was he able to offer in return? Since their arrival in South America and India, the Portuguese had resented other Europeans attempting to trade and set up their own colonies, particularly if those Europeans were Protestants spreading blasphemous ideas. Trade with Portugal, and with the territories Portugal controlled, was a rich prize. On 8 February 1641, three ships provisioned for long journeys sailed from Lisbon. They presented favourable terms to France, England and the United Provinces, including access to Portugal's lucrative spice trade. Later in the year, two more ships set off for Denmark and Rome.

Treaties gave João arms, munitions, cavalry and trading partners with an interest in one another's affairs. But what he really needed was allies strong enough to support him in war. And this was where having children was useful.

England and Portugal had negotiated a treaty of trade and friendship in 1642.[37] Encouraged by this, João approached England two years later with terms for a more significant alliance, proposing to seal the deal with the marriage of his serious five-year-old daughter Catherine to the dashing fourteen-year-old Prince of Wales, Charles. However, all discussions soon ceased. Civil war had broken out in England in 1642. At first it was thought the war would be over quickly and the king would keep his throne, but that belief was shattered by Parliamentarian victories, particularly the Battle of Marston Moor in 1644. The Portuguese embassy was stuck in London, having to apply for permission to leave. The embassy's secretary, António de Sousa de Macedo, decided to stay on, and allowed Royalists to hide their mail among the Portuguese diplomatic post, including correspondence between Charles I and his wife, Henrietta Maria. When the Parliamentarians inevitably found out about this partisanship, they viewed Portugal as a potentially hostile country, not helping João's fragile position on the international stage.[38]

Since Spain and France were at war, France seemed to be a natural ally for the new Braganza dynasty, and João proposed an incredible alliance with the French, suggesting that his eldest son, Teodósio, marry a niece of Louis XIV, while his elder daughter, Joana, would marry Charles Manuel of Savoy, Louis' cousin. João would then abdicate the throne of Portugal in favour of Teodósio and his new wife, and take as his own territory part of northern Brazil. This remarkable suggestion shows the importance of international alliance in bolstering Portugal's new regime. The negotiations continued for a tense four years, from 1643 to 1647, but no agreement was struck.

2

Only one thing about the balance of power in early-modern Europe could ever be relied upon: it was always changing. In November 1648, Catherine celebrated her tenth birthday. A month later, the Dutch gained independence from Hapsburg rule. Four years later, the Catalan revolt ended (at least militarily; it's still going in the hearts of the Catalan people). Spain's forces, instead of being split between four fronts, were now fighting on only two: Portugal and France. The possibility of a French marriage was still open, but eventually it became clear that France had been prevaricating. There was not going to be a double marriage, or a safe retirement for João in Brazil. The question of Portuguese independence had been a bargaining chip to be used in negotiations with Spain.

In 1648, Portugal was excluded from the discussions that saw France and her allies end many of the conflicts of the Thirty Years War, signing the Peace of Westphalia.[39] Aside from some smaller sorties, the Spanish colossus was now engaged on only one front: Portugal. The war for independence had begun in desperate earnest.

As if he didn't have enough problems, João was about to be swept into another set of difficulties. Or one difficulty in particular. His name was Prince Rupert, and he was bearing down on the coast of Portugal with a fleet of ships of questionable provenance. Dashing, brave and favouring the flowing locks of the Cavalier, Rupert was the thirty-year-old son of Charles I's sister, Elizabeth of Bohemia, who was known romantically – or mockingly, depending on the speaker – as the Winter Queen, since she ruled for only one winter.[40]

As one of the few living royals with actual experience of war, Rupert had gained a quasi-mythical reputation as a leader in the English Civil War, quickly becoming commander-in-chief of the Royalist forces. After Royalist defeat, exile and the declaration of a Commonwealth in England, he decided to turn to the high seas, following the grand tradition of English privateers (no matter that he was half German, and frequently referred to as Rupert of the Rhine). Fleeing Ireland hotly pursued by the Commonwealth fleet, he and his forces were, as one member of his crew put it, like Noah and his ark, 'driven to begin the world anew, with seven sail'.[41]

Rupert had already sent word to João asking for access to his ports and rivers for refuelling and repairing his small fleet, alongside permission to sell his captured prize booty on the Portuguese market. This put the cautious João in a difficult position. Being a king himself, and a traditionalist in a traditionally minded country, he supported the cause of royalty against that of self-appointed governments like the new Commonwealth. And there was always a possibility that Charles I would return to power. A grateful King of England, Scotland, Wales and Ireland might be a useful tool in the future. However, he had no desire to upset the newly established Commonwealth, since England was Portugal's biggest trading partner. To make matters worse, Rupert was brave and dashing, but entirely lacking in tact. His hot-headed impetuosity had left many a plan in disarray in the past, even if it occasionally won the day. His tendency to make things happen, whether for good or ill, had led his brothers and sisters to call him Rupert the Devil growing up.[42] Personality-wise, he was João's polar opposite.

João's councillors disagreed on the best course of action – whether to side with Rupert or the Commonwealth – but they all agreed that they did not want to be dragged into a foreign war. The only dissident voice was Teodósio, now fourteen and stirred by the worthy cause of hereditary right. He was also just the right age and temperament to espouse any military cause that promised some glamour, revelling in the romanticism of royalty in exile now pursuing a life on the open sea.[43] Teodósio was the people's favourite, and Catherine's too, a serious young man of tall, slim build, with a round face, a rosebud mouth and a close crop of dark curling hair.[44] The siblings shared a love of learning and a facility with languages, alongside an intense piety. Teodósio was said to begin his day with holy exercises, and spent many hours contemplating the divine, just as Catherine did in both youth and later life.[45]

He loved astrology, could read Greek, Latin, French and Italian, and spoke Spanish with notable energy. All the siblings spoke Spanish, since it was their mother's native tongue, and their ease with language was also perhaps inherited from Luisa. Teodósio's other interests included the latest advances in science, maths, theology and philosophy. He was respected by Portugal's intellectual elite for his learning, and by the general population for his piety and valour.[46] He was so desperate to be at war that he actually fled the comfort of the Ribeira Palace to join the front lines of battle at Alentejo, fighting for independence against Spain.

However, his hot-headed support for Rupert was overruled. Instead, João equivocated: he promised the Royalists safe harbour in Portugal without actually taking their side.

The English party anchored in the clear waters of Cascais Bay (famous in later history as the setting for *Casino Royale*), and went onshore, where they were feasted and entertained. João welcomed them at the Ribeira Palace with great generosity and all due ceremony (Rupert's younger brother Prince Maurice was also of the party).[47] Although there is no evidence that ten-year-old Catherine met the dashing German princes – she might have been in a convent at the time – she would certainly have been aware of their glamorous presence. She was close to her elder brother, and may even have taken his side – we know that she believed strongly in the divine right of kings, and would likely have been horrified by the state of affairs in the kingless Commonwealth England. Perhaps some of the ideas she was to advocate later in life were discussed first with her elder brother on the advent of Prince Rupert and his extensive, expensive entourage.

Rupert and Maurice quickly made themselves popular in Lisbon, dispensing largesse to the people. They were glamorous figures, with great masses of black hair, long aristocratic noses, and free manners that appealed to the *povo* as well as the clergy – the English aristocracy were much less formal than the Portuguese at the time. João could not leave the palace without hearing exclamations of support for Rupert from the citizens of Lisbon, while even the councillors who were against the princes' continued stay in their city did not outwardly criticise him for fear of getting on the *povo*'s bad side.[48] Their popularity was naturally helped by Rupert's request that the leading Parliamentarian merchants in Portugal be imprisoned, which João agreed to do. Dissent safely removed, all seemed set for a profitable career in piracy, with profits funnelled into the Royalist cause.

Both Rupert and João enjoyed the company of practical people who knew what they were talking about, and respected one another's ability to ride hard and track game. Rupert far preferred physical activity to sitting about diplomatically. As a young man, he had once been so focused on the hunt that when his dog went down a hole after a fox, the prince followed him and got stuck himself. His manservant managed to pull him out by the legs, to find Rupert holding onto the dog, which in turn was gripping the fox with its teeth.[49] João, Rupert and Maurice hunted daily, whiling away their days in the slaughter of deer and tawny mouflon (wild sheep). In their defence, they and their sailors and courtiers did eat what they had killed.

There were a few harmonious months, but a pirate–king alliance was always a naive idea. By supporting Rupert, João had somewhat accidentally been drawn into taking sides. Early in 1650, the Parliamentarian general at sea Robert Blake set off from England in pursuit of what the Commonwealth called, 'treacherous fugitives, renegados and sea robbers'.[50] Blake's fleet was sighted at the mouth of the Tagus in March, and he demanded that João release Rupert to them. It was an uncomfortable situation. The Commonwealth fleet had anchored only two miles away from Rupert's fleet, the sound of the crews easily carrying across the open water. They came into even more contact in the port, with multiple brawls breaking out between the sailors on either side.

João's hands were somewhat tied: his Secretary of State, Count de Miro, had long been urging a neutral policy, suggesting that 'His Majesty should rather equally entertain and receive all of the English nation, since with them he had renewed the contracts of peace and friendship that have always been between the two nations'. He reminded João of 'the king's custom-house', which would suffer a huge loss in revenue if English trade continued to be disrupted.[51] They certainly could not afford war with the new Commonwealth. But João had also agreed to offer Rupert his protection. He could hardly give him up to the first threat of violence. Luisa and Teodósio urged him to support the Royalists, arguing that he had given his word, and could not go back on it now.[52] Besides all this, it would have made him look weak on the international stage, and that would have been a deadly move. With his customary caution, he decided to negotiate with the new arrivals. He quickly found out how difficult this would be.

Rupert's fleet was safe in the Tagus, but their funds were at an all-time low, and anticipating a Commonwealth win, few in Lisbon were willing to extend credit to the prince's party, popular as Rupert and Maurice might be. The Commonwealth negotiator, Charles Vane, tried to reason with the English merchants in the city, but since all the Parliamentarians had been locked up at Rupert's request, he had little success in getting them to take his side. Most merchants wanted to stay out of the conflict, and for the powers-that-be to leave them in peace. It was a tense stalemate, which quickly devolved into name-calling, Rupert issuing a declaration that Parliamentarians 'are nothing else but tumultuous, factious, seditious soldiers, and other disorderly and refractory persons conspiring together'. He spread fear of their forces through Lisbon, insinuating that the Commonwealth fleet was in secret league with the Spanish.[53]

In response, the Commonwealth began their own propaganda effort, scattering papers through the city to sway popular opinion and thus force João into supporting their cause. They called Rupert 'this Vagabond German, a Prince of Fortune, whose highness is nothing else but haughtiness, his Principality mere piracy'. Reversing the charge of being in league with the Spanish, they accused Rupert of siding with Spain and trying to undercut Portuguese independence.[54]

Tension escalated when Commonwealth sailors (according to the Royalists, at least) tried to ambush Rupert and Maurice as they were returning from a hunting trip. Small, easily manoeuvrable ships waited just offshore with crews ready to kill them as they tried to get back to their own boats. Luckily for the princes, the attack failed. In a typically daring move, Rupert responded by sending a boat masquerading as a fruit seller to the Commonwealth frigate the *Leopard*. The disguise hid a firebomb, which almost succeeded in destroying the ship. There is another, slightly less dramatic version of this story, in which Rupert sent one of his own men dressed in Portuguese clothing to plant a bomb disguised as a barrel of oil on Blake's ship. However, the man was recognised and the enterprise failed.[55]

By this point, João had had enough of both sides, the assassination attempts and the bombings, and must have deeply regretted dipping his toe into the never-ending round of English bickering, propaganda and counter-attack. He offered Portuguese protection to Rupert if the prince agreed to leave Lisbon and get out into the open sea. The governor of the fort at the mouth of the Tagus promised to help the prince's fleet to slip away, but word spread to the enemy and they moved to block an escape.[56]

Trying to lure Rupert out from Portuguese protection, Robert Blake finally ordered his fleet back out to sea, where they seized ten merchant ships bound for Brazil with the intention of forcing João to give up Rupert in exchange for the vessels. This was too much like provocation to João, and he began to arm and provision his own fleet, stationing it ready in the wide, deep waters of the Tagus.[57] When they were fully victualled and supplied with gunpowder, Rupert let fly his standard and weighed anchor, giving chase to the Commonwealth fleet, closely followed and supported by the Portuguese. However, according to one of Rupert's crew, the enemy had 'the weather-gage of us' and got away.[58] The wind died down and they anchored again, sailing around the next day in a fog until Commonwealth ships were finally sighted emerging out of the blanketing mist. Both sides fought, fired and gave chase.

As the days continued, João was being dragged further and further into a war he had no desire to be a part of, fearing equally that the Commonwealth forces might make an alliance with Spain. Finally, he bargained with Blake for peace, and signed a treaty that would allow free trade, with the condition that Rupert would no longer be made welcome in Lisbon. The Portuguese also had to pay a yearly fine to the Commonwealth for the incident. The accidental war was at an end, for João at least, and he could breathe a sigh of relief, whatever dreams Teodósio might have had about storming the Commonwealth fleet and fighting them off single-handed.

At Michaelmas, with the vine leaves turning red, Rupert sailed for Spain, planning to pursue his career as a pirate there. His reception was much less welcoming. A Royalist captain melodramatically recalled, 'now misfortunes being no novelty to us, we plough the sea for subsistence, and, being destitute of a port, we take the confines of the Mediterranean Sea for our harbour; poverty and despair being companions, and revenge our guide'.[59] They were 'now flattered, now fired upon . . . according to the ups and downs of Commonwealth prestige: finally the ups gained the day', and the bedraggled fleet fled to Barbados, where they could enrich themselves without Commonwealth interference.[60]

But this brief interlude of Portuguese friendship towards the Royalists would not be forgotten, and it would prove significant in the course of Catherine's life.

The death of Teodósio three years later, at the age of nineteen, was the great tragedy of Catherine's younger life. She was only thirteen when he was taken by tuberculosis, and watched as his already slim frame reduced until the formerly energetic, war-mad young man could barely get up, his body racked by coughing. She undoubtedly found comfort in prayer, but the experience taught her that the world could be an unfair and arbitrary place.

Teodósio's death was not just a personal but a national tragedy. He was famed for his learning, his wit and his courage, and contemporaries mourned the young man as their 'perfect prince'.[61] One last *beija-mão* was performed for the prince who never would be king, hands kissed in a great public orgy of grief. A hole was left both in the national consciousness and in the Braganza family. At the end of her own life, Catherine asked to be buried next to her beloved brother. Fifty-two years later, she had not forgotten Portugal's Teodósio.

For now, her younger brother, Afonso, was next in line to the throne, and attention would fall on Catherine as the Braganzas desperately tried to make alliances and survive in their war with Spain.

3

The Bridegroom Hunt

NOW THAT HE had successfully disentangled himself from an awkward and unwanted conflict, João's attention, of necessity, turned back to France for an alliance. Catherine's elder sister, Joana, Princess of Beira, died in 1653, aged just eighteen, another family tragedy, leaving Catherine as the only remaining daughter of the House of Braganza. Her value as a piece in the political chess game was raised accordingly. Preoccupied with securing their dynasty and fragile monarchy in the face of European indifference and Spanish antagonism, both João and Luisa bargained with Catherine's hand.

In 1656, João offered his daughter in marriage to the seventeen-year-old King of France, Louis XIV. To sweeten the deal, he promised an enormous dowry of one million cruzados, as well as either Tangier or Mazagão (a North African port, now El Jadida). France, still locked in war with Spain, was wary of antagonising the European superpower any further. It certainly did not want to become embroiled in a doomed conflict, as Portugal's ongoing war for independence looked likely to be. The powerful Anna of Austria, Louis' mother and queen regent, was herself a Hapsburg, and had favoured the idea of a Spanish alliance since her young son was in his cradle.[1]

After some coming and going, Louis' advisers refused Catherine's hand, preferring to leave France open to either oppose or side with Portugal. The young King Louis was later to blame his mother and her chief adviser, Cardinal Mazarin, for this policy, describing Catherine as 'a Lady of great Beauty and admirable Endowments'.[2]

In 1656, João died. The next in line to the throne, Afonso, was only thirteen, so Luisa became regent. Ruling was not new to her, and she steered Portugal successfully through the difficult next few years. On a personal level, the residents of the Ribeira Palace, including Catherine, had rather an uncomfortable time of it during Afonso's wild youth. He had suffered from meningitis as a child, which left lasting health effects.[3] His distraught parents had thought he was going to die, trying every medicine and relic they could think of to preserve the life of their son.[4] There are theories that his wild behaviour was a result of his illness, but he may have simply been a typical teenager, more interested in partying than in being king.

Afonso's portraits show light brown, almost burnished-looking hair, heavy-lidded eyes and a pale complexion. Despite an attendant sleeping in the corridor just outside his room, he would sneak out of the palace in the dead of night using rope ladders. According to the clergyman and court visitor, John Colbatch, the young man enjoyed meeting 'with a lewd rabble of grooms' so that they could box, throw knives, watch dog fights and wrestle. He had a hot temper and preferred the company of 'lewd women' to the sheltered ladies of Lisbon's formal court, which was presided over by Luisa's iron grasp and where strict etiquette was the order of the day.[5]

Afonso's younger, stockier brother, Pedro, was not very different, though he was thought to be quicker and more thoughtful than Afonso. As Colbatch put it, Pedro did 'not like persons of quality, and does not hide his pleasure when he has got rid of them'. He loved to fight, and also enjoyed gossip and the company of 'all the gay girls in the town'.[6] Both brothers were probably escaping the iron hand of their parents; before he died, João was afraid that, if given the chance, they would run off like their elder brother Teodósio to join the fighting. They had to climb out of windows if they wanted to have any fun.

Luisa was left in charge while her sons partied. Only Catherine obeyed their mother, not that she had much choice, since female behaviour was much more constrained. Her value was in her ability to marry a head of state and forge an alliance for her country, and she would have had this drilled into her throughout her childhood, along with all the etiquette and diplomatic skills a queen would need. However, like her siblings, she loved music and parties, and had a great sense of fun, which became apparent as soon as she escaped from her loving but controlling mother. For now, Luisa and Catherine were almost continually together in the Ribeira Palace, and since Catherine had a docile temper, she was most likely content to follow her mother's rules – she certainly did not complain later in life about this period.

Then disaster struck. The year 1659 began well, with the Portuguese gaining their first major victory in their war with Spain, capturing 5,000 Spanish troops. But in September, Europe's two greatest powers – France and Spain – signed the Treaty of the Pyrenees, ending the war between them and allying the countries. It was sealed with marriage between King Louis XIV and the Infanta Maria Theresa of Spain.

Luisa once again turned to England as a possible ally, buying arms and horses and negotiating permission with the Commonwealth government to recruit up to 12,000 men from England for the Portuguese army. Believing that Cromwell would be crowned king, she sent 3,000 cruzados to Francisco de Melo, her ambassador in England, so that he could throw a lavish coronation party and cosy up to the new monarch.[7] De Melo was a pale, thickset man with impressive dark mustachios. His sturdy physique belied his habit of retreating to bed with some dramatic ailment whenever things got too much. He was a capable ambassador and a canny politician, able to accurately read the winds of change, which happened all too often.

Luisa and de Melo's plans were upset when, on 3 September 1658, at the age of fifty-nine, Cromwell died from a return of the malarial fever that had long plagued him. The money was instead spent on celebrating the succession of his son, Richard. But Richard was no Oliver. By the time Luisa's letter of congratulation reached him, he had already resigned as Lord Protector.[8]

Then came yet another spoke in the wheel, this time from the Portuguese Inquisition. De Melo was quick to try to calm the situation when the Inquisition arrested the English consul, Thomas Maynard, in Lisbon, almost provoking war with the Commonwealth. Tensions were always high between the zealous Inquisition and the Protestant consul, but the dispute flared over a sixteen-year-old English girl who had converted to Protestantism after visiting Maynard's house, for which he was blamed. Busy negotiating in London, de Melo thought he would be arrested in retaliation, and lamented, 'Wretched Portugal, miserable negotiations, unfortunate ambassador! England was Portugal's last hope.'[9] The Inquisition, of course, did not care whether Portugal remained independent or not, since they would be serving the same masters either way – God, and the Pope in Rome.

The Portuguese ambassador was right to despair – matters were pressing, and the agreement was delayed by two years. Finally, however, on 8 April 1660, he signed a treaty agreeing that the Portuguese could buy their armaments in England, as well as promising 2,550 cavalry troops (fully furnished with horses), 12,000 foot soldiers and up to 24 warships.

This was a hugely significant breakthrough, guaranteeing an ally, supply chains and fresh men for the war effort. De Melo and Luisa must have rejoiced at finally coming to terms, despite the lengthy interruption. Five weeks later, their rejoicing was at an end. The treaty was void. England had a king again.[10]

The event was 'to the astonishment of all the Christian world', being 'past imagination both the greatness and the suddenness of it'.[11] Oliver Cromwell had, after all, been dead for two years, and there had been no sign of Charles II being recalled, much to the latter's frustration. The country wanted the stability that Cromwell had brought, a comparatively conservative figure in his latter years. When he died, the land was plunged into confusion. Many began to think longingly of the monarchy once more, and Charles had been sensible enough to remain a Protestant, the essential requirement for a reigning king. By 16 March 1660, people on the street were beginning to 'talk loud of the king', and the traditional insult 'kiss my arse' had morphed into 'kiss my parliament'. In mockery of the successive rump Parliaments, rumps of beef were roasted on bonfires along the wide thoroughfare of the Strand.[12]

It was General Monck who made the decision to end the uncertainty and, for better or worse, the Republic. A moderate obsessed with the establishment of law and order, he decided to play the part of the strong man, marching his troops down from Scotland in February. With an army behind him, he set about replacing influential Parliamentarians with Royalist sympathisers, carrying out his self-appointed reforms with ruthless efficiency. He communicated secretly with Charles, the king-in-exile, but mostly played his cards close to his chest.

On May Day 1660, traditionally a day of dancing and disorder, the populace celebrated the return of their king, getting down on their knees in the street to drink his health, lighting bonfires and crying out their approval. As Charles processed through his kingdom, diarist Samuel Pepys recorded, 'The shouting and joy expressed by all is past imagination.'[13] The few staunch Parliamentarians left were sickened by a people so willing to put on harness once more for a king. But they were overruled. A Charles Stuart was back on the throne, and the politics of Europe shifted once more.

Thanks to this seismic event, the still-wet ink on their treaty of friendship with the Protectorate looked grim for Luisa and de Melo. The treaty was not a binding document of mutual support, but almost evidence of a crime. De Melo, an astute politician, immediately asked to be recalled to Lisbon, so that a new, untainted ambassador could take his place and hopefully have better luck negotiating with the Royalists. Luisa chose to ignore his request. There was no one so able at delicate negotiation, nor so conversant with the complicated state of British politics. For both players, it took a tremendous amount of grit, dusting themselves off and venturing into diplomatic negotiations yet again, trying to gain English support, arms and troops for the war with Spain.

But who would this new England side with? Charles had just been in Spain and had been financially supported by the Hapsburgs during his exile, however slow they were in their payments. He had also signed a treaty with Spain promising support against Portugal should he be returned to the throne, something the Portuguese were unaware of.[14] De Melo believed it might seem ungrateful of Charles to make an alliance with Portugal now, and the new king had refused to see the Portuguese ambassador to the United Provinces while he was in the Hague.[15] This boded ill. Despite the fact that Luisa had hotly supported Prince Rupert against the Commonwealth while he tried his hand at piracy in Lisbon, an alliance with Charles' regime now looked a distant prospect.

Attempting to make the best of a bad situation, de Melo began networking like mad among those of his allies who were still in power, including the influential Monck, now Duke of Albemarle. De Melo's credentials from Luisa to act as her ambassador to the new regime had not yet arrived, but he did not let this hinder his diplomatic progress, simply forging new ones and presenting himself to the great and the good.[16] It quickly became a race between de Melo and the Spanish as to who could win over the most allies, with enormous sums changing hands to try and secure the new king's ear. In this, de Melo was inevitably out-spent by Spain, who handed out 400,000 cruzados to his 40,000.[17] Some fine Andalusian horses with their distinctively luxuriant manes, enormous chests and incredible stamina were presented to Charles, while the new Spanish ambassador disbursed gifts of money wherever he could, on the pretext that these were unpaid wages for services rendered in exile in Spain.[18] Gone were those painfully poor days, when money due to Charles was paid grudgingly and with excruciating slowness. He had frequently been an object of pity, dressed practically in rags, a king with nothing but the name. He would never forget the straits and humiliations of exile, and it produced in him a cynicism, a love of luxury, and an intense dislike of being told what to do.

Whenever he could, de Melo brought up Portuguese support of Prince Rupert's forces, reminding the new regime that it was a support that had cost Portugal dear – up until the last days of the Protectorate, they were still paying an annual sum as compensation.[19] He rallied the Portuguese merchants resident in London to his cause, assembling a petition of 200 signatures to remind England of the extent and value of trade with Portugal, worth around £200,000 a year, as well as all the English living in Portugal and vice versa.

But there was scope for closer alliance yet. Charles – at the grand old age of thirty and still unmarried – needed a queen. Luisa had a daughter of marriageable age. In fact, it was a match that had been proposed by their fathers. Surprisingly, however, it was neither de Melo nor Luisa who resurrected the scheme. Instead it was the Portuguese ambassador to France, who mentioned the marriage to Luisa as a 'bad alliance' but a political necessity.[20] But once he had suggested the idea, all agreed that 'for security, we should marry Lady Infanta Dona Catherine to the king'.[21] Otherwise, Charles might accept payment from Portugal, then immediately turn around and sign another treaty with Spain.

(*above*) Catherine's mother
Luisa de Guzmán as a teenager.
The dog is an emblem of
fidelity, and her pink-and-white
face is a stark contrast against
her fashionable black dress.

(*right*) A young João, matching
his future wife Luisa in the severe
opulence of his dress.

The acclamation of João 'the Restorer'. Painted in 1908, this image showcases the importance of this act of independence in Portuguese history.

The Vila Viçosa, Catherine's birthplace and home of her very early childhood.

The dashing young Prince Rupert, who Catherine
possibly first met as a pirate in Lisbon.

Catherine very shortly before her marriage, sporting fashionable Portuguese clothing and hair. The dark gloves draw attention to her elegant hands.

Edward Hyde, Charles II's dour Lord Chancellor, who advocated for the Portuguese match.

The Ribeira Palace in 1662, the year that Catherine departed Lisbon.

James, Duke of York, the first courtier to greet Catherine on her arrival in England. This portrait celebrates his role as Lord High Admiral, dressed as Mars, god of war.

Catherine by Peter Lely early in her reign, before setting court trends for herself.

Tunbridge Wells in around 1719, after Catherine had helped popularise the town as a bathing place.

Catherine's new husband Charles II at his coronation. Noted for his
excellent figure and severe expression, this portrait projects
confidence the new regime sorely needed.

Barbara Palmer, Countess of Castlemaine, the reason for Catherine and Charles's first argument as a married couple and later Catherine's sometime-ally.

Mary of Modena, Catherine's close ally in later years. Mary was frequently painted with a dog, representing marital fidelity.

(*above*) The acid-tongued John Wilmot, Earl of Rochester, and his monkey, representing human folly.

(*right*) Catherine posing as her namesake, Catherine of Alexandria, complete with Catherine wheel. Huysmans' picture started a trend of women posing as the saint.

But a marriage with Catherine was not to be entered into lightly. France had prevaricated for a reason. Any husband of hers would automatically be drawn into war with Spain. What could Luisa and de Melo possibly offer that would entice Charles into such a marriage?

Portugal's saving grace was that Catherine, now twenty-four years old, was a pretty woman. A contemporary portrait shows her rosy-cheeked, with the same delicately arched eyebrows of childhood, a long, slightly tip-tilted nose and large dark eyes. Charles was extremely particular about who he married, and unwilling to countenance anyone unattractive. He declared that the German princesses – which meant most of the Protestant candidates of marriageable age – were universally 'dull and foggy' and 'I cannot like any one of them for a wife'.[22] The other excellent Protestant contender, the Dowager Princess of Orange's youngest daughter, Maria, unfortunately had a beautiful and vivacious elder sister, Henriette-Catherine, who shared a history with the new king. During his exile, the pair were perhaps not in love, but were at least very much in like, exchanging love letters with the code names 'Infanta' and 'Don Lauren' or 'Loran'. However, when Oliver Cromwell died and no immediate move was made to reinstate Charles to his kingdom, Henriette-Catherine's mother rethought the relationship and eventually married her to a German prince, who, while not quite so high-ranking, at least had a country of his own.

When Henriette-Catherine's younger sister Maria was proposed as a match after the Restoration, Charles expressed a firm 'no'. While he had had to chafe at the shifts and humiliations of life at someone else's court during his period of exile, he had promised not to forget either his injuries or those who had done him a good turn. He would not be offering advantageous terms of alliance to the Dowager Princess of Orange. This was not the first time he had been overlooked as a suitor; a match with France's most fabulously wealthy heiress had been the dearest wish of his mother, Henrietta Maria, but that lady had felt she could do better than a king without a country.

So the German princesses were out, as were the ladies both French and Dutch who had been connected to Charles's humiliations on the continent. The court was at an impasse. De Melo, of course, had a solution ready. But it was a tricky negotiation. After much careful deliberation, and using his customary tact, he approached the pro-Portuguese Edward Montagu, Earl of Manchester, about a potential match with Portugal's last surviving infanta. Manchester was mild-mannered and sensitive, his saving grace in the eyes of the new regime was that, despite having been a Parliamentarian commander in the war, he had argued vehemently against the trial and execution of Charles I, leading to his retiring from public office. Since 1659, he had been paving the way for Charles II's return, and had become an important supporter of the new king – in other words, an excellent ally for de Melo to have onside.

Attracted by the picture de Melo painted of a Portuguese alliance, Manchester quickly sought out Charles, telling him '*That there was in* Portugal a Princess in her Beauty, Person and Age, was very fit for him, and who would have a Portion suitable to her Birth and Quality.' He was careful to stress in as tactful a way as possible that Catherine, though a Catholic, was no Henrietta Maria, being 'totally without that Meddling and Activity in her Nature, which many Times made those of that Religion troublesome and restless, when they came into a Country where another Religion was practiced'. Of course, 'a Protestant Queen would in all Respects be looked upon as the greatest Blessing to the Kingdom', but if a Protestant to suit the King's tastes could not be found, Catherine was surely the best type of Catholic princess they were likely to find.[23] There were only so many unmarried princesses, after all, of marriageable age. Moreover, Manchester hinted, the Portuguese were willing to pay out a very generous dowry.

Hearing a flattering description of Catherine, and always ready to accept a source of income that did not have to be approved through bargaining with Parliament, Charles met the next day with the Portuguese ambassador for an informal audience. De Melo made the terms of negotiation clearer: in exchange for the alliance, Charles was to receive £100,000, along with Tangier and Bombay (now Mumbai), two places that 'might reasonably be valued above the Portion in Money'.[24] The ambassador also offered free trade in Brazil and the East Indies, assuring the king somewhat spuriously, given João's policy of trade concessions, that this was a privilege the Portuguese 'had hitherto denied to all Nations but themselves'.[25] Maintaining trade with Portugal was extremely valuable, both nations dependent on the other as vast quantities of goods moved between them.

Besides the cash sum, Charles was especially excited by the idea of owning Tangier, the naval commander Sir John Lawson having told him that, if they could build a fort there, 'they would keep the Place against all the World, and give the Law to all the Trade of the Mediterranean'.[26] He gathered a secret group of trusted advisers to consult about the idea of marriage to Catherine, bidding them speak their minds openly on the subject. All agreed that a Protestant would be preferable, but if one could not be found, Catherine's enormous dowry made her far and away the best option.

The final term of the marriage was a clever one, proposing that England and Portugal renew the treaty made with the Commonwealth, minus the yearly charge that Portugal had had to pay as a penalty for assisting Prince Rupert.[27] The treaty included an article that promised Portugal 6,000 foot soldiers, levied and outfitted at English expense. The additional soldiers would aid Portugal against Spain, but Charles wanted to avoid actually committing himself to war, particularly since he was far from being on completely firm footing at home. His Lord Chancellor, Edward Hyde – later the Earl of Clarendon – sententiously remarks in his *History* that this was 'A Resolution very prudently made; and if it had been adhered to, much Evil which succeeded the Departure from it, might have been prevented.'[28] However, in characteristic fashion, seeing the world the way he wanted to see it, Charles declared that he could 'help a Brother and Ally with a Levy of Men at their Charge, without entering into a War with the other Prince'.[29] If King Philip IV chose to see a marriage between Charles and Catherine as a declaration of war, that was his problem, and nothing whatsoever to do with Charles's actions.

The Portuguese ambassador was duly sent back to Portugal with full approval to negotiate the marriage, pretending to look dissatisfied as he boarded the ship in order to try and stop too much gossip about the match flitting around London. This, of course, was always a losing gambit: gossip to Londoners was practically a currency. He carried letters written by Charles to Luisa, Afonso and Catherine. The one addressed to Catherine was particularly charming, with Charles looking forward to sharing their married life together. From the tone of the letters, the match was almost a done deal. It certainly seemed so to the ambassador, and most likely to Catherine, receiving such a confiding note. But in English court life just as in Portuguese, there was always another plot waiting to be sprung at just the wrong moment.

In this instance, things began to go awry when Charles revealed his plans to George Digby, Earl of Bristol. Bristol was a dashing loose cannon, memorably painted by van Dyck in a swirl of apricot silks and flowing blonde locks. Having been born in Spain and living there until he was eleven years old, he was no friend to Portuguese independence. Ever ambitious but possessing almost no common sense, he had a silver tongue, which got him into difficult situations as frequently as it extracted him from them.

Bristol immediately tried to convince Charles that the Portuguese match was a terrible idea, telling him that Portugal was on the verge of annihilation, with Spain amassing a crushing force ready for invasion. What was the point, therefore, of allying with them? He added that the Portuguese people were weary of their government, 'so that that miserable Family had no Hope, but by transporting themselves and their poor Party in their Ships to *Brasil*, and their other large Territories in the *East-Indies*, which were possessed only by *Portugueses*, who might possibly be willing to subject to them'. This, he asserted, was common knowledge. The idea of ever receiving a dowry payment from such a beleaguered country was laughable.[30]

Presumably hoping to add further persuasions to his own, Bristol confided the secret of the proposed marriage to the Spanish ambassador, Luis de Haro, who was incensed by the idea and spoke with great passion wherever he went, telling Charles that it would 'prove ruinous to himself and his Kingdom; for the King of *Spain* could not but resent it to such a Degree, as would bring great Inconvenience to his Affairs'.[31] This argument did not carry much weight with Charles, who was brave perhaps to a fault, and moreover hated being dictated to, even by his closest advisers. However, de Haro then embarked on another strain of argument that seriously alarmed the king, suggesting that Catherine was unable to have children, and that she was 'deformed, and had many Diseases'.

The Earl of Bristol, scenting victory, enlarged on this theme, contrasting Catherine's allegedly frightful appearance with the beautiful Italian ladies he had known on his travels. He and de Haro told Charles that 'there were many beautiful ladies in *Italy*, of the greatest Houses; and that his Majesty might take his Choice of them, and the King of *Spain* would give a Portion with her, as if She were a Daughter of *Spain*, and the King should marry her as such'.[32] Bristol's colourful descriptions of voluptuous Italian women, alongside their joint disparagement of Catherine, began to have their effect.

Thankfully for Catherine, however, the earl, 'ever restless and ambitious', went off to Italy to find some acceptably attractive Italian lady of birth high enough to pacify the English.[33] Above all else, he needed to confirm the 'Persons, Beauties and good Humours of the Princesses'.[34] As far as he was concerned, the Portuguese match was off, and the Italian ladies only needed to be persuaded that what they really wanted above all else was to be Queen of England, Scotland, Wales and Ireland. In leaving the country, however, Bristol took himself out of the race, leaving the field open for the persuasions of Charles's other councillors.

The more sober-minded among them pointed out that the king could hardly begin negotiations with another principality when he was so committed to Portugal. He would at least have to tell the Portuguese that he had changed his mind.

Despite his letters declaring as much, Charles no longer thought of Catherine as his wife. When de Melo returned to the English court, he was shocked by his cool reception. He had brought letters with him for Charles from Luisa and Afonso, but kept them back, confused by this unexpected hostility. Unable to fathom what on earth had happened, he dealt with the problem by taking to his bed, since he was 'naturally a hypochondriac'.[35]

It is here that the affairs of men took an unusual twist. Significantly, in the brief time he had been in Portugal, Luisa had raised de Melo to the new title of the Marquis de Sande, in thanks for his devoted service. This rise in status inflamed the petty jealousy of de Haro, who pressed Charles for assurances that he was not going to marry Catherine. Otherwise, de Haro announced, war would be declared. This was a fatal miscalculation. Bridling, Charles declared 'that He would not receive Orders from the *Catholick* King, how to dispose himself in Marriage'.[36] Seeing that he had perhaps gone too far, de Haro came back the next day with an offer to amply dower any Protestant lady, using Spain's deep coffers. Charles could have the best of both worlds: cash in hand and a Protestant bride, sure to be popular with the people.

However, the damage had been done. It was perhaps more to spite Spain, rather than any other reason, that Charles and Catherine ended up married. If anything was more likely to encourage Charles to enter a war that he had no particular inclination for, it was telling him that he could not engage in such a war. Such are the accidents of history. It helped, of course, that while umming and ahhing about the decision, he spoke to someone who had actually met Catherine, who assured him that she was not the frightful, disease-ridden creature Bristol and de Haro had described. He looked at her miniature and decided 'that Person could not be unhandsome'.[37] France had also intimated that a match with Portugal would be an excellent idea, looked on favourably by Louis XIV, who offered to stand the money for England's first military engagement there. The French envoy reassured Charles as to Catherine's good looks.[38]

Attempting to secure an insider at Charles's court, the same envoy offered a bribe of £10,000 to Clarendon, which the Chancellor indignantly refused, saying he would accept no one's wages but his master's. When he told Charles about the offer, the king laughed and called him a fool, telling him to take the money. It is entirely characteristic of both men's temperaments – and Clarendon's constant shock and disapproval that Charles could be so unconcerned with morals that he himself could not live without.[39] Almost everyone else at court was accepting bribes from any foreign power that felt like handing them out.

Finally, despite some unexpected twists and turns, the alliance with Portugal had been decided upon. The Privy Council and the Lords were let in on the secret, advising Charles 'with all imaginable Chearfulness to this Marriage', their unusual unity something Charles 'looked upon as very wonderful, and even as some Instance of the Approbation of God himself'. The Commons, which in this early period of Charles's reign was overwhelmingly Royalist, told him that the news 'had exceedingly rejoiced their Hearts'.[40] It is clear how seriously everyone took the marriage, preserving as it would the stability of the Stuart dynasty and the country.

Comically, the Earl of Bristol was still wandering about somewhere in Italy judging the appeal of potential wifely candidates. Perhaps fortunately, their beauty was not found to be up to scratch. Bristol viewed both princesses of Parma on their way to church and judged one lady to be so fat and one so plain that Charles would never have consented to the match – they were just as bad as the German dowds.[41]

Refusing to accept defeat, de Haro tried propaganda, printing pamphlets that listed all his arguments against the match with Catherine and scattering them about the streets. His anger made him highly indiscreet, dropping pamphlets from his own window to soldiers passing below. Charles, incensed, sent him from the kingdom, 'carrying with him the Character of a very bold rash Man'.[42] In contrast, de Melo was out of his sickbed and making merry. The glee he felt at finally pulling off this coup is palpable in a letter to the young King Afonso, in which he describes the great state visit the pompous Clarendon made to his apartments, bearing all the seals of office and approval from both Lords and Commons. Apparently, everyone rejoiced at 'the wise choice which this prince has made of the most serene lady infanta'.*[43]

There was a secret but important article in the marriage treaty that de Melo must have congratulated himself over particularly, and it was to have a profound impact on both countries concerned. It promised to protect all of Portugal's colonies and

---

* The title of Portuguese monarchs is always 'serene' or 'most serene' – unfortunately for the poor historian with little to go on, this is not a statement about Catherine's character.

conquests, to mediate peace between Portugal and the United Provinces (but to defend Portugal against the Dutch if peace could not be agreed on), and to send help to the Portuguese-controlled East Indies in the next monsoon, when the trade winds were favourable.[44] It was a fabulous coup, securing the kind of alliance that João and Luisa had been plotting since they ascended to the throne twenty years earlier.

It wasn't only Charles's support they had gained. Louis XIV, fast securing his place as the most powerful monarch in Europe, smiled on the marriage, and he was closely allied by blood to the Stuarts; Charles's younger sister, Henriette-Anne, was married to Louis' only brother, while the two kings also shared a grandfather in Henri IV. The match set Portugal firmly within a network of French-leaning alliance. Its importance cannot be overestimated.

As such, nothing could be allowed to upset it. In readiness for the marriage, Luisa had resorted to desperate straits to raise the huge sum dangled in front of Charles as a dowry. She sold her own jewels and plate (much of this provided by her own family on her marriage), as well as borrowing plate and jewels from the Church (the likelihood of this 'loan' being repaid was doubtful). To effect the handover of Tangier, the intractable old governor had been removed, since his moods could not be depended on, and replaced with 'a Creature of the Queens, who could not deceive her'.[45] Luisa promised to do the same with Bombay.

The marriage has been seen as 'the crowning achievement of Luisa's life'. Not only did it draw Portugal into the pro-French network of Stuart alliances, it also secured military support for the war for independence.[46] A contemporary in Lisbon stated that the treaty was 'the only thing under heaven left them to keep them from despair and ruine'.[47] The cruzado rose on the Roman currency exchange. Even the Pope paid attention; perhaps Portugal was not a Spanish province after all.[48]

Whatever actual benefit Portugal received in the long term from the marriage between Catherine and Charles, the news was greeted with profound relief across the country, particularly close to the border with Spain. The treaty promised that England would come to Portugal's defence by sea and land, prompting the governor of the Algarve to muse hopefully that 'We shall all be thankful to God for the wedding of Her Serenity Queen of England, thanks to which we shall be protected, by having such a powerful ally, not only against Spanish power but also against any other enemy, hopefully bringing great joy to Portugal.'[49] He ordered that the main squares of towns 'close to the enemy's border, should echo with gun salvos, to lift people's spirits'.[50] The contested border towns had now experienced twenty years of raids, lack of trade and grudging warfare. They needed something to boost morale. But it was not just the border towns celebrating. This was an exciting time for Catherine to be living in Lisbon, as the *povo* spontaneously filled the streets, cheering '*il rey di Gran Britannia*'. Sparkling trails of green and citron filled the sky as the citizens let off fireworks, while dancing groups gathered in the squares.

To ensure that Catherine would settle into her new role as queen, letters were dispatched, with Charles addressing her as 'my wife and lady' and declaring that 'for me, the signing of the marriage has been great happiness', as though no thought of backing out in favour of an unspecified voluptuous Italian had ever occurred to him. Twitchily anxious for her arrival, he was off on a progress of his newly acquired kingdom, 'seeking, in vain, tranquillity in my restlessness; hoping to see the beloved person of your majesty in these kingdoms, already your own'.[51]

A servant was also sent with clothes and shoes to match the French-inspired fashions of the English court. Like the language and high culture of the Portuguese court that Catherine had grown up reading and learning about, Portuguese court fashions were distinctly Spanish. She and the other court ladies wore *guardinfante*, considered scandalous garments back in the late sixteenth century since they were effective in covering up unwanted pregnancies. Gradually they evolved into court fashion de rigueur, worn by even the most modest of maidens.[52] Rolls of padding were secured around the hips, followed either by layers of petticoats or hooped skirts that held the outer garment well away from the body and totally obscured the legs, giving the impression that the wearer was floating along the ground. It was elegant as long as one did not try to move too much, since *guardinfante* were rather cumbersome for getting through doors or navigating around furniture.

Catherine must have been glad to leave the contraption behind, as it was excessively uncomfortable. However, the garments that arrived for her to wear in her new home were rather shocking. Unpacking the boxes must have provoked confusion and some trepidation, particularly at the way some of the garments hugged her slight figure and dropped disconcertingly low at the front. While black predominated at the Spanish and Portuguese courts, this strange shipment from England introduced her to a riot of colourful clothing.

High heels were another odd fashion that were shipped over. Admittedly not stilettos, they were nonetheless precarious, with pointed toes and a blocky heel, tapering to the ground.

Gorgeous gold-thread embroidery, outsize silk pompoms or diamond-studded buckles showed off the wearer's social status. The sole or even the whole shoe was often bright red, the expensive dye showing off the wealth of the wearer. And unlike our more restrained palettes, late-seventeenth-century ladies had no problem with clashing colours, often wearing green or other dyed stockings to contrast with their red shoes. Gamely willing to try this odd new fashion, Catherine practised walking up and down the corridors of the Ribeira Palace in heels. Finding the balancing act a little difficult to master, she strained and bruised her foot.[53]

She had already begun familiarising herself with the language and culture of England. Becoming queen of another country was after all a serious business, and it would be advantageous for her to adapt and integrate with her subjects and court as quickly as possible: constantly dressing as a foreigner or not speaking the language would work against her political interests, not to mention her social ones – she needed, as do we all, to make some friends.

To pick up Catherine and bring her to England, Charles chose the ardent-Parliamentarian-turned-pragmatic-Royalist Edward Montagu, Earl of Sandwich, who had purged the navy of Republican officers in advance of his restoration. Sandwich was fair, upright and much starchier than his cousin Samuel Pepys (his mother being Paulina Pepys). The Montagu family were to play an important part in Catherine's queenship.

In a telling action that was not exactly complimentary to the young bride, after the marriage treaty had been signed by both sides, Sandwich immediately skipped Lisbon, dropping off a letter to Luisa announcing himself via one of his ship's smaller boats on 23 June 1661 and then heading straight off to agree peace treaties with Algiers, Tunis and Tripoli aiming to stop English vessels being confiscated and their crews enslaved.[54] This was not so extensive a problem as it had been a generation before, when slaving galleys had come as far as the Thames estuary, and frequently raided England, Wales and the Irish coast. However, it was a huge problem for shipping, and both Christian and Muslim vessels aggressively attacked one another for cargoes and men, with the lines of engagement delineated around religious differences (although only the Spanish went as far as mounting slave raids, and corsair slaving was in general undertaken by townspeople along the Barbary coast). Around this time, Pepys met two former slaves who had been captives in Algiers, who recounted their horror stories to him of 'how they eat nothing but bread and water . . . How they are beat upon the soles of the feet and bellies at the Liberty of their *Padron*.'[55]

Catherine, profoundly religious herself, was deeply concerned about slavery that was so starkly divided on religious lines. Even Christians would torture and enslave one another; one English Protestant escaped Turkish slavery only to become a prisoner of the Spanish Inquisition, which was 'now more cruel than the Turks, not knowing any cause why'.[56] It was a brutal and unforgiving world for sailors, although occasionally slaves would be treated well, and even freed if they converted to the 'correct' religion. However, if these converts were returned to their country of origin, they were termed 'renegados' or 'renegades', and subjected to intense hostility.

Terms not being agreed, Algiers bombarded the English fleet, which returned fire. In his journal, Sandwich recorded drily that the masts were damaged and some men killed, as though the damage to the ships was the more important of the two pieces of news. Leaving his second, Sir John Lawson, in charge to deal with the problem, he returned to Lisbon. Lawson (who had unknowingly promoted the marriage with his enthusiastic ideas about building a fort at Tangier) eventually dealt with the corsair problem in Algiers by capturing Algerian ships, releasing the British captives and taking the ships' crews as slaves instead. Eventually, the Algerians capitulated and signed a peace treaty. However, the whole enterprise was an exercise in futility. As soon as Lawson left for Lisbon, piracy began again; from 1672 to 1682, between 280 and 420 British slaves were taken annually by Algerian ships.[57]

But this was a future problem. By 9 September 1661, some three months after his message had arrived via boat, Sandwich was kissing Catherine's hands, granted an audience with the 'Queen of England' and the 'Queen Mother'. He was greeted with great magnanimity, particularly by his new young queen, who he described as gracious and supremely at ease in her surroundings. She was able to counsel him on matters of etiquette (unlike in England, earls in the presence of the King of Portugal wore their hats), her own manners exquisite.[58] Catherine was fully conversant with both the etiquette and minutiae of court life, alongside the perils faced by both her family and her country. Offset by the opulence of the palace, the Braganza wealth displayed in bright tapestries and gilt-edged tables, she made for a slim, elegant figure, made paler-looking by the fashionable Spanish black.

Sandwich had returned to Lisbon in the nick of time. Soon after his arrival, a large, well-equipped Spanish fleet had appeared at A Coruña (in Spanish, La Coruña), a sprawling port city in Galicía, the Spanish province touching northern Portugal. Ominously, the fleet continued sailing closer to Portugal, reaching one of the small islands off the coast of north-west Spain. There, they stopped. They had heard the news that the English fleet was at Lisbon. The advantage of surprise they had sought was gone. For 'jealousy of the English fleet', the Spanish were forced to turn back. Sandwich found out about these events some time later from the master of an English merchant vessel.[59] (The role of merchants is worth noting here: they were often the bearers of news, trying to make a living as they slipped between warring factions, but held hostage or their business confiscated when the political situation went wrong.)

Finally, after two years of negotiation and delay, the ships were readied for Catherine to leave. Luisa orchestrated celebrations that would both emphasise Portugal's wealth and importance to their foreign guests, and showcase the advantages of the marriage to the people. An outpouring of Portuguese texts celebrated the union, while the engraver Dirk Stoop created a series of popular etchings of the festivities. Bullfights, Masses and dancing enlivened the days and nights. For one such occasion, the ground was watered by a specially decorated cart so that dust didn't plume to choke the spectators. Tumblers and musicians then cavorted about the damp ground, followed by a bull, which footmen struck with darts, enraging the animal. Eventually they killed the tired beast to the sound of trumpets, repeating the process with another three or four animals. The next entertainment was the fabulously dressed Conde de Sarzedas, his servants decked in silver lace.[60] He marched up to Afonso, then Catherine, showing his obeisance, before killing any number of bulls with a lance.

Sandwich drily remarked, 'When all was killed that ought to be, then the Conde went up again and made his respect to the King and Queen as before and went away.'[61]

Luisa was anxious for her daughter to leave for England before winter set in and crossing by sea became more dangerous, but Sandwich had other priorities. Three days later, he was off on the second of his North African errands, this time securing part of Catherine's dowry: Tangier. He arrived on 10 October and celebrated the alliance with three nights of festivities, the town's guns firing to match those of his fleet. The citizens also 'hung out abundance of torches of light'.[62]

Tangier would be the focus of governmental ambitions, perhaps to the advantage of the rising 'Alawi power in North Africa, since the English made rather a hash of organising themselves. To put it crassly, Charles II was most interested in his new bride's money. After that, he liked the idea of owning Tangier, as we have seen, referring to it poetically as 'a jewell of immense value in the royal diadem'. The potential of Bombay, a deep-water port with close proximity to Surat – at the time 'the subcontinent's most important port' – was not widely appreciated at first.[63] Instead, Tangier was considered the more valuable possession. Located at the western entrance of the Strait of Gibraltar, the city overlooked the Mediterranean, 'the world's greatest center for commerce'.[64]

In the early stages of British possession, Pepys wrote that Tangier was 'likely to be the most considerable place the King of England hath in the world'.[65] In Portugal, its loss was as unpopular as its gain was popular in England. A Portuguese presence in North Africa was a particularly emotive topic, as it had long been policy to station troops there 'to project Portuguese power into Morocco'.[66] In 1550, far back in the time of the Aviz dynasty, Manuel I's son, the Infante Luis, described the walls of Tangier as 'living stone' soldiers, creating a kind of Christian barrier to police the boundary between Christendom and the Islamic world.[67] Luisa ordered that any references to Tangier be cut from the final reading of Catherine's marriage treaty, fearing that objections to its loss would upset the whole scheme.[68]

But the rising power of the 'Alawi dynasty in North Africa was making Tangier increasingly difficult for the Portuguese to hold onto (the 'Alawis remain the royal family to this day). And the English did not find it any easier. From 1661 until its loss in 1684, they poured two million pounds into the city, only to be forced to abandon it.[69] The plan was for Tangier to be a free port, meaning tax and customs rules did not apply, thereby undercutting other nearby ports where heavy duties were levied. The ambitious enterprise was funded partly by Catherine's dowry payment, and partly by the selling of Dunkirk back to the French – a deeply unpopular move in England, where the sale would sour Charles's reign almost from the very beginning.

The British attempted to pursue peace with Morocco and were rather surprised when the Moroccans did not wish to pursue it with them. The underfunded garrison at Tangier was always in danger of being overwhelmed.

English possession of Tangier was yet another afront to Spain, and they moved a huge number of troops from the border with Portugal to the coast of Andalusia, preparing for war should it break out.[70] The Spanish banned trade with Tangier, and settled for a kind of war-by-proxy, supplying arms for the north Moroccan leader Khadir Ghailan's attacks on the city.[71] When the English finally concluded a treaty with Ghailan, allowing them to use large strips of land around Tangier to grow their own food, Ghailan's armies were defeated weeks later by the new Sultan of Morocco, Mawlay Rachid. It was an unmitigated disaster. This 'Alawi sultan would eventually drive the English out of Morocco, forcing them to abandon Tangier. None of the plans to create a free port full of bustling trade would come to pass, but at the time of Catherine's wedding negotiations, it was the most glittering jewel in her dowry.

Finally, on 18 February 1662, 'About 5 o'clock in the morning, as soon as the west tide came', Sandwich 'weighed for Lisbon',[72] dropping off the 800 Portuguese who wished to leave Tangier on his way.[73] Naturally, many were angry at the peremptory way they'd been turfed out of a city that had been their home. On arriving to take possession, the English complained that the former occupants had taken everything with them, including what was nailed down, 'the very fflooers, the Windowes and the Dores', leaving Tangier 'very little better than a ruin of walls and full of spoile, scarsity and want as to all such materials and utensils as could have given assistance to English souldiers'.[74] It sounds uncannily like a student house of today.

Considering Luisa's desire for her daughter to be on her way to England four months earlier, Sandwich rather hypocritically sent Catherine 'a paper of reasons for her speedy voyage'.[75] Catherine and Luisa had no objections to his reasons, and made preparations to leave.

But in the saga of Catherine's marriage, nothing was ever simple. The first half of the dowry payment, for which Luisa had sold her plate and jewels, was supposed to be sent with Catherine to England. But war with the Spanish had become ferocious and help from England had yet to appear. Luisa had been forced to spend the money she had raised on troops and supplies. She therefore ordered the equivalent sum to be loaded onto Sandwich's ships in sugar, merchandise and bills of exchange. Sandwich, seeing what was being hauled up from the port in great crates, but also in mere notes of paper, immediately protested, saying that this went against the terms of the treaty, and he must have the payment 'in money, jewels, sugars or other merchandises'.[76] The truth was that this was impossible for Portugal to do, her funds having been so exhausted by war.

Sandwich went to see Catherine, who – sensible of the awkwardness of her position – was very 'gracious', receiving him with smiles and every appearance of friendly feeling. She attempted to conciliate him into accepting the bills of exchange and what merchandise they could cobble together instead of cash, arguing that she herself 'had overcome almost impossibilities to hasten her voyage' and that Sandwich should overcome this slight hiccup too, in order for them to be off. She also pointed out 'the poverty of the Portugal nation caused by the oppression of their enemies'.[77] Having narrowly escaped one Spanish fleet, she was concerned that the Spanish would attack as soon as Sandwich left with her for England, and urged him to move Sir John Lawson from Algiers to Lisbon for their better protection. Sandwich wrote that she 'assured me that both the King and the Duke of York would take it well at my hands', approving of such an action.[78] He duly did what she had asked.

She was already acting like a queen, personally escorting some of the dowry to Sandwich's quarters in Lisbon, doing all she could to smooth what could easily have become a diplomatic incident.[79] She was clearly trusted by her shrewd mother to have difficult conversations, and confident in being accepted as a powerful co-partner by Charles. She had all the assurance of a much-loved daughter and sister, but she had never been required to leave the comfortable aura of the family circle. It would be a sharp shock when she did so.

Meanwhile, there were renewed celebrations for the marriage. The evening before Catherine's departure, the Regiment of the City of Lisbon had organised a horseback show, riding with stirrups shortened, knees resting on the horses' shoulders, in order to showcase the regiment's prowess, the theory being that they could leap to their own defence better by riding in such a way. Competing against one another, they tried to unseat other riders in a display of athletic ability.

St George's Day was the date fixed for Catherine's departure. On the same day, Charles II was due to be crowned in Westminster Abbey. It had been agreed that it was best for this to happen before he and Catherine were married, avoiding the awkwardness of a Catholic queen going through a Protestant ceremony. When the day arrived for Catherine to set off to meet her new husband, she processed through Lisbon on the way to the ship via hastily erected fountains, columns and magnificently decorated arches, as well as a bridge built specially for her. Appropriately, the English arch was embellished with a statue of St George. It was a time of great excitement mingled with fear; Catherine only spoke a few words of English, and she had no idea what was waiting for her in her new country, never having left Portugal in her life, and confined mostly to the palace in Lisbon.

Unusually for royal marriages of the time, Catherine and Charles were not married by proxy, as the Pope – bowing to Spanish pressure – had yet to recognise Portugal as a country independent from the Hapsburg Empire. Sandwich, as Charles's representative in Lisbon, accompanied Catherine through processions and blessings in Portugal, but did not stand next to her in a proxy marriage.

Over in England, de Melo was suitably melodramatic about the terrible risk Portugal was taking by sending off a technically unmarried infanta; this 'was such a Trust that had never been reposed in any Prince'. If Charles broke his word and did not marry her, there would be 'an everlasting Reproach upon their Nation'.[80] He possibly emphasised this so the king did not make a fuss about the dowry. The Portuguese had put their trust in Charles; he could not give Catherine back over such a minor thing as money.

As soon as Catherine boarded the *Royal Charles* on 22 April 1662, the fleet fired gun salvos, while rockets and squibs (fireworks that hiss as they burn) were set off through the night in the run-up to her early-morning departure, cracking and fizzing through the sky and filling the air with smoke. The ship had been quickly and tactfully renamed on her husband's restoration to the throne: its original title was the *Naseby*, after the decisive Parliamentarian victory that marked the beginning of the end for Royalist forces during the Civil War. Tapestries picked out with threads of gold, vermilion and lapis-lazuli blue lined Catherine's staterooms, the ship a statement of power and prestige as much as it was a functioning boat. Her brothers Afonso and Pedro came aboard to say goodbye, Afonso returning incognito in a barge to serenade his sister, a typical Braganza gesture since they all loved music.[81] The young princes seem to have delighted in the celebrations, enjoying the festival atmosphere and their own importance in seeing their elder sister off.

Catherine and Luisa kissed one another on shore for the last time. They both knew that this was the end. After twenty-four years of almost constant companionship, it was unlikely that they would ever see one another again. Catherine had already lost her father, brother and sister, and now she said goodbye to her closest living relative. Luisa later lamented, 'My daughter And all my love, without you . . . my pain . . . increases with the lack of seeing you.'[82]

At six o'clock in the morning of 23 April, the *Royal Charles* weighed anchor and set sail. Catherine was journeying to an unfamiliar land with strange new customs. It would be one of the most challenging periods of her life.

4

Marriage and the Mistress

AFTER THE EMOTION of celebration, leave-taking and boarding the sumptuous *Royal Charles* to sail for new shores, Catherine and all her ladies were promptly seasick, with storms delaying the journey.

Catherine was attended by a vast suite of servants and companions, including six chaplains, four cooks, a barber and her own personal perfumer, should any scent emergencies occur on the month-long voyage from Lisbon to Portsmouth.[1] Although the *Royal Charles* was luxurious, no seventeenth-century ship was perfectly comfortable. The smell of salt-soaked timber mingled with rotting food and chamber pots that were sometimes emptied into the bilge by lazy servants, creating a disgusting soup of odorous organic matter that even the world's greatest perfumer could not obliterate. The boat was rocked by storms and most of the passage was extremely unpleasant.

While Catherine was busy being seasick, there was almost immediately trouble on board. The source was her dowry, in large part chests of expensive sugar, which she had personally seen loaded as cargo. At the end of April, these were broken into, and a council of war to try the men responsible was held. Their fate is not recorded, but most likely they were flogged.[2]

On 7 May, the ship was finally in sight of English soil, approaching St Michael's Mount in Cornwall. In the morning, the owner of the island 'came on board and brought the Queen a present of fresh provisions'.[3]

At sunset on 11 May, the king's brother, James, Duke of York, was the first to greet Catherine. As the *Royal Charles* sailed towards Portsmouth, James steered his trim yacht alongside and hopped between their boats to visit her every day. He was attended by a panoply of notables from the court, including the Duke of Ormond and the Earl of Suffolk, all jostling to catch a first glimpse of their new queen. Catherine was gracious in her reception, despite still feeling horribly seasick. Despite her having possibly met Prince Rupert in Lisbon, the courtiers informal manners are likely to have surprised her, as well as the competing colours of their silks and satins – all would have been dressed to impress. As the whole party came towards Portsmouth, the sea calmed and things began, finally, to look up. They sailed slowly into the harbour, passing grass-ringed marshes and glossy mudflats, with long-legged plover searching for cockles, accompanied by the cries of gulls overhead.

Legend has it that, wobbly-legged and haggard after the journey, Catherine was offered a mug of ale immediately on her arrival at Portsmouth. She was not impressed with the idea, requesting a simple cup of tea instead, much to the surprise of the English who had gathered to meet her. It was a common beverage at her own court in Lisbon but was more often seen as medicine in England rather than a sophisticated drink. Her request created a sensation, and the court quickly picked up the new habit. Catherine's tastes helped to popularise tea, making its pouring, consumption and display a fashionable pastime that has defined British life for centuries.[4] A later tribute to her in honour of her birthday hailed it as her crowning achievement, with poet Edmund Waller writing:

> Venus her myrtle, Phoebus has her bays;
> Tea both excels, which she vouchsafes to praise.
> The best of Queens, and the best of herbs, we owe
> To that bold nation, which the way did show
> To the fair region where the sun doth rise,
> Whose rich productions we so justly prize.
> The Muse's friend, tea does our fancy aid,
> Repress those vapours which the head invade,
> And keep the palace of the soul serene,
> Fit on her birthday to salute the Queen.[5]

Now that the seasickness had abated, Catherine was beset by a dreadful cold, only able to peep her head over the covers to greet her new husband when he arrived to meet her in Portsmouth. She was staying at the governor's house, greeted with bonfires and the sound of every bell in the town ringing to celebrate her arrival. The couple conversed amiably enough in Spanish, which Charles had picked up while in exile. Impressively, he seems to have learned the language from reading a Spanish New Testament.[6] His first impression of his new wife was good; he wrote that 'her face is not so exact as to be caled a beuty, though her eyes are excellent good, and not anything in her face that can shoque one, on the contrary, she hath as much agreeable-nesse in her lookes althogether as ever I saw, and if I have any skill in visiognimy, which I thinke I have, she must be as good a woman as ever was borne'.[7]

Along with many of the more legitimate sciences, Charles was fascinated by physiognomy, believing he could tell a person's temperament and character traits from looking at their head. The pseudo-science was an odd combination of religion and contemporary interest in anatomy, and closely associated with the science of chiromancy, or palm-reading.[8] Charles was too polite to mention it, but the English found Catherine's hair distinctly odd: resembling a heavy noughties side fringe, a quantity of hair was teased from a side parting to cover her forehead, giving her a peculiar air despite her adoption of English fashions in dress. Charles reported that 'Her conversation, as much as I can perceave, is very good; for she has witt enough, and a most agreeable voyse.'[9] While this praise may seem somewhat tepid, it was not a bad beginning as royal marriages went – compared with the French king Louis XIV's match with his wife, it was positively doting. Looking back over his long life and many lovers, Louis wrote that 'Of all the women I have ever known . . . she was the only one I never loved.'[10]

We do not have a record of Catherine's immediate reaction to Charles. She was a short woman, and at just over six feet in height, he must have loomed over her. Portraits show a man with deep-set eyes, a wide mouth and a Roman nose. His face was serious in repose, but softened, eyes sparkling, when he spoke. Years of anxiety junketing about the continent, unsure of his status as an exiled king and practically begging at foreign courts for two buttons to rub together, had turned his boyishly handsome face grave and lean, with lines carved about his mouth and cheeks. He was reported to be 'a black grim man', 'black' meaning dark or olive-complexioned at the time, the seriousness of his countenance at odds with his legacy as the 'Merrie Monarch'.[11]

His figure was generally considered excellent, with long legs and finely shaped hands; 'so exactly formed, that the most curious Eye cannot find one Error in his shape'.[12] He and Catherine shared an abundance of hair, his 'of a shining black, not frizzled, but so Naturally Curling into great Rings, that it is a very comely Ornament'.[13] As for the qualities of his mind, one observer wrote that, 'his most Transcendently Symmetrical Organs are full stretcht'.[14] Charles was indeed a clever man, with a quick person's impatience for stupidity and slowness. He was reluctant to put sustained hard work into any project, relying instead on flashes of brilliance. Catherine likely appreciated that her new husband was an excellent, relaxed conversationalist. He also swore seldom, his favourite expletive the mild 'oddsfish', a corrupted blasphemy from 'God's flesh'.[15]

Catherine and Charles had a private Catholic ceremony in Catherine's room before an almost entirely Portuguese audience, followed by a public Protestant ceremony at the house of the governor of Portsmouth. Compared with the royal weddings of today, it was a low-key affair. The new queen wore a rose-coloured dress made in English fashion, a much racier style than that permitted to noble ladies in Portugal: a low-cut, rounded neck-line that exposed breast and shoulders, with enormous puffy sleeves and a tiny, corseted waist.[16] Her outfit was embellished with love knots of blue ribbon that – as was Portuguese trad-ition – were snipped off and given to those present, a sign of the enduring ties of love and marriage. So many had crowded in to see the couple married that the ribbons had to be snipped into minuscule pieces to be handed around. Catherine's dress was overlaid with a lace wrap covered in crowns, Tudor roses and oak leaves – a symbol of monarchy as well as a possible nod to Charles's narrow escape from Parliamentary forces, hiding in an oak tree after the Battle of Worcester.[17] Everything about the occasion was carefully curated to project the right political associations. Poor Catherine smiled through her residual sickness at the huge crowd of gawkers assembled to watch her marriage.

The storms that had made the journey so disagreeable had also delayed the date of sailing, upsetting the carefully calculated wedding date, meaning that Catherine was on her period on her wedding night and unable to sleep with Charles. Usually, weddings were timed to avoid the awkwardness of periods, but the king joked to his beloved sister Henriette that 'the curse that followes our family is fallen upon me', as she had had a similar experience on her own wedding night. He explained, 'car Monr Le Cardinal m'a fermé la porte au nez' ('because the cardinal closed the door in my face') – the phrase playing on the traditional red of a cardinal's outfit and its association with blood – and wrote that 'he was content to let those [courses/ period] passe over before I go to bed my wife', believing that he had been so jolted in the carriage ride down to Portsmouth that he probably would not have been able to perform to his satisfaction anyway. However, he hoped to do better than his sister's husband during that couple's first attempt at sex – Philippe, Duc d'Orléans, had apparently put in a disappointing performance, possibly because he was gay, although he may have been bisexual.[18]

When Catherine and Charles's bedding did eventually happen, it was instantly common knowledge, discussed as casually as them supping together. In his journal on 25 May, Sandwich

records, 'The King at night first bedded the Queen.'[19] This public interest in her intensely private life would not have shocked
Catherine, accustomed as she was to a similar atmosphere in
Lisbon. Signs of consummation and evidence of periods were
openly discussed. A monarch's body was not, after all, ever really
their own; it was always in part public property, however much
they might wish to be private.

After their Portsmouth wedding, Catherine and Charles toured
the country on honeymoon. It was cold and wet in her new
home, and having to smile along to a foreign language (French
rather than Spanish was the language of the educated), with no
real friends or allies, could be at times a trial to endure. So many
people thronged the dining hall at Hampton Court hoping to
see her that she had to rush out of the room, her make-up threatening to run off her face with sweat.[20] On a magnificent parade
of gilded barges and boats on the Thames from Hampton Court
to Whitehall organised in her honour, one observer recorded
that Catherine looked like a captive in a Roman triumph, being
shown off to the curious.[21] Her doll-like figure remained stiff,
teeth gritted, as she was taken to the university towns and celebrated there. One congratulatory verse recorded:

> See how unmov'd She views the Crowd and show
> As stars above men's toils below.[22]

Another from the same volume of Oxford notables cried, 'You
are already a goddess to me Catherine!'[23] While she may have
been a little stiff, her public was overjoyed to see a new queen
installed, and wherever she travelled, the streets teemed with
curious well-wishers.

Charles was charming, using the caresses and expressions of affection that came naturally to him. Catherine was happy to finally have done her part in completing the treaty. Whatever grumbles the English might make about her dowry payment, they could not go back on the agreement now. Her mother had told her while still in Portugal that Charles had a mistress, and was not likely to be entirely faithful, but she had grown up with such things and expected to be treated with the same respect in public that Luisa had been. She had yet to understand the primed powder keg waiting at her new home, Hampton Court.

Catherine was hailed by the people as a sister-in-arms, a 'persecuted maid' that Charles had been right to rescue from Spanish oppression.[24] Rumours of her fabulous dowry also boosted her popularity; it was hoped that it would bring prosperity to the country, especially since many Royalists were still impoverished from the Civil War and their loss of property afterwards. A popular ballad called 'The Cavaliers Comfort' hoped that 'Cavaliers may all be paid' with the proceeds of Catherine's dowry.[25]

When Catherine arrived, an heir was expected to follow soon after, and was as much a theme of the panegyrics celebrating the marriage as was victory against Spain. On first seeing Catherine at the queen dowager Henrietta Maria's residence of Somerset House, Pepys recalls the new couple's jocularity on the subject of the succession: 'The King and Queen were very merry; and he would have made the Queen-Mother believe that his Queen was with child, and said that she said so. And the young Queen answered, "You lye;" which was the first English word that I ever heard her say which made the King good sport; and he would have taught her to say in English, "Confess and be hanged."'[26]

At least in public, then, Catherine and Charles appeared to be pleased with one another, joking together as Catherine became more comfortable both with English and with the public display inherent in British court life. But this relatively easy transition into a new and alien culture was to suffer a severe setback with the entrance of Charles's long-time mistress Barbara Palmer, Countess of Castlemaine.

It goes without saying that Castlemaine was beautiful. But she had something beyond beauty. Graceful and voluptuous, she practically patented the heavy-lidded look that was de rigueur for ladies of the time, as though they were all perpetually either thinking about the bedchamber or just emerging from it.

Charles and Castlemaine had met in 1660 when Castlemaine and her long-suffering husband, Roger Palmer, hearing news of Charles's imminent arrival back in Britain, had gone to the Hague to seek favour from the soon-to-be king. They certainly found it, although not quite in the way Roger Palmer had hoped.

Beautiful, tempestuous and strong-willed, Barbara Castlemaine was possessed of sexual appetites that were the subject of many a bawdy verse, including the Earl of Rochester's claim that she 'has swallowed more pricks than the nation has land'.[27] Samuel Pepys felt a frisson of desire merely seeing her petticoats and smocks drying outside Whitehall.[28] By the time of Catherine's arrival on the scene in 1662, Castlemaine had already presented Charles with two children: a daughter, Anne (although another of her lovers also claimed parentage), and a son, Charles. She had actually given birth to Charles during Catherine and Charles II's honeymoon, insisting on doing so at the royal couple's future home of Hampton Court. This did not bode well for a harmonious married life. Unlike the rest of the nation, she had refused to light a fire outside her bedroom door to welcome the queen, the lack of fire very noticeable when the whole country was ablaze.[29]

For reasons best known to himself, Charles believed that the way to avoid temptation now that he was a sober married man was to place Castlemaine as near as possible to his new wife, perhaps hoping to remove her voluptuous appeal by daily association with the stodginess of married life. Whatever his motivations, Catherine was outraged when he suggested that his mistress serve her as a lady of the bedchamber, a prestigious position with duties that included dressing the queen. Typically this role was taken by some of the highest-ranking women in the land, and those whom the queen particularly favoured.

Catherine had promised her mother that not only would she not meet with Castlemaine, she would never have the lady's name even alluded to in her presence, let alone allowing her husband's mistress to help dress her every day.[30] She scratched Castlemaine's name from Charles's suggested list of attendants and refused to meet her. In response, Charles took an exceptionally theatrical stance, asserting that 'I wish I may be unhappy in this world and in the world to come, if I faile in the least degree of what I have resolved, which is, of making my Lady Castlemaine of my wive's bedchamber.' Not only did he hope to have an unhappy afterlife if Castlemaine did not become a lady of the bedchamber, he promised that 'whosoever I find use any endeavour to hinder this resolution of myne . . . I will be his enemy to the last moment of my life'.[31] He had found it in his heart to forgive most of the people connected to his father's beheading, so this was an extreme statement indeed. Perhaps a self-conscious awareness of his own unreasonableness led to this melodramatically entrenched position.

Catherine and Charles were quickly at loggerheads with one another, and neither was willing to compromise. As Charles became more unreasonable, Catherine grew melodramatic in her own statements: she asked not to see Castlemaine, 'or that he would send her from whence she come'. The king raged, while Catherine was 'discontented a whole day and night upon it', Charles promising to have nothing more to do with her. Pepys did not believe Charles's histrionics, thinking that he loved Catherine too well already to throw her off, and indeed it would have created not only a very awkward social dynamic but a precarious diplomatic situation.[32]

Far from the reception she had expected as a new queen – and been led to expect by Charles's charming letters – Catherine was plunged into the worst court intrigue, before she had managed to make alliances or master anything but the bare minimum of the new language. In Portugal she had known every nuance of the language and etiquette; it was a steep learning curve to earn back some of that knowledge when she reached England, and she would have to fight tenaciously for it.

Castlemaine's supporters, on the other hand, stoked Charles's determination to do as he wished with his mistress by reminding him of his French grandfather, Henri IV, who was known as 'Le Vert Gallant' or 'the vigorous man' for how much he enjoyed the company of women. Being a renowned philanderer did not impact Henri's public reputation negatively: his other appellation was 'good King Henri'. Charles, so this reasoning went, was perfectly justified in having as many mistresses as he liked, and displaying them as publicly as he wanted. The reasoning was not, in fact, wrong: during his reign, he was called 'Good King Charles' and, for his sexual escapades, 'Old Rowley', after one of his prize stallions that sired many foals.

In an attempt to persuade Catherine to accept Castlemaine, Charles resorted to trickery. He assured her that he would not press her and would let the matter lie, before bringing Castlemaine into her presence and introducing them at a public event. Catherine, not recognising this stranger, greeted the other woman politely. When she discovered who she was, her nose started bleeding and she fell into a swoon, before being carried out of the room. Later, she and Charles had a screaming row, which was so loud that – according to the Lord Chancellor Clarendon – 'the passion and noise of the night reached too many ears to be secret the next day; and the whole Court was full of that, which ought to have been known to nobody'.[33]

Catherine was friendless in a strange country, and Charles made this worse by sending many of her attendants back to Portugal. At public events, she 'sat untaken notice of', and court gossip simmered maliciously. The king was openly affectionate towards Castlemaine, and indeed, anyone other than Catherine. Clarendon tells us, 'She alone was left out of all jollities, and not suffered to have any part in those pleasant applications and caresses that she saw made abroad to everybody else.' Even her attendants abandoned her, showing more respect to Castlemaine, who, unlike their neglected and unpopular queen, could advance them socially and politically.[34] In a letter to her brother Pedro, which may well have been alluding to the bedchamber incident and other similar humiliations, Catherine wrote that 'my only Consolation' is 'I suffer on your behalf & for my mother Country which I love soe much'.[35] She threatened to return to her beloved

Portugal if she had to acknowledge Charles's mistress. She was intensely patriotic, referring to Portugal alternately as her 'native land' and 'fatherland'.[36] Anyone who talked about Portugal positively found favour with her, and anyone who insulted it was instantly in her black books.

Losing patience, Charles sent Clarendon to reason with her. This Clarendon did with extreme reluctance, believing that 'flesh and blood could not comply with' the scheme.[37] Himself a conservative and a staunchly upright Anglican, he would not let his own wife consort with someone as disreputable as Castlemaine. Catherine did not bend immediately, but the tremendous social pressure that was already bearing upon her may have combined with Portugal's urgent need for military aid. Her mother remained unable to pay the full dowry from her war-weakened coffers but desperately needed British troops to fight the Spanish. With one side of the bargain unfulfilled, Charles could easily have prevaricated in fulfilling his side had the marriage not proved successful.

If Catherine had carried through on her threat to return to Portugal, the Anglo-Portuguese alliance would have been at an end, and the history of Portugal as we now know it may have been very different; the war her brother and mother were fighting for independence against Spain would certainly have been an even harder fight. Perhaps in an alternate dimension where she did return to her homeland, the whole Iberian peninsula speaks Spanish.

To make matters worse for Catherine's precarious situation at the English court, the news was just filtering through that her mother, the formidable Luisa, had been ousted from power by a palace coup in Lisbon, and effectively replaced by the Count of Castelo Melhor. Pale-complexioned and perturbed-looking,

Castelo Melhor was ostensibly taking the part of her son, King Afonso, convincing the young monarch that his mother was trying to steal his throne. To be fair, she was: she had already held onto power beyond the age of Afonso's majority, and by 1662, he was nineteen.

Luisa retired to a convent. So far, so simple. Castelo Melhor retained close ties with England, but also sought an alliance with France in order to unite the Portuguese court, which was riven with infighting between pro-French and pro-English factions. There was little Luisa could do. To what extent Afonso was capable of kingship has been hotly debated: his childhood meningitis left lasting health effects that may have hindered him in his rule and caused overreliance on his advisers, in particular Castelo Melhor.[38]

Losing the political support of her mother made Catherine's position in Britain even more tenuous: Afonso, with mistresses aplenty of his own, was unlikely to offer any diplomatic aid should she refuse to do what her new husband told her to and recognise his mistress. Bowing to political necessity, she finally accepted the scandalous Countess of Castlemaine's presence as one of her ladies of the bedchamber. The Anglo-Portuguese alliance was maintained, and later the same year, British troops were sent as promised to support the Portuguese Restoration War.

Thankfully, Charles had many well-trained and experienced troops who had fought through the Civil War. The war against Spain proved a convenient way for him to get rid of a large group of potentially destructive demobilised soldiers, many of whom had fought for Cromwell and were not exactly ideologically sympathetic to their new monarch.[39] Since his restoration, observers noted that radical 'ill humours' had rippled through the mostly Parliamentarian army that had brought down his father. On swearing fealty to the new king, the troops' faces 'did sufficiently manifest, that They were drawn thither to a Service They were not delighted in'.[40] Ex-soldiers around the country, meanwhile, had been re-arming in case of a second civil war. Soon, so many weapons had been confiscated from these stockpiles that even the cavernous Tower of London ran out of storage space.

It was a relief for Charles and his government to have somewhere to send these ambiguously loyal soldiers, and possibly an external enemy at which to direct some of the tense animosities and ill humours that still simmered in a long-divided Britain. War with Spain was always going to play well with the British people, and declaring any kind of war is almost always a popular political move in the short term. Between 1662 and 1668, 4,500 British soldiers were sent to relieve Portugal.

Within the year, British musketeers had helped prevent a Spanish incursion into the heart of Portugal. They followed this up by storming San Antonio, the strongest fort in the outworks of Évora, a strategic Portuguese frontier town, and putting their enemies 'to the sword'.[41] The troops' Cromwellian reputation for ruthlessness proved helpful on the battlefield; one contingent of Spanish cavalry is said to have fled crying, 'There come the British redcoats, who give no quarter.'[42] The Portuguese Restoration War was to provide the greatest military successes of Charles II's reign, and the news of every victorious battle was celebrated with bonfires and strong drink all over Britain, even as it was becoming increasingly hard to keep up the supply of troops.

The English soldiers were led by the Catholic Earl of Inchiquin, who had little faith in the conflict ending well, his eldest son already having lost an eye in the fighting against Spain.[43] Treated by some of their Royalist commanders as 'Cromwells whelps and rebels', banished to Portugal 'for murdering the late King', the rank-and-file troops were badly paid and poorly fed. They died in great numbers, only about 800 surviving to see an end of the conflict.[44] Recruiting more soldiers to replace the dead proved difficult: in 1663, many new recruits ran away after rumours spread that they were being sold as slaves in exchange for sugar.[45] Diplomatically, Britain began to press Spain for peace, and helped finally to negotiate the end of the war in 1668.

Most historians agree that Catherine's capitulation to Charles's melodramatic demands over Castlemaine soured their relationship, with Ronald Hutton claiming that it ended the 'secret respect' her husband held for her and finished any hope of a loving marriage. There is little evidence for this other than the assumption that a man must be faithful to his wife in order to love or respect her.[46] Charles may not have loved Catherine like a conventional faithful hero from a romance, but he did feel genuine affection for his wife. After the bedchamber incident had blown over, he spent almost every night in her bedroom, however often he may have supped with his mistresses. In this incident as in many others, Charles was insistent on getting his own way, but was indulgent as long as his pleasures were not thwarted.

After Catherine's capitulation, he was openly affectionate towards her, and became fiercely jealous. Following a rumour that her newly appointed Master of the Horse, Edward Montagu, had squeezed the queen's hand, Charles ordered him away from court. Ironically, the autocratic and rather brazen Edward was replaced by his brother Ralph, generally known as a ladies' man. Ralph, however, learned from his brother's mistakes. He decided not to fix his attention on the queen, focusing instead on a succession of mistresses and latterly wooing a second wife, whom he allegedly courted in disguise, pretending to be the Emperor of China, since she had vowed to only wed a royal.[47] For ever after, the lady's servants treated her and served her meals as though she really were the Empress of China.

The bedchamber incident was a defining moment in Catherine's tenure as Queen of England, teaching her of the precariousness of her position. However unreasonable Charles's behaviour – and even his doting sister Henriette believed that he had acted entirely unfairly – the court would side with him.[48] Catherine needed friends, she needed to be able to communicate with the court, and she needed to keep the king on her side. She had tried arguments and tears with him, and neither had worked. Instead, she would need a new strategy if she was to prosper in her role as queen. This would involve assimilation within the court on the one hand, and tactfulness with Charles on the other.

She strove thereafter to be on excellent terms with her husband's mistresses and many illegitimate children. Although there was friction and jealousy to spare at the beginning of their relationship, she and Castlemaine eventually rubbed along pretty well, riding out to take the air in the queen's carriage, attending the same balls, and dining together. Catherine also showed favour to Charles's eldest illegitimate son, the Duke of Monmouth (son of an earlier mistress, Lucy Walter). To prove that the quarrel was well and truly over, she ostentatiously shared a coach with both Castlemaine and Monmouth in public, and spoke kindly about Castlemaine. Catherine had learned that acting a part was the way to secure social and political harmony. And she had achieved her aim of securing aid for Portugal, which was always the most important objective of her political life.

But being Old Rowley's queen was never entirely easy: in 1664, Pepys recorded that 'the King still do doat upon his women, even beyond all shame; and that the good Queen will of herself stop before she goes sometimes into her dressing-room, till she knows whether the King be there', dallying with one of his paramours.[49] Catherine was careful to avoid situations that would embarrass both her and Charles, whatever mortification it cost her. Maintained by her steadfast tact, this relatively amicable situation was very unlike the relationships between some of Charles's mistresses. Actress Nell Gwyn went as far as putting laxatives in her rivals' food when she knew the king was due to visit them.

Thanks to Catherine's compromising, by 1663 she and Charles were well and truly reconciled. He attended her personally during her illness that year, when Samuel Pepys described her 'as full of the spots as a leopard'. It was probably an attack of typhus, whose symptoms can include delirium, fever and a red rash all over the body.[50] The disease is transmitted by lice and is generally associated with poor sanitation; no surprise considering Catherine's environment at Whitehall. Although she was surrounded by fashionable luxuries, washing the rich fabrics of her wardrobe, particularly heavy velvets, brocades and delicate embroidery, was almost impossible to do thoroughly. Accordingly, like any Restoration nobleman or woman, she wore fine linen garments under the richer fabrics, often changing these several times a day. But the outer layer could be worn for years with only cursory washing, harbouring any bug that cared to make its home there. Lice were commonplace, even for the queen.

As she lay delirious in bed, Catherine believed she was going to die, and the king was openly grief-stricken. She became so ill 'as to be shaved and pidgeons put to her feet, and to have the extreme unction given her by the priests'.[51] Pigeons were the Restoration medical treatment of last resort, showing that her illness was serious indeed.[52] The cure involved a bird being killed, swiftly sliced open and placed on the feet of the patient while still warm, its blood continuing to pump from the heart. The live, healthy body of the pigeon was thought to draw out the pestilence of the wound. For all we know, the semi-mystical cure worked in Catherine's case: she survived, and the attending physician, Sir Francis Prujean, was acclaimed for his virtuoso pigeon-slicing skills.

By the end of 1663, Catherine had survived court politics and a near-death brush with typhus. She had ensured that Britain continued its war against Spain for her homeland's independence. But the war in Portugal had not yet been won, half her dowry remained unpaid, and there were no whisperings of a hoped-for heir. She still barely spoke English, and had no allies to warn her of potential pitfalls, politically or socially. Most of her familiar Portuguese followers had been sent home, and her husband's mistress was one of her chief attendants. Her position remained extremely tenuous.

5

Fashion and Frivolity

IN SEVENTEENTH-CENTURY BRITAIN, it was almost impossible to keep a secret. Rumour and gossip spread faster than an internet connection, often becoming strangely garbled between one overheard conversation and another. Speakers might try to escape to a park or garden for privacy, but even then confidentiality wasn't guaranteed.

Amongst this society of inveterate chatterers, the single greatest gossip of the time was the Irish-born courtier Anthony Hamilton. Obsessed with the complex social interplay of courtiers, royals, their hangers-on and their servants, he reported that 'The queen was a woman of sense, and used all her endeavours to please the king, by that kind obliging behaviour which her affection made natural to her: she was particularly attentive in promoting every sort of pleasure and amusement especially such as she could be present at herself.'[1]

Catherine put on masques, ballets, dances, plays; anything to amuse a group of jaded courtiers, some of whom had experienced more adventure during the Civil War than anyone could wish for. In doing so, she sought to gain allies: her arrival, friendless and unpitied as she fought her husband, had been a baptism of fire. Moreover, if she was to claim any political benefit for her home country, she needed a complacent king and court who would continue to support the war for independence.

When she had arrived, shy and pious, in England in 1662, Catherine had been overwhelmed by the public display and noise of British court life. However, the new queen was blessed with a naturally lively disposition, and swiftly adapted to living her life under scrutiny. She also quickly made one crucial ally: Charles's mother, the dowager queen Henrietta Maria, who had set up her own residence in Somerset House. She was fifty-two at the time of Catherine's marriage, full of life and – most importantly – influence. Admittedly, Charles had been known to avoid her on awkward occasions as he did not enjoy being taken to task by his mother, but she was a loved and respected force to be reckoned with.

Not only did Henrietta Maria offer her public support to Catherine, she would also serve as a model for the new queen in terms of her social power, developing a practice called a 'circle' – essentially a precursor of the great eighteenth-century salon. Before the Civil War, Henrietta Maria had been England's premier hostess, gathering around her the great and the good, the interesting and the important. As soon as she returned to England, she had reintroduced these circles – so termed because everyone circled around the queen dowager, as though she were the star and they the planets. In practice, the circles were convivial evening assemblies where – as the French ambassador put it – 'all the people couldn't fail to find themselves'.[2] Catherine could be found there frequently, sitting next to the dowager queen in great favour, watching as the king mingled informally with ambassadors, statesmen and even lowly civil servants like Samuel Pepys.

Seeing their utility and their popularity, Catherine very soon instituted her own daily circles, and they would be an important step in her path towards gathering alliances and taking back her place in English court life that had been wrested from her in the earliest days of her queenship. Initially she copied her mother-in-law, using her own presence chamber to host these assemblies. Catherine seated herself under a velvet dais embroidered with England's coat of arms, a celebration of royal status. However, this was rather formal, not suiting either her husband or her own love of cards and high jinks – as we shall see later. She quickly changed the venue to her withdrawing room (later the 'with' was dropped, and in great houses these more relaxed chambers were just called 'drawing rooms'). This was close to the most private sanctum – her bedroom – meaning that on at least one occasion the circle still went ahead while she was ill, Catherine presiding over the whole thing from her bed. During the summer, guests spilled out onto the terrace facing the Thames.[3]

There was no formal canopy of state or raised dais, but instead two armchairs and ten stools – the armchairs were of course reserved for royalty. At the beginning of the evening, guests would stand around Catherine's armchair, entertaining her on various subjects. Ambassadors were frequent visitors, since – as the Danish envoy reported – Catherine's circle featured 'many high ladies and cavaliers who ordinarily assemble every evening in her majesty's room to wait upon their majesties, who usually find themselves there'.[4] The king came most evenings, as did the next in line to the throne, the Duke of York. The presence of the regal brothers was a draw, and could even provoke undignified jostling. In 1673, Ralph Montagu was elbowed aside by the Duke of Buckingham as the latter tried to get the king's attention. Such a lapse of manners was hot gossip at the time.[5]

Almost every evening throughout Catherine's reign, circles were a staple, only cancelled altogether when she was too ill even to direct the occasion from bed. That she adopted the practice so quickly and adapted it to both her own preference and her husband's love of informality reflects her tactics throughout her reign: she strove to win friends and assimilate people, often quietly but with a steely determination to preside over court life and adapt herself to the strange manners of the time that can only be admired.

The circles – as the great elbowing incident of 1673 indicates – were not just social affairs. They were political. And they had one great advantage over other political affairs: they were informal. Many a deal or a treaty was likely to be discussed at Catherine's circles, but unfortunately because of their unofficial nature we only have the barest snippets, hints of gossip and news exchanged. On multiple occasions, Charles or James would take a favoured or particularly useful person into Catherine's bedroom to have a more private chat.

One of the clearest examples of the circles' under-the-radar political value was the visit of Cosimo III de Medici, Grand Duke of Tuscany. Hearing the Medici name, a reader might think of wealth, power and the notorious excesses of one of the most famous families ever to have lived. Cosimo's forebear Lorenzo the Magnificent, for example, had a pet giraffe. But Lorenzo was also not very good at the family industry – banking – which brings us to the unfortunate Cosimo III. His ancestors had run through much of the family money, and most unfortunately, he had married a French princess called Marguerite Louise, who was spoiled, frivolous and possibly having an affair with her cousin when they wed. On the other hand, Cosimo had decided to stop smiling in public by the time he met his fun-loving new wife. Not exactly a match made in heaven. Marguerite Louise seemed to enjoy humiliating him: on one notable occasion, she tried to smuggle the crown jewels out of Tuscany, and also refused to employ local cooks, complaining that her husband was trying to poison her. Cosimo, despite his intense religiosity, was not a saint either – he put forty guards on his wife to watch her day and night in case she escaped back to France.

This is all to say that, by 1667, Cosimo had had enough, embarking on a series of European travels. In March 1669, he sailed from Portugal to England – where he was probably doubly welcomed by Catherine, bearing the latest news from her home country. But as soon as he arrived, he presented a problem: he was not travelling on an official state visit, but rather semi-incognito. He could not be received with all the trappings that were usual for the very rare visit of a foreign ruler. Catherine's circles provided the perfect middle ground: Charles, Catherine and the nobility could receive Cosimo daily, but informally. He sat on her recently reupholstered sky-blue stools, brocade and jewels glittering under a chandelier, and did not have to declare some definite diplomatic intent.

Catherine adored ombre, a card game of Spanish origin that is something like bridge, only with *matadores* – cards that serve as additional trumps and are laid down to triumphant cries of '*Matadores!*', livening up the game. She liked to 'rule over the chatter of the women for three or four hours a day, leaving this at times to play ombre in the same room',[6] and calling out to any passer-by to come and join the game, regardless of the etiquette supposed to govern a queen and her subjects.

This observation of an entirely leisured life given over to gambling and pointless talk is not quite accurate. The apparently meaningless chatter included audiences for both domestic and foreign visitors, an important ambassadorial function. Foreign diplomats in particular were received with a display of ceremony designed to dazzle them with the wealth and power of the court. French diplomat Balthasar de Monconys recalls being ushered into Catherine's presence for the first time, where he saw her sitting at the centre of a large room lined with luxuriant tapestries, perched in an enormous armchair atop a dais of red velvet embroidered with gold thread.[7] He was sufficiently impressed by the spectacle to stay in the room for some hours, despite not being able to communicate with the queen, she not speaking French and he not speaking English. If Catherine really approved of a visitor, she might stand and take several steps forward, or even kiss them. If they were of similar status to her, they would be offered a stool; otherwise, visitors stood in her presence, unless she invited them to a game of ombre, when the rules of social status went out of the window.[8]

On his visit to London, de Monconys proceeded from the queen's audience to a formal dinner, watching as the king handed Catherine into the dining hall. Dinners were another highly public occasion: almost anyone who had the right clothes could watch the royal couple eat their meal together. Admitted to the banqueting hall at Whitehall Palace were 'Persons of good Fashion and good Appearance that have a desire to see Us at Dinner'. Only the unfashionable were left out in the cold, specifically 'any Inferior, Mean, or Unknowne People'.[9] There was a rail between the table and the public to ensure that the crowd did not overrun the feast. It also protected the food from being stolen; at one royal feast without a dining rail, a course of ruinously expensive fruit from all over Europe was served, which was immediately plundered by the crowd, leaving the besieged royals to defend their own portion of 'delicate viands' as well as they could.[10]

In England generally, 'dinner' was taken in the early afternoon, and was the biggest meal of the day. As one French visitor remarked, 'the English eat a great deal at dinner; they rest a while, and [return] to it again until they have quite stuffed their paunch. Their supper is moderate: gluttons at noon and abstinence at night.'[11] For the first and second courses of a state banquet, gluttony took the form of heaping portions of meat, with '*Chickens* fat', '*Chickens* fine' and '*Turkey Chickens*' competing for space among the – to us – more unusual animals like leverets (young hares) and godwits (long-billed wading birds). These were of course spiced and often served as pie or with lashings of butter and cream, with the very occasional vegetable like artichokes, peas or asparagus making a token appearance. Other delicacies included udders, eel and tripe.[12]

Things got even more adventurous when it came to dessert, thanks to the availability of ever-cheaper sugar for experimentation in culinary creations. Old-fashioned Tudor gingerbreads were served alongside creamy syllabubs, candied oranges and sea holly roots (thought to be a powerful aphrodisiac). Even ice cream made an appearance at the royal table during the 1670s.[13] The spread of sweet treats was partly thanks to the adaptability of the sugar cane plant: European colonists took it from India and Andalusia to Jamaica and Brazil, and it became a source of

Portuguese wealth and power as it took root in South America. The cheapness of sugar also owed much to the availability of African slaves, who performed the hard field labour: preparing the ground, planting, weeding and harvesting the cane, and applying fertiliser after the soil had become exhausted. Although slaves were only expected to live for seven years, mortality figures for English labourers were around four times higher, as they had no natural resistance to malaria.[14]

Sugar was all very well, but a newer and more exciting food served at state dinners was the pineapple; diarist John Evelyn encountered his first explosively sweet-sour taste of the fruit when observing a dinner in 1668. He was somewhat disappointed, as it differed from the fabled magnificence he had heard of, but enjoyed its 'grateful acidity'.[15] Catherine would have eaten her own pineapple from a silver plate, servers tasting a tiny portion of each dish to prove that it wasn't poisoned, before presenting it to her on bended knee.[16] The royal couple used forks, something that the rest of the country was still catching up on, and which would only become widespread by the 1690s. Until then, meat was steadied with a napkin and cut with a knife, which diners sometimes brought to dinner with them.[17]

Charles kept his hat on to eat, while everyone else would be bare-headed, seated on a chair if they were of really high status, on a stool if slightly less so. Above the feasters in Whitehall's dining hall sprawled Rubens' masterpiece, three paintings celebrating the union of the English and Scottish crowns, including a portrayal of virtue triumphing over vice, with Hercules clubbing Envy to death while Minerva spears Ignorance.[18] Central to all is the apotheosis of James I, who ascends to heaven on Jupiter's eagle, to be crowned by the goddess of war and wisdom,

Minerva.[19] State dining in these surroundings was symbolic of the continuity of the Stuart dynasty, regardless of any inconvenient interruptions, and the divine right of the monarch to rule, something Catherine believed in as fervently as her husband.

Such banquets were an important ritual act of monarchy in and of itself: to be a legitimate monarch, the logic went, one must act like a legitimate monarch. If the couple chose to dine alone, food was sometimes still served to an empty throne in whatever residence they were staying in, signifying the royal presence.[20] However, it was not all unparalleled luxury: food was so expensive that even royalty sometimes had to cut down on their dishes at dinner and reduce the enormous number of different types of meat served.[21]

After dinner came dancing. Catherine's first ball was soon after her arrival in England, and she sat merely watching the merry commotion, unable to join in the dance. She quickly ordered the dancing master to her rooms, and picked up with ease the unfamiliar English country dances that finished each ball. These were lively, fast-paced and often a little racy, some involving kissing or scandalously allusive partner-swapping. Reflecting their risqué tone, each dance had a tongue-in-cheek name, such as 'Take not a Woman's Anger ill, For if one won't, another will', or one of Charles's favourites, 'Cuckolds all a-row'.[22]

Once she had mastered the art of dancing, Catherine often hosted small, relatively informal balls, using her suite of apartments as a venue. These were a way for her to be at the centre of the social and political action, for the socially and the politically influential were often one and the same person. One of de Monconys' more interesting recollections of his visit, in an account otherwise filled with his unhelpfully detailed observations on English architecture, is of attending '*un petit bale en privé*' (a little private ball) in Catherine's rooms, which lasted only until midnight. It opened with Catherine dancing the branle with the Duke of York, who was accounted a less graceful dancer than his brother.[23] However, he cannot have gone too far wrong with a branle, which was a very simple set of steps. Dancers linked hands and swayed penguin-like in a circle or line. Even at this relatively informal ball, etiquette was carefully observed, the ladies of the court standing while Catherine or Charles danced. If the Duke of York was dancing, the women would stand when he started the dance, sit during, and stand once again when he sat back down. It must have been very tiring.

De Monconys was amazed by the quantity of blazing silver chandeliers in the room, surrounding a central crystal chandelier that reflected rainbows of light on the dancers below. It was the royal bodyguards' job to hold enormous torches up at the back of the room, illuminating the dance still further and showing through all this conspicuous consumption of expensive white tallow that Catherine begrudged no expense.[24] If there was trouble with gatecrashers or over-rowdy guests, the bodyguards were ready to spring into action, although this was a somewhat impractical arrangement, as they would have had to first ask someone to hold their torch.

This kind of dance was the most basic of Catherine's balls: she also threw a spectacular annual birthday ball, organised masques and ballets, and on occasion held elaborate themed parties, like one 'splendid masquerade' in which the dancers 'had to represent different nations'.[25] Catherine picked who would dance, and made sure countries were not double-represented. Costumes were ordered, and tailors and mantua-makers worked

night and day to have extravagant outfits ready. The Chevalier
de Gramont, representing France, sent his valet to Paris for his
suit of clothes, promising that 'if I do not show you at his return
the most splendid habit you have ever seen, look upon mine as
the most disgraced nation in your masquerade'.[26] However, the
valet – after allegedly commissioning the most fabulous outfit
in Paris – took a shortcut on the way back and ended up to the
top of his head in quicksand. He and his horse had to be hauled
out with great difficulty, but the outfit was never found. The
chevalier was so outraged and embarrassed that he claimed he
would have killed the valet if it would not have made him late
for the ball.

Finding an accurate costume for more distant climes could
also prove a challenge: one attendee lamented that 'if you knew
what a plague it is to find out, in this cursed town, in what manner the people of Babylon dress, you would pity me for what I
have suffered . . . besides, the cost which it puts me to is beyond
all imagination'.[27] Managing for the most part to surmount these
difficulties, guests arrived in their finest interpretations of Rus-
sian, Italian or Babylonian dress. Candlelight glittered from
diamonds bedecking women and men, their costumes so shot
with silver and gold thread as well as sequins (made with silver
and gold rather than the plastics of today) that the whole assem-
bly sparkled with the movement of the dance and the flickering
of flames.

While Catherine's balls were respectable events that even the
most prudish could attend, they were not always sedate affairs,
often carrying on until the early hours of the morning. Although
Catherine personally was abstemious, the British were then – as
now – a nation of binge drinkers. At this particular masquerade

of the nations, one lady, to much hilarity, accosted every man on the way into the rooms and claimed that the queen was waiting for him to dance with her. Spoiling the fun, her husband found her and took her home, leaving a sentry at her chamber door so that she could not return to the ball.[28]

Balls were busy and often chaotic, with running, jumping and kissing all important parts of various dances. Such was the confusion at a particular event that one of Catherine's maids-of-honour was said to have given birth in front of the whole court in the middle of a dance. The story goes that the child was wrapped up in a handkerchief and carried from the room.[29] The identity of the mother is uncertain: Pepys believed it to be Winifred Wells, 'a tall girl, exquisitely shaped', who 'walked like a goddess' but had an expression 'of careless indolence that made her look sheepish'.[30] Those who saw her had 'a bad opinion of her wit: and her wit had the ill-luck to make good that opinion'. Charles, not overscrupulous in his expectations of his bed partners' intelligence, made her his mistress. Since 'she was of a loyal family; and her father having faithfully served Charles the First, she thought it her duty not to revolt against Charles the Second'.[31]

However, Anthony Hamilton claimed that it was not Winifred Wells but another maid-of-honour, Miss Warmestre, who had given birth so scandalously. Miss Warmestre had a somewhat more flattering review from Hamilton, who claimed that she 'had no shape at all, and still less air; but she had a very lively complexion, very sparkling eyes, tempting looks, which spared nothing that might ensnare a lover, and promised everything which could preserve him'.[32] Catherine was very solicitous – sometimes too much so for a jaded and sophisticated court – and attempted to discover the mystery of the father of Miss Warme-stre's baby, sending for her supposed lover and asking whether he planned to marry her. He denied his involvement emphatic-ally, and Miss Warmestre was left to disgrace. (Both Miss Wells and Miss Warmestre eventually escaped scandal by marrying respectable country gentlemen who cared not for court politics.)

After the austere, but expensive, black of Puritan fashion, Restoration balls saw an explosion of colour, sparkling jewels covering any inch of flesh not draped in heavy velvets, brocades or lighter silks. Silk, with its sensuous sway, was colourfast and newly affordable, thanks both to renewed trade with Portugal and Britain's expanding foothold in the East Asian market: it came mostly from China, but was also manufactured in India. Early Restoration fashion made the most of this glossily extrava-gant material, being characterised by enormous puffy sleeves that sat slightly off the shoulder, and an excess of flounces. On clothing for both men and women, if tailors were in doubt of the perfection of the garment, the answer always seems to have been to add another ribbon, perhaps topped by some lace and maybe a feather if they really wanted their client to sit up and pay their bills on time. A loose ribbon or an artlessly draped silk wrap finished the look, as Cavalier poet Robert Herrick put it:

> A sweet disorder in the dress
> Kindles in clothes a wantonness.[33]

Fashion was designed to mirror the ladies' languishing looks, suggestive once again of having just left the bedroom. However, undergarments were still awkwardly close-fitting, and the arms so tight that women 'could not so much scratch their heads for the necessary removal of a biting louse'.[34] And despite an expanse of décolletage being on display, it would have been disgraceful to reveal too much of the upper arm.

What the court wore, so (eventually) did everyone else. For well-to-do Londoners, the court was the place to go and check out the latest fashions before having any new clothing made up. Silks, feathers and the brightly printed cottons from India known as 'calicoes' were the height of aspirational fashion, with some disquiet as to the new availability of such things for people of the middling classes. Rich dyes from New Spain were also changing wardrobes, although these remained expensive: the indigo plant (a member of the bean family) produced a luxurious blue, and cochineal (a dried insect) resulted in a deep blood red.

Catherine revelled in Restoration court fashions, straying increasingly far from the modest Portuguese garments she had grown up wearing. By 1663, she felt comfortable enough to sit in public 'exposing her breast and shoulders without even the glaze of the lightest gauze', while the modest piece of cloth that she had formerly worn over her low-cut dresses was 'with licentious boldness' folded over the neckline, exposing a scandalous expanse of flesh quite comparable to any of Charles's mistresses' garments.[35] For women, the derrière was back in fashion, and Catherine wore a 'bum roll', a pad sometimes reinforced with wires that was attached to the lower back and hips, making the waist appear smaller and the derrière bigger in relation to the rest of the body.

Portraits show her in dresses that are practically falling off, mimicking the flow of drapery in classical sculpture as well as alluding to a state of undress. This kind of garment, however, was reserved for the home, more a nightgown than a ball dress.

Her eyes are heavy-lidded, similarly allusive to undress and eminently fashionable. It was said that one court lady's long custom of showing 'languishing tenderness' in her looks meant that she could no longer fully open her eyes.[36]

Every ruler needs a good propagandist, and Catherine's choice of portraitist to commemorate her fashions and her languishing looks showed a keen eye for the necessity of advertising. When she first arrived in Britain, any court lady with aspirations towards beauty or fashion was painted by Peter Lely, a Dutch 'genius' with an eye for colour. By 1660, he was sworn in as Charles II's principal artist.[37] Lely was so popular that usually he only painted the head of his sitter, with the rest finished by assistants, and – lest anyone take his title of premier portrait painter away from him – he was immensely secretive about his techniques.[38]

Catherine was painted once by Lely in the early years of her reign, possibly as early as 1663. Like almost every other Lely portrait, the gorgeousness of her clothing – fringed with pearls – and the play of light on silk takes up most of the canvas, although her forearms are bare, reflecting the contemporary fashion away from longer sleeves, which were thought to be impractical. Like most of Lely's work, the focus is on magnificence, of both the sitter's looks and the sumptuousness of dress. While this suited her husband and most court ladies, it did not suit Catherine, who wanted to send a more complex message with her portraits. Casting about for a painter who could tell a story through his work as well as flatter, she alighted on the young Jacob Huysmans, another Dutchman, who was new to Britain. By 1664, he had painted what he considered his greatest work: Queen Catherine as St Catherine of Alexandria.[39]

There is more to this choice of portraying the queen as St Catherine than the fact that they shared a name. St Catherine was inspired to convert to Christianity by a vision of the Madonna and Child. The blue and gold of Catherine's dress in her portrait seems to deliberately evoke the iconography related to this pairing, as does her pearl earring; pearls are often associated with the Virgin Mother. The silvery colour of her gown might indicate that the painting was originally a much more vivid indigo blue, echoing images of Mary, as indigo tends to fade to a silvery blue. (Just like in fashion, new trade links were making themselves felt: indigo was now commonly used in oil paint, replacing the prohibitively expensive lapis lazuli.)[40] Like her namesake, Catherine of Braganza was a princess, and the sun sets over a contemporary scene behind her, with a baroque bell tower outlined against the light. One cherub looks up towards heaven, another looks at Catherine and the third, lowest figure looks directly at the viewer. We are shown three levels – the divine, the divinely appointed and the human. Catherine's visit from heavenly intercessors shows Queen Catherine, like the saint, as divinely appointed, associating her with the broader ideals of a divinely appointed monarchy.

This portrait can be read as a statement not only of personal power, but of political intent. Catherine was firmly allying herself with divine monarchy, answerable to God rather than to any secular body. Copies were widely circulated, as were engravings, suggesting a propaganda function tying Catholicism and divine, absolute monarchy to the queen's image, at least for those who wanted to read into it.[41] For those who did not, it is a beautiful woman draped luxuriantly in costly garments, sending a message of a different kind of power and wealth.

After the success of the Catherine of Alexandria painting, Huysmans began styling himself as 'her Majesty's Painter', and favourable comparisons were made with Lely, some critics arguing that the younger man exceeded the king's official painter.[42] Huysmans' paintings relied heavily on the new Italian trend sweeping Europe: the baroque. Originally a jeweller's term for lumpy, irregularly shaped pearls (this term may even further back have come from 'verruca' or 'wart'), the baroque celebrated unusual shapes, eclectic combinations and abundance.[43] In architecture, domes, curves and the broken arch became popular, injecting movement and vitality into buildings, while painters and sculptors sought to convey emotion via expression, movement and dynamism in a way never before attempted.

In Huysmans' portrait of Catherine as St Catherine, one knee rests on a low platform, while the other leg is extended, as though she is ready either to kneel in prayer or leap into the service of her god. Huysmans' other portraits all convey some of this restless energy, this double meaning. In his portrait of Catherine as a shepherdess, she is serene, a lamb resting its head on her knee, content to soak up her majesty, suggesting a peaceful and fruitful life.[44] But the cherub to her left, presenting an offering of flowers, is arrested mid-motion, caught in an act of adoration, while Catherine's silver robes shimmer with light, themselves moving, as though they are the glowing raiment of a goddess.

After Catherine helped bring Huysmans into fashion, he painted other courtiers, including her maids-of-honour and ladies of the bedchamber. On a visit to his studio in 1664, Pepys recalls seeing Frances Stuart dressed 'in a buff doublet like a soldier'. In the portrait, Stuart power-poses masterfully with one hand touching her sword hilt, the other atop a cane. The look was completed by magnificent slashed sleeves and a cascading grey-brown periwig. Catherine loved the trend, and coordinated with her ladies to show it off. Masculine style was a political statement as much as a fashion, and it infuriated social conservatives of the time. One disapproving voice commented, 'Women would strive to be like men, viz: when they rode on horseback or in coaches weare plush caps like monteros, either full of ribbons or feathers, long periwigs which men used to weare, and riding coate of a red colour all bedaubed with lace which they call vests.'[45] Monteros were Spanish hunters, who wore neat pleated caps with a crown-like central band.

Lace, feathers and even indulging in new fashions at all were signs of wealth, but women like Catherine and Frances Stuart also enjoyed the access to power this fashion gave them, its potential for subverting the normal order. The poet and libertine John Wilmot, Earl of Rochester, alluded to this in an extempore poem he is said to have jotted down for his wife after she sent a servant to him asking how much longer he meant to stay in town:

Yielding to your fair bum the breeches,
I'll show myself, in all I can,
Your faithful, humble servant, John.[46]

The poem refers to the power play within this type of fashion; Rochester's wife, Elizabeth, literally wearing the trousers in their relationship. Catherine most likely enjoyed playing with this idea too, taking back some of the power and agency she had lost at her marriage. Elizabeth Wilmot was a noted fan of masculine fashion and a close friend of Frances Stuart.

Catherine had an eye for drama as well as for fashion. She liked her ladies to coordinate in a particular theme, which made a public sensation and offset her own ultra-fashionable attire. On several occasions she had her ladies of the bedchamber fitted out in silver lace, shimmering in the sunlight as they paraded on their daily walk and drawing all eyes to the queen and her entourage. Despite eschewing many of the trappings of excess, she was not unwilling to spend to make the right impression.

On the same visit to Huysmans' studio, Pepys also saw incarnations of Catherine as both a shepherdess and a saint, and declared them to be 'most like and most admirably' done.[47] Since he had seen her in person on multiple occasions by this time, we can be fairly sure that the portraits are accurate representations; good enough at least for one eyewitness.

After Catherine had patronised Huysmans, he became a popular portrait painter for the rich and famous of Restoration society, particularly those allied with the queen or those who wanted to tell a story about themselves through portraiture. Another famous – or rather infamous – sitter was the Earl of Rochester. His cruelly funny pen mocked anyone he came into contact with. He called Catherine 'Cuntagratia' in his play *Sodom: The Quintessence of Debauchery*, in which the randy King Bolloximian has had so much sex with women that he has become bored, turning to sex with men instead. No one was exempt from mockery, Castlemaine featuring as the sex-mad character called Fuckadilla.[48]

Just as Catherine had done, Rochester carefully arranged the story told by his own portrait, replete with double and even triple meanings. Next to the bewigged and orange-silk-draped earl sits a monkey, ripping leaves from a book and presenting them to his master. Monkeys were a motif Rochester often used in his poetry to satirise the condition of mankind, but this one also specifically mocks the Poet Laureate of the time, John Dryden, whose rather boring and sententious rhymes were the opposite of Rochester's quick, satirical style. The monkey also commemorates Rochester's own pet monkey. Allegedly, he trained the animal to defecate on his guests, perhaps his ultimate mockery of the human condition.

Using Huysmans as her propagandist, Catherine commissioned a series of paintings, but her portrait as St Catherine was the most influential – the Countess of Castlemaine was so impressed that she too had herself painted as St Catherine. Mostly, the painting has been seen by history as a deliberate, cruel mockery of the queen. However, this version of events is unlikely. By this time, the two women were friends and lived quite contentedly alongside one another. Castlemaine had also converted to Catholicism three years earlier, giving her an interest in Catholic iconography and common ground with Catherine's desire to spread the good news about the religion. There is no evidence that her driving obsession was to rival the queen. In fact, Catherine had started a popular trend for being painted as a saint, and particularly as St Catherine, perhaps in homage to the queen and perhaps because the saint represented a universal ideal, being both learned and beautiful. In 1664, two years before Castlemaine's painting was completed, Pepys' wife Elisabeth was also painted by Huysmans as St Catherine.[49]

Whatever the motivations of her copyists, Queen Catherine's own St Catherine portrait primarily seeks to celebrate the Catholic faith, with Catherine declaring 'I am not moderate' in terms of religious belief.[50] St Catherine was scholarly, winning a debate against pagan philosophers when she was only eighteen, her arguments so eloquent that many of her opponents converted to Christianity. In Huysmans' portrait, the quill in the queen's right hand points to her intellectual claims: Catherine took an interest in science, Britain's increasingly significant navy and theology. It also asserts her interest in promoting Catholicism in her new country, although through more subtle means than outright conversion – she did not share her patron saint's interest in being beaten to death on a spiked wheel (in the legend, St Catherine actually had to be beheaded, as the wheel mystically broke at her touch).

Rather than martyrdom, Queen Catherine chose instead intellectual and aesthetic forms of conversion, spending a good portion of her annual £30,000 allowance on making her chapel at Somerset House on the Strand dazzling to any and all visitors. Catholics were allowed to worship there, but even Puritan-leaning Protestants like Pepys nosed their way into a service to see what all the fuss was about. They were greeted with a tabernacle of gleaming silver, a dais of red velvet and gold embroidery that Catherine had brought with her from Portugal, and priests in the most splendid vestments money could buy. Even the chests were held together with silver nails.[51] It was a chance to show off the splendour and ritual of Catholic worship. Catherine also enjoyed spending on relics, acquiring for example a fragment of St Thomas à Becket's pastoral staff, a simple piece of wood that she had contained in an opulent silver cross engraved with her monogram and the royal crown amidst fleur-de-lis, cherubs and a very droopy Jesus.[52]

The music at Catherine's chapel was also some of the best and most innovative in the country, bringing the baroque style to

English ears and introducing a new form of tonality – the minor and major keys we know today were invented in the baroque period. Music had a special power in Restoration Britain, exciting emotion and – so some thought – accessing the divine part of humans directly. Its effect was inexplicably entrancing; it could calm, soothe, excite and charm like no other art form, and Catherine made full use of it in her aesthetic battle for souls.

She brought some of her own musicians with her from Portugal, who at first sounded alien and discordant to English ears. This was probably thanks to their use of wind instruments, the reedy sound of pipes mingling with the deeper resonance of the bassoon.[53] These instruments were only used for outdoor entertainments in England, so the sound was unexpected for church music. Their phrasing and tonality may have also veered towards the baroque, meaning that phrases ran into one another without pausing, while minor chords may have shocked English ears. Diarist John Evelyn remembered hearing 'very ill voices', while Pepys 'heard their Musique . . . which may be good, but it did not appear so to me, neither as to their manner of singing, nor was it good concord to my eares, whatever the matter was'.[54]

However, this all changed when the successful theatre manager Thomas Killigrew attempted to set up an Italian opera company in London. Killigrew had been so obsessed with the stage as a child that he had frequently performed as a devil – a kind of extra – in order to see plays for free.[55] Despite his theatrical successes, the opera company was not to be. When the venture failed, Catherine snapped up his troupe of talented Italian musicians, with voices ranging from 'eunuche' (high-voiced castrato) to deep bass.[56] Gradually more Italians were added to her ensemble, and the Queen's chapel became one of the finest and most innovative places to hear music in the country. Pepys, a passionate devotee of music and no mean player of the lute himself, recorded in 1668 that the music of Catherine's chapel 'did appear most admirable to me, beyond anything of ours – I was never so well satisfied in my life with it'.[57] Later in the year he recorded the same set of musicians drawing up in a barge next to Catherine's apartments at Whitehall and serenading the queen and her ladies for almost an hour with their lovely voices.[58]

Despite these popular innovations in fashion, music and dancing, Catherine was beginning to be seriously worried. The predictions of Huysmans' portraits for fertility and abundance had not yet come to pass. Her husband's brood of children from his many mistresses grew ever larger, but no legitimate heir to the throne had materialised. Catherine had possibly been pregnant and miscarried during her attack of typhus in 1663; it was said that 'the Queen hath much changed her humour, and is become very pleasant and sociable as any', although this is likely to have been her finding her feet in an alien court.[59] Thereafter she was generally counted as sociable as anyone else at the heart of court life. More certain evidence is her change of dress. At that time, she had altered her style of dressing to a popular mode signalling pregnancy, wearing 'a white laced waistcoat and crimson short petty-coate and her hair dressed a la negligence, mighty pretty'.[60]

In order to help conception, Catherine was careful not to drink too much wine, most oddly (according to the English) 'taking a very large draught of water' instead at the end of a meal. There was also a rumour that though by 'nature she is very susceptible to pleasures, but whether through virtue or ineptitude, not only does she content herself with those she has with the King, but is as temperate as she can be in these'. She may deliberately have conducted a 'temperate' sex life in order to conceive, and might also have found sex an excruciating ordeal. She certainly bled afterwards.[61] It is possible that she had endometriosis, a common condition where tissue from the womb lining grows outside the womb. It can make conception difficult, and both periods and sex intensely painful.

To augment the effectiveness of piety, prayers and lifestyle, she began an annual pilgrimage around 1663 to Tunbridge Wells, known for its iron-laced waters 'often prescribed by Physitians against many Diseases; as *Palsies, Tremblings, Ulcers of the Stomach, Reins, Bladder and Womb, Tenesmus, deprav'd Months, Abortion, &c.'*.[62] One contemporary, pondering at length on the power of the waters, suggested that if they could not save a patient, 'the Grave' was the only other option.[63] Thankfully, Catherine's case was not so desperate.

Signalling her increasingly dominant position at the heart of court culture, where she went, the rest of the court followed. When she decamped for Tunbridge Wells, all the houses for several miles around the small town became full to bursting with nattily attired courtiers the like of which this sleepy part of England had never seen. During the late summer and early autumn, Tunbridge Wells became 'the general rendezvous of all the gay and handsome of both sexes'. A holiday atmosphere was encouraged by Catherine, who decreed that the normal formalities and strict etiquette practised in her presence could be dispensed with. Alongside meeting to take the waters every morning and dancing on the bowling green at night, Catherine 'even surpassed her usual attentions in inventing and supporting entertainments'. It was a heady atmosphere – Anthony Hamilton claimed, 'Never did love see his empire in a more flourishing condition than on this spot: those who were smitten before they came to it, felt a mighty augmentation of their flame; and those who seemed the least susceptible of love, laid aside their natural ferocity, to act in a new character.'[64]

In the late summer or early autumn of 1666, Catherine had sent to London for the theatre players from the company known as the King's Men to provide more entertainment for a quickly bored court. The haughty mathematics fan and courageous Civil War general Prince Rupert (the same Rupert Catherine may have met as a child in Portugal) promptly fell in love with the actress Margaret Hughes, proving Hamilton right about the love-laced atmosphere of the place. Hughes is believed to have been the first ever actress to perform on the English stage.

Catherine may have had an ulterior motive in setting up this particular entertainment: Charles had for some time been pursuing Frances Stuart, a distant relative and one of Catherine's maids-of-honour. Known as La Belle Stuart, with the long, large nose so in vogue at the time, 'sweet' dark eyes and extreme grace, Frances caused a sensation when she first arrived in England from France in 1662.[65] She began to catch the king's eye almost immediately, although courtiers who expected some political gain from this connection were disappointed. Anthony Hamilton commented acidly that 'it was hardly possible for a woman to have less wit, or more beauty'. However, he admired her perfect 'air of dress . . . which cannot be attained unless it be taken when young, in France'.[66] Charles's chief mistress, the Countess of Castlemaine, made a favourite of her, often sleeping next to her so that Charles found them in titillating semi-undress

together the next morning. One night, Castlemaine even orchestrated a pretend marriage ceremony between La Belle Stuart and
the king. It was here that matters became dicey for Catherine,
as by 1666 rumours began circulating that Charles was going
to divorce his childless queen in order to marry the young and
lovely Frances instead. Inviting the players to Tunbridge Wells
diverted his attention from the beautiful Frances Stuart, and
Prince Rupert's startling love affair became the focus of gossip,
at least for a few weeks.

The king's relations with La Belle Stuart came to a head soon
after this visit to take the waters, when he found her in bed
with the Duke of Richmond. Fearing that Charles was about
to throw him out of the window into the unsavoury waters of
the Thames, the duke beat a hasty retreat, leaving Frances and
Charles to engage in a screaming match. The king was not at all
pacified by her angry arguments, and the Duke of Richmond
was ordered from the court. Stuart 'threw herself at the queen's
feet', who 'mingled her tears with those of Miss Stewart' and
promised to take her part.[67] Soon afterwards, Stuart eloped with
Richmond, causing yet another explosion from the king, who
only reconciled with her after she almost died from smallpox
(so called to distinguish it from the sexually transmitted 'great
pox', or syphilis, that afflicted many courtiers, including the Earl
of Rochester).[68] Charles was profoundly thankful that Frances
Stuart 'is not much marked' by the blisters typical of the pox,
although her eyesight was troubled ever after.[69] She became
a lady of the bedchamber to Catherine, and the two remained
intimate companions.

Alongside the reputation of its waters and for inflaming
love, leafy Tunbridge Wells had something of a reputation for

providing children to marriages that had so far lacked issue. The Earl of Rochester described the man walking confidently about town:

> With brawny back and legs and potent prick,
> Who more substantially will cure thy wife,
> And on her half-dead womb bestow new life.[70]

Jesting and Rochester's vulgarities aside, there was great pressure on women to provide an heir, and with fertility being inadequately understood, it was generally seen as the woman's fault if a couple remained childless. Some women certainly looked outside the marriage bed for the children they desired. If Catherine tried the services of other men, however – an unlikely circumstance considering her chaste reputation – it did not have the required effect. She miscarried again in 1666, 1668 and 1669. However, Frances Stuart's controversial marriage at least ended the speculation about the king's potential divorce and remarriage to this most eligible of ladies.

While Frances Stuart did not become Charles's mistress, he had no shortage of women willing to fill the position. For the first half of his reign at least, he proved a popular king, but the great criticism levelled against him was his susceptibility to 'petticoat government', or being unduly ruled by the women around him. As the Earl of Rochester put it, Charles was:

> The easiest King and best-bred man alive.
> Him no ambition moves to get renown . . .
> Peace is his aim, his gentleness is such,
> And love he loves, for he loves fucking much.

Nor are his high desires above his strength:

His scepter and his prick are of a length;

And she may sway the one who plays with th'other.[71]

This is one of many bawdy verses on the subject of Charles's mistresses, many of whom became vastly unpopular with a large part of the court, and with the people of Britain, who believed that the king both wasted money on these women and was led into political decisions by them.

Although Catherine was vastly wealthy, and displayed Charles's extravagant gifts to her in her private rooms, she was careful to distance herself from the profligacy, waste and negative political influence associated with mistresses like Castlemaine. Her bedroom – a room accessible to many and therefore a kind of showcase for the curious who wanted to see her apparently 'private' personality – was decorated with simple devotional pictures, lacking the gilt and oil paintings ornamenting the rooms of most great ladies and gentlemen. Similarly, on her annual birthday ball in 1666, she was remarkable for her lack of ostentatious jewellery. Most other ladies had their 'head and shoulders dressed with Dyamonds', a stark contrast with Catherine's intended message: wearing no jewels showcased her own piety, simplicity and lack of ostentation.[72]

In the Restoration, as now, fashion often contained a political message. Catherine was well aware of the political associations of her relatively simple outfits. To help the beleaguered British wool industry, Charles announced a radical change in style. On 8 October 1666, Pepys recorded that 'The King hath yesterday in Council declared his resolution of setting a fashion for clothes, which he will never alter. It will be a vest, I know not well how.'[73]

It was a knee-length garment that fitted tightly over the chest, billowing into a skirt at the waist and ornamented by a long row of tiny buttons all down the front.[74] Originally it was pinked or cut to show the fine cloth beneath, but Charles thought this made him look too much like a magpie, and the shirt remained firmly beneath the vest.[75] Louis XIV, perhaps resenting Charles's pretensions in daring to set a fashion not already begun in France, had a set of these vests commissioned for his footmen.

Allegedly the garments would 'teach the nobility thrift', being made of plain wool rather than costly satins or brocades, but quickly this was adapted, and some bejewelled versions may have been worth upwards of £1,000.[76] John Evelyn lamented this return to extravagance, recalling, 'It was a comely and manly habit, too good to hold, it being impossible for us in good earnest to leave ye Monsieurs vanities long.'[77] The whole episode sounds like an exaggerated furore, but the importance of the new style was clearly felt by Charles, who announced it as a political matter in his Privy Council, which was usually reserved for state and foreign affairs. Eventually these vests were raised from thigh-length to the waistline, becoming waistcoats, and the three-piece suit was born, which even the French have long adopted – Britain's great contribution to fashion history.

To coincide with this in a kind of joint press release, amplifying the dubiously exciting news of woollen vests with something a little more reliably exciting, Catherine announced that she was breaking with French trends and their superfluity of trailing fabric by introducing the short skirt, thereby revealing a risqué peep of ankle and silken shoe.[78] Of course, this fashion suited her particularly well, showing off well-turned ankles and fashionably tiny feet. However, it was quickly adopted by the rest of the court, just as the trend for her maids-of-honour to wear masculine riding habits had been. Short skirts were a popular innovation, but unless we somehow relate the 1960s miniskirt to Queen Catherine, the impact on global fashion was less long-lasting than that of the three-piece suit.

Catherine remained close friends with Frances Stuart, now the Duchess of Richmond, as well as Mary Villiers, the Duchess of Buckingham, whose husband was to become one of the most influential ministers of Charles's later reign. While staying at Audley End, a sprawling royal residence that Charles had mainly bought so that he could be close to the horse-racing at Newmarket, the three friends came up with a 'frolick'. At a fair being held nearby for the farmers and yeomen of the neigh-bourhood, the ladies decided to disguise themselves as simple country folk, wearing red petticoats, waistcoats and plain blouses. Gentlemen of the court on carthorses preceded them as their escorts. However, the group of courtiers had 'all so over done it in their disguise, and look'd so much more like Antiques than country volk' that they drew the entire fair's attention. Since Catherine's attendant, the mercenary-turned-merchant Bernard Gascoigne, was, like the queen, not a native English speaker, the men's attempts to jokingly buy gloves for their sweethearts aroused further suspicion: 'they were soon, by their gebrish, found to be strangers'. This drew even more people to flock around the courtiers, and one woman recognised Catherine, leading the entire fair to try and catch a glimpse of the queen. The courtiers fled on their horses, but they were pursued to the gates of Audley End by curious country people, anxious 'to get as much gape at they could' at the bizarrely dressed royal party.[79]

This undignified end to their day of merrymaking did not dissuade Catherine from using disguises or taking part in frolics. It had become fashionable for courtiers to follow strains of music drifting through the streets of London, and to gatecrash any party they found at the other end of the trail. Wearing the black masks popular at the time, they would disguise themselves in relatively humble apparel and merrily join in the feasting and dancing of their social inferiors incognito. The next day, the court would laughingly recount their experiences among the great unwashed. Slipping into strangers' parties exactly suited Catherine's humour and appetite for novelty. She travelled from the hallway of one private house to the next in a litter, borne by two strong men, so that she never had to set foot on the wet, muddy streets. Unfortunately, one evening she took her cunning disguise so far that her bearers did not recognise her, and abandoned her in the middle of the city. She had to actually place satin-shod feet on the dirty streets, and return to the palace in the first carriage that came along – quite shocking behaviour for a queen.

The whole episode showed almost unrecognisable boldness from the shy, pious woman who had first landed at Portsmouth in 1662.[80] Catherine was to need all the humour and confidence she had acquired so far for the years of plague, fire and war that were coming.

6

Plague, Fire and New York City

ENGLISH COLONISTS IN the Americas had long looked
avariciously at the rich port city of New Amsterdam (now
New York). And the marriage between Charles and Catherine
caused global ripples that would inevitably reach this city halfway
round the world. The leader of New Amsterdam, director general
Peter Stuyvesant, was a conscientious man who did his best to
warn old Amsterdam of the trouble brewing on the other side of
the Atlantic. Perturbed by England's alliance with the House of
Braganza, he wrote home predicting 'imminent rupture between
our own government and the lately crowned King [Charles II]
on account of his marriage and close connection with the Crown
of Portugal'.[1] With England and Portugal made allies, the two
naval powers might turn against the United Provinces, their principal competitor in international trade and colonising, leading to
war in North America. The international balance of trade and
alliance was a finely threaded web, changes to one thread having
repercussions across the whole structure.

Stuyvesant was to be proved right, at least as far as his fears
of hostile English takeover went. In March 1664, two years
after his marriage to Catherine, Charles granted James, Duke

of York, much of the American East Coast, 'together also with
... Hudson's River and all the land from the west side of the
Connectecutte River to the East side of De la Ware Bay'.[2]
At the stroke of a pen, he had changed world geography, or
at least begun to. After this pronouncement, James organised
four warships, headed by his close personal supporter and
arch-Royalist Captain Richard Nicolls, to take New Amsterdam.
As a side mission, Nicolls was ordered to assert royal authority in
Massachusetts, which had been showing a worrying inclination
for independence. By August, his small fleet was anchored near
Nantasket, near Boston.

Meanwhile, the New Netherlanders set about preparing for
the inevitable clash with the English settlers, hauling rocks to
create defences around their city and watching day and night
for signs of attack.[3] By 'shovel, spade or wheelbarrow', citizens strengthened the city's defences, but they were woefully
unprepared for a conflict. Old Amsterdam, wilfully blind to the
signs of rising conflict, had provided no support. There was so
little gunpowder in the colony that one artilleryman gloomily
announced, 'were I to commence firing in the morning, I should
have all used up by noon'.[4] In their off hours, they drank their
troubles away, breaking the law so that they could drink on
Sundays.[5] They knew the English were coming.

On 26 August 1664, Nicolls landed 450 soldiers, who
marched to the ferry at Brooklyn. His ships dropped anchor
at the battery, blockading the harbour. The citizens prepared
for a massacre – they were not soldiers. Nicolls' master stroke
was a letter. Asking for the surrender of 'the Towne, Scituate
[situated] upon the Island commonly knowne by the Name of
Manhatoes',[6] he promised in exchange that the Dutch could

go on with their lives as before.[7] The city's grain reserves were dwindling to almost nothing, and the people were restive at the idea of inevitable slaughter to defend – what? The name New Amsterdam? They were promised rights and freedoms if they surrendered, only having to change the name of their master, and what difference did that make for most people? With four warships ranged against them, the citizenry had little hope of victory, more used as they were to trading than to fighting.

Stuyvesant, however, was determined to fight. Citizens ceased their work building up the city's defences and mobbed City Hall, asking him to surrender New Amsterdam. He remained unmoved. The next day, ninety-three of the city's most influential citizens petitioned their leader, imagining the inevitable outcome should they not surrender: 'misery, sorrow, conflagration, the dishonor of women, murder of children in their cradles, and, in a word, the absolute ruin and destruction of about fifteen hundred innocent souls, only two hundred and fifty of whom are capable of bearing arms'. They added, attempting to save face, 'These threats would not have been at all regarded, could your Honors or we, your petitioners, expect the smallest aid or succor. But (God help us!) whether we turn us for assistance to the north or to the south, to the east or to the west, 'tis all vain!'[8]

Finally, accepting that his people had no wish to fight and no hope of winning, Stuyvesant surrendered the city. New Amsterdam had fallen without bloodshed. It was renamed New York, after the duke, while Kings County, after Charles II, was decided upon for the borough now more popularly known as Brooklyn (naming something after an English king suddenly became quite unpopular after the revolution). The adjoining borough became Queens County, after Catherine, sitting side by side with her husband on the city map.

It has since been contested whether Queens County (now just called Queens) was in fact named after Catherine. It was named in 1683, when Catherine was still Queen of England, so although there is no record directly linking her with the place, there is no other possible candidate; why would English colonists have renamed the area after the Queen of France or Spain? At the time, it was a popular gesture of patriotism to name places after Charles and Catherine, and there has been no dispute over Kings County. This was part of a more general trend: several English streets were christened in Catherine's honour. In the area of St James's, in central London, Charles II Street still exists, but Portugal Street, named for Catherine, has been renamed and is now Jermyn Street. Another Portugal Street still exists near Lincoln's Inn.

With the English in power and the city renamed, the Dutch citizens continued with their lives remarkably unchanged. They retained their rights and New Amsterdam prospered as a trade hub. The United Provinces, on the other hand, was shocked by these events, and finally jarred out of its long inaction. It sent a fleet to New York, but the sailors were not a large enough force and after a brief recce decided that they were unable to retake the city, returning home to Europe instead to ready themselves for the war that was now inevitable. The English ambassador to the United Provinces, Sir George Downing (after whom Downing Street was named), did nothing to ease the tense political situation now bubbling over into talk of war. He was widely disliked; a 'perfidious rogue' or 'a crafty, fawning man' depending who you talked to.[9] He, in turn, disliked the Dutch and managed a spy network that frequently one-upped Dutch leader Johan de Witt, bragging that he frequently 'had the keys out of de Witt's pocket when he was a-bed, and his closet opened and his papers brought to him and left in his hands for an hour, and carried back and laid in the place again, and keys put into his pocket again'.[10] Such blatant disregard for political niceties forced the prospect of war ever closer.

In England, the people were clamouring for war. Pepys, in his role of naval administrator, did not feel very sanguine about the prospect. He wrote in his diary on 28 June 1662: 'Great talk there is of a fear of war with the Dutch, and we have order to pitch upon twenty ships to be forthwith set out; but I hope it is but a scare-crow to the world, to let them see we can be ready for them; though, God knows! the king is not able to set out five ships at this present without great difficulty, we neither having money, credit, nor stores.'[11]

Somehow or other the ships were outfitted, although the supplies were not up to scratch; the commissioner of Chatham Dockyard, Peter Pett, complained that, of the oars delivered to him, 'not one in eight is worth anything'.[12] The condition of the men who were to fight and crew the ships was a good deal worse. Unlike in the United Provinces, where there was a ready supply of men willing to go to war, the English rank-and-file had to be impressed. Men were seized from taverns and streets, and even plucked from the decks of ships after long months or years at sea. It was no wonder that naval volunteers were not forthcoming; the navy was chronically underfunded, and pay was almost always late, when it came at all. As was to be expected, impressed men often had no knowledge of ships or warfare, being trained in entirely different skills.[13] An angry Pett wrote that the men were 'in no way fit for service, being made up of all sorts of country trades, and such a ragged crew as never was seen'. He decided that 'those pitiful pressed creatures . . . are fit for nothing but to fill the ships full of vermin'.[14]

In these preparations for war, Catherine was in as fervent as any English-born courtier in support of the English side, perhaps even more so, since the United Provinces was locked in a long on-again off-again war with Portugal, ongoing since 1602. Her old friend the Earl of Sandwich, who had picked her up from Portugal and accidentally saved Lisbon from Spanish attack in 1662, was in charge of fitting out the English fleet, and Charles wrote to him that 'My wife is so faraide [afraid] that she shall not see the fleet before it goes, that she intends to get out from hence on Monday next, with the afternoone tide.'[15] Since she was from a seafaring nation herself, and well able to appreciate the importance of the navy, her enthusiasm matched her husband's.

Bishop Burnet rather disapprovingly noted that the king 'understood navigation well; but above all he knew the architecture of his ships so perfectly that in that respect he was exact rather more than became a Prince'.[16] A king, of course, should take an interest in the activities of his people, but Burnet thought Charles's obvious passion for one particular subject rather unbecoming. Wanting to show off the fleet to Catherine, the king commanded Sandwich to 'tell all the youghts except that which the French ambassador hath to be ready at Gravesend by that time'.[17] The royal party, including Catherine's ladies and her ally Henrietta Maria, duly travelled in the royal barge, coasting down the Thames on the afternoon tide, to the busy port town of Gravesend.

From the luxurious setting of the barge, they marvelled at the assembled fleet. The bow-shaped ships with rows of white sails stacked on top of one another enabled quick sallies, the sterns of these fabulously expensive vessels blocky as though cut through the middle, and often lavishly decorated and gilded. Catherine and the royal crew were thorough in their patriotic tour, inspecting the ships a second time a few days later. However, Charles carelessly left his periwig off and caught a cold (his natural hair would have been cropped very close to his head, not providing much warmth). Applying the seventeenth-century remedy for all ills, his doctors bled him, and all was well again some few days later.

The royals with attendant hangers-on interested themselves again in naval affairs on 25 October, witnessing the launch of the *Royal Katherine* at Woolwich, named as a compliment to the queen and ready for the war. At the bow flew the Union Jack, with pennants streaming dramatically in the wind from every mast. Catherine was already fond of sailing. Aside from this new ship, Charles had already built a yacht in her honour when their marriage was decided; the *Katherine* was a low, long vessel built for a snip: £1,335 (around £250,000 today).

Instead of today's bottle-smashing ceremony, when christening ships Charles or one of his representatives would sprinkle wine on the deck and drink from a goblet, the cup frequently presented to the captain as a souvenir after the ceremony. When the *Royal Katherine* was being launched, Pepys shoved the goblet into the Duke of York's hands, as everyone else was having too jolly a time and had forgotten about it. The ceremony may refer back to medieval ship blessings, where the ship was consecrated in the same manner as a church, in the hope that this would provide extra protection against enemies. The *Royal Katherine* was an elegant vessel, equipped with seventy guns that Catherine admired as she sailed alongside in her elegantly appointed state barge. Charles declared that 'she had the best bow that ever he saw'.

At the time of the launch, the river was extremely rough, causing many of the royal party to be seasick. One of Catherine's closest companions and ladies of the bedchamber, Mary Villiers, the Duchess of Buckingham, was decidedly ill. She and Catherine had likely bonded over their husbands' notorious and public infidelities. The duchess actually had to leave her marital home after the duke killed his lover's husband in a duel, and then proceeded to set up house with the new widow. It was the second time a duel had been fought over Anna Talbot, Countess of Shrewsbury, and the second man to have died for her. She apparently enjoyed the drama and was present for the scene, dressed like a boy and holding the duke's horse.[18] Like Catherine, the Duchess of Buckingham was the opposite of her flashy husband; well-mannered and discreet, she was remembered for being virtuous and pious.[19] While Catherine could not choose exactly who to surround herself with, she was careful to maintain relationships with well-connected but devout women like Mary Villiers.

Perhaps Catherine had found her sea legs during the long voyage from Portugal to England, for she herself suffered no ill-effects despite the rolling of the waves increasing through the leisurely lunch the courtiers enjoyed as an accompaniment to their military sightseeing. Pepys was very disappointed with the ribaldry and coarse jokes the courtiers made about the suffering ladies, thinking it beneath royal dignity. The waters continued so rough that Catherine finally decided to leave the royal barge, take over the king's coaches and return to London by road. Charles was left to hire horses to get back himself.[20]

Fuelled by the taking of New York as well as territory in the Gambia, on 4 March 1665 England and the United Provinces were officially at war. There was an early victory for the English; they only lost one ship in the Battle of Lowestoft, while the Dutch lost eight. The *Royal Katherine* had her first outing at the battle. The Duke of York was commanding the central force, and a chain shot came perilously close to hitting him, killing several courtiers who had been standing in the wrong place at the wrong time, including the sweet-natured but slow Earl of Falmouth. The poet Andrew Marvell described Falmouth's decapitation as 'the last first proof that he had Brains'.[21] Despite their losses, the majority of the Dutch fleet escaped to fight another day. The short, decisive war that both sides had hoped for was impossible. Shipyards on both sides of the Channel rang with shouted orders and the sound of planks being hammered into place.

By 1666, the Dutch had rebuilt with heavier ships better able to withstand cannon fire. The two warring factions were now more evenly matched. In early June, one of the longest naval engagements in history followed, known as the Four Days' Battle, at which the *Royal Katherine* was again present. The air quickly became thick with smoke, movement difficult to track as cannon boomed and tar-coated fireships were loosed into the water to try and set other ships ablaze. It was a near-impossible job to simultaneously sail, avoid fireships and try to keep in disciplined lines. There were inevitable impacts, and as two Dutch ships collided with an almighty crashing of timber and cursing of crews, the English vice admiral Sir William Berkeley set a course for the tangled ships. The attack was quickly repulsed, and Berkeley was killed by a musket ball. His lieutenant was found with his throat cut; apparently he had tried to blow up the ship rather than be taken prisoner, but the crew, not keen to die so heroically, had poured water on the gunpowder supplies, making them unusable.

The battle raged – as its name suggests – for four days, and this time ended in a Dutch victory, with ten English ships destroyed to four Dutch. However, neither side had been able to bring a quick, decisive end to the war, each battle bringing about a reversal of fortune. The tides would turn yet again on 25 July 1666, when the English won a victory partly thanks to the bull-headedness of Dutch admiral Cornelis Tromp, who separated his ships from the main body to fight a skirmish on his own. However, the outcome was not decisive as, again, most of the Dutch fleet escaped. The war was not over yet. Attempting to capitalise on their advantage and gain booty and glory for themselves, the English raided merchant ships that had taken refuge in the treacherous waters of the Vlie estuary, sandbanks and half-hidden islands waiting to trip the unwary navigator. Making their way through the difficult waters, the English burned over a hundred ships, smoke choking the sky. This was perfectly normal within contemporary rules of military engagement.

What was not normal were the actions of Sir Robert Holmes, who led a force ashore onto the islands of Vlie and Schelling on 10 August, destroying local stores and houses. The English – long inured by propaganda into thinking that the Dutch were subhuman – were not repentant, terming the action 'Holmes's Bonfire' and grandiosely declaring that:

The Startled States (again) shall never boast
Of things nere done, bravad'ing on our Coast.[22]

Holmes was painted shortly after by court favourite Lely, showing off his achievements. One arm is braced against a cannon, the other points with his mark of office – a commander's baton – towards belching smoke some way in the distance. A hint of flame flickers behind a Doric column. The portrait is an odd mix of war leader and fashionable fop; Holmes wears a brown silk turban, studded with jewels, perched atop a glossy head of curls, almost certainly an expensive wig. Pepys described him as 'a cunning fellow, and one (by his own confession to me) that can put on two several faces and look his enemies in the face with as much love as his friends'.[23] The diarist did not like him much, and relations soured further after Holmes made a pass at the lovely and youthful Elizabeth Pepys, Samuel's wife.[24]

The raid on Vlie and Schelling may have been a victory for the English, but they did not celebrate for long.

In December 1664, a large white-tinged comet had been seen throughout Europe and the Americas. Interested in the new scientific discoveries of astronomy, Catherine sat up for two nights at Whitehall Palace looking out onto the frozen Thames. That winter was exceptionally cold, and she and Charles were well wrapped up as they awaited the spectacle. The second night, they opened the thick-paned glass windows to see the bright comet blaze across the sky, making a great arch and seeming to almost touch London before disappearing abruptly into the blanket of stars overhead.[25]

Watching the comet at the same time was a young man

called Isaac Newton, who initially confused it with a star or nebula. By 17 December, he had finally worked out what the object was, describing the tail as pointing towards the North Pole, and the whole comet as setting over the horizon about two minutes after the Dog Star, Sirius.[26] Both Catherine and Charles were interested in the theories of scientists like Newton and his contemporary Robert Hooke, who was attempting to measure the comet, ingeniously designing new devices to more accurately calculate angles, critical to measuring distant objects. Science, for Restoration courtiers, was a fashionable interest, and Catherine was not to be outdone when it came to keeping up with the court.

Others saw the comet not as a scientific opportunity but as an omen of evil to come. To many it presaged:

> Famine, Plague and War:
> *To* Princes, death! *To* Kingdoms, *many* Crosses;
> To *all* Estates, *inevitable* Losses![27]

Tales of nature overturning itself proliferated; at the same time as the comet there were apparently strange births and odd weather patterns, and the devil was believed to be on the loose, possessing victims.[28] A thorn tree spontaneously bore five types of fruit, lightning and earthquakes were reported, and Oxford don Anthony Wood recounted that a child was born in Oxford 'having one hand, one leg, one eye in the forehead, noe nose, and its 2 eares in the nape of the neck'.[29] A coffin appeared out of thin air in Hamburg, its ghostly outline a terrible prediction of dark times to come.

The comet was greeted with a similar reaction in North

America. In New England, astronomer and Puritan minister Samuel Danforth predicted 'great Calamities' and preached against eccentric personalities that mirrored the odd orbit of the comet.[30] The factual reality of a coffin appearing out of thin air is questionable, but something terrible and devastatingly destructive was undoubtedly making its way through the world.

Plague. The name itself brought fear.

While the comet was the talk of the town in December 1664, plague was already creeping through London, from rats to fleas to humans, enlarging the lymph nodes and causing painful red swellings near the site of infection. One of the worst symptoms of plague is necrosis, or decay of the skin while the sufferer is still alive. The affected area turns black from the build-up of decomposing tissue. However, even while the sickness crept through the streets, its symptoms were mostly attributed to some other disease. At the time, the plague was much more virulent in Amsterdam, and – much like the beginnings of the Covid pandemic in 2020 – people in England were content to go on as normal, in the sanguine belief that what happened overseas would never reach them.

For now, the icy winter kept it relatively at bay. The Thames froze and people huddled together for warmth. But the whole country was in a flurry of anxiety about what would happen in the warmer months, when rats came out of hibernation and the heat provided the perfect conditions for fast-growing bacteria.

It was already hot by spring, and on 30 April 1665, Pepys cried, 'Great fears of the Sicknesse here in the City . . . God preserve us all!'[31] By early June, he had seen the first houses with red crosses painted on their doors, marking them out as plague-struck. 'Lord Have Mercy Upon Us' was the phrase frequently printed and pasted next to these crosses.[32] In some market towns, 'vinegar stones' were erected so that the inhabitants could continue their trading; a depression in the stone was filled with vinegar, and money was placed there before being taken out by the seller/buyer, a Restoration alternative to hand sanitiser. Fearing the effects of the plague on the navy, currently at war with the Dutch, sailors were ordered to remain on their ships rather than risk infection by coming ashore. Since this had little effect, with men sneaking off to dockside taverns to game, drink and debauch themselves, the ships were sent out to sea, proving a much more effective quarantine measure.[33]

The summer was already one of the hottest in memory, plague cases rising with the heat, and on 25 June, Catherine left for Hampton Court, joining the throng of people escaping London in coaches, on horseback, or even carrying their worldly goods in wheelbarrows and sleeping in the countryside under makeshift tents.[34] She hoped to escape infection in the red-brick Tudor palace nestled in a looping meander of the cleaner part of the Thames, west of Whitehall and the City of London. But it was no use: only a month later, the plague reached the small villages surrounding Hampton Court. Worse still, one of the sentries guarding the palace fell ill at his post, his body covered in raised, angry-looking buboes. The disease was terrifyingly close. Catherine and Charles turned south, heading to Salisbury.

Although busy and inevitably somewhat chaotic, their departure was not a panicked exodus, as one might expect. Spectators gathered, eager for a glimpse of the elite, and Catherine and her ladies of the bedchamber, all attired in the masculine riding dress of the time, did not disappoint. Pepys

was part of the crowd who saw them off before he returned to
the plague-stricken city, recalling that 'it was pretty to see the
young pretty ladies dressed like men, in velvet coats, caps with
ribbands, and with laced bands . . . Only the Duchesse herself
it did not become.'[35] Catherine was one of the 'young pretty
ladies', at only twenty-six years old and slender – unlike her
unfortunate sister-in-law Anne, Duchess of York, whose depression led her to being – as arch-gossip Anthony Hamilton put
it – 'one of the highest feeders in England'.[36] Catherine went
the other way, unable to eat when she was depressed, and since
she was often depressed, she stayed enviably slim. She probably
would have preferred to be plumper and happier.

Even the court's relative exile in Salisbury was not safe. By
September, the pustules of plague had permeated its close grid
of medieval streets. Catherine continued her slow flight from
disease, journeying with her retinue to Oxford. The residents of
Salisbury, in fear of plague, nonetheless breathed a sigh of relief,
spared from further payments for the dubious pleasure of housing the king and queen, and able to return to the quarters that
Catherine, Charles and their retinues had taken over as their own.[37]

Catherine entered her new home in pomp, as Oxford don
Anthony Wood recalled, 'with great acclimations following
her'.[38] She stayed at Merton College, just as Henrietta Maria had
done when Charles I's court was forced to flee from London
during the Civil War in 1644. Most likely she was assigned
the same rooms, above a Tudor arch of mellow sand-coloured
stone, with views over both quads, now known as the Queen's
Room. Her reputation must have been flying high at this time,
since she proved to be immediately popular with the members
of the college and the citizens. Her arrival was greeted with

celebrations and versifying, even in this time of fear and plague. One poem praised 'Your rayes and luster madam'.[39] She had a special reception from the vice chancellor, mayor and aldermen on 27 September, and later in her stay became godmother to the child of the college's doctor. The fact that the girl was named in her honour suggests Catherine continued to win approval even after the first flush of excitement at housing the queen had worn off, and despite the upheaval she caused as dons were shipped off to other colleges in order to accommodate her substantial entourage.[40] Other ladies, including Anne, Duchess of York, were not nearly so popular; the dour Anthony Wood recalled that a speech of praise to Anne was 'done against a great many will'.[41]

As always, it was one rule for the rich and another for the poor: since July, a watch had been posted at Oxford's gates to keep out refugees from London who might bring plague, but Charles and Catherine were, of course, allowed into the city. The royal couple were just as paranoid about the disease reaching them, and probably exhausted from their constant packings and unpackings. The servants certainly could not have been thrilled at the idea of moving yet again. Quarantine measures were adopted, with anything that came from plague-ridden London being avoided. Despite all this, it was a mostly happy time for Catherine, who was visibly pregnant again and enjoying Charles's attention. Thinking that an heir to the throne was about to emerge, Charles was attempting somewhat to rein in his excesses, filled with good intentions to be a model husband, although he was still visiting Frances Stuart and a heavily pregnant Countess of Castlemaine every morning before breakfast.[42]

The royals, followed by the whole court, set themselves up among Oxford's university buildings. Crenellated New

College was converted into the Spanish embassy and castle-like Magdalen the French. The whole city, in fact, was transformed, down to the less desirable courtly hangers-on, the con artists and the thieves drawn to the potential profits to be made from the wealthy elite. One such was a man calling himself Major Clancie, who 'wore a red coat with silver buttons; looked sharkingly' and would steal cloaks or other possessions after church services.[43] The confusion of people as they left the church was the perfect cover for absconding with a few garments, to be resold on the country's thriving second-hand clothes market. In addition, the ever-irascible Anthony Wood complained that local tradespeople favoured courtiers over Oxford dons like himself. But slower deliveries and some light pickpocketing was not much to put up with compared with what London was suffering.

The capital had become a city of the dead. If someone caught plague, they were shut up with their entire household, with the others allowed out forty days later if no one else fell ill. Frequently locked in with their suppurating dead relatives, however, supplies of food dwindling, everyone in the house was doomed. Some tried to kill the watchman assigned to guard each plague-stricken house. One man used a bomb made from gunpowder he had on hand for making fireworks, while others lowered nooses onto unsuspecting necks from upper storeys, pulling upwards to hang the watchman if he did not agree to open the door for them, the family escaping while the man kicked his feet. It was kill or be killed for the desperate, and at least forty watchmen were murdered by the people they were guarding.[44]

The hot summer produced an unimaginable odour, the smell of the dead mingling with piled-up excrement and the stench of the river, the rubbish dump of the city. Fear lurked everywhere as the plague made its inexorable advance. Clergyman John Allin breathlessly recorded the progress of the disease from house to house: 'I am, through mercy, yet well in middest of death and that, too, approaching neerer and neerer: not many doors off, and the pitt open dayly within view of my chamber window.'[45] This was a burial pit, corpses piled up unceremoniously and dumped in great heaps, with arms and legs haphazardly atop one another. Victims were avoided 'like a Basiliske or Salamander, which kill all they see or touch', healthy Londoners too scared to speak to one another for fear of infection, while supplies of food and coal dwindled as ships were afraid to dock into the port.[46]

The city became quiet, punctuated by the doleful sound of church bells ringing and wagon drivers calling, 'Bring out your dead!' The only crowds that gathered were for funerals, a form of public entertainment for an alternately suffering and bored population. In their desperation, some people believed a wild rumour that contracting the French pox (syphilis) would immunise them against plague, and rushed out to consort with prostitutes. Unsurprisingly, many were successful in contracting syphilis, but this did not give them the longed-for immunity: instead, they had two diseases to contend with.[47]

Some plague victims, aware of the hysteria attending their dire condition and perhaps becoming delirious, tried to bring the healthy down with them, spitting at them in the street. Acts of selfishness contrasted with those of heroism, like Pepys' doctor, Alexander Burnett, who survived the first wave of plague and went on to treat many sufferers, causing him to be reinfected and finally die himself.[48] Kentish apothecary William Boghurst tirelessly travelled 'out of one house into another, dressing soares and being allwaies in their breath and sweate', helping sufferers to sit up and breathe even as they vomited in his face.[49] Of those who had not fled, so many doctors and apothecaries died that there were barely any left in the city by the time the plague had run its course. Many sufferers died avoidable deaths from dehydration and lack of food, neglected for fear of the disease. While some turned to helping others or to God and penitence, others drank and sang in the taverns, crying out blasphemies.

Merrily ensconced at Oxford, the court continued its usual round of dancing, gossiping and scandal while London died. Inevitably, tales of its scandals travelled from mouth to mouth, eventually reaching the city, where Pepys was predictably outraged at 'the wantonnesses of the Court', hearing that Charles 'do spend most of his time in feeling and kissing them [women] naked'. Rather hypocritically considering Pepys' own sex life, he was saddened that 'this lechery will never leave him'.[50] Pepys and Catherine at least had that sentiment in common.

The courtiers' raucous way of life was not much approved of in Oxford. Anthony Wood recorded that 'The greater sort of the courtiers were high, proud, insolent, and looked upon scholars noe more than pedants, or pedagogicall persons . . . To give further character of the court, they, though they were neat and gay in their apparell, yet they were very nasty and beastly . . . Rude, rough, whoremongers; vaine, empty, carelesse.'[51] There is not much of substance to Wood's complaint here, other than offence that courtiers did not respect 'pedagogicall persons' very much. He himself was a great pedant, so it is no surprise that the courtiers thought him so.

In December 1665, while lodging at Merton College with Catherine and the rest of her ladies, Castlemaine gave birth to the third of her sons with Charles. As soon as the news spread through the small city, a libel was pinned to her door that ran:

The reason why she is not duck'd
'Cause by Caesar she is fuck'd.

It is an inversion of Thomas Wyatt's sonnet, presumed to be about Anne Boleyn, whom he describes as a hind with 'Noli me tangere, for Caesar's I am' written in diamonds around her neck. Noli me tangere means 'do not touch me', the implication being that no one can touch Castlemaine because of Charles. The ominous libel suggests that, without Charles's protection, Castlemaine would have been punished in a humiliating ordeal that was visited on sex workers – the ducking stool, a kind of see-saw with a chair on one end that was lowered into water, 'ducking' the sitter.

Catherine, on the other hand, remained exempt from criticism and continued to be one of the few popular courtiers who had descended on Oxford. However, her stay in the beautiful suite of rooms with their clear-paned windows overlooking Merton's dual quads was not without its trials. Like Castlemaine, she was pregnant in late 1665, but suffered a miscarriage on 4 February 1666. She had been married for almost three years now, watching in despair while her husband's mistress celebrated and recovered from the birth of yet another healthy boy.[52] Catherine had so far been unable to have any children, and the pressure was mounting to produce an heir. A child would secure not only the future of the Stuart dynasty, but her own place as queen consort; without a child, she would never be entirely safe from calls of divorce, and always forced to defend her place.

After her devastating miscarriage, Catherine picked herself up and left for London on 16 February 1666, joining the rest of the court in the capital, where the plague had mostly run its course. Charles met her at the blocky Tudor palace of Syon, perched on the north bank of the Thames, and they sailed majestically to Whitehall together on the royal barge.[53] Catherine put on a good show of stateliness, but continued to be unwell through March and April, possibly fuelled by low mood. Her appetite, as usual, suffered. One of her attendants theorised that 'the profound depression and melancholy which so often assail her causes her stomach to fail in its function'.[54] She was undergoing a 'course of physique'[55] when word reached London of her mother's death.

Charles and Catherine's doctors feared that she was too ill to bear the news that the woman to whom she had been so close, who had educated her (albeit not very comprehensively), loved her and taught her how to be a queen, had died. When Catherine was finally well enough to be told, she was thrown into despair once more. As a mark of her status, the whole court followed her into deep mourning, which included not dressing their hair in elaborate curls or wearing fashionable black patches on the face, otherwise known as 'mouches' or flies; these signs of vanity were thought to be disrespectful to the dead. Pepys was disappointed to see Castlemaine without them, and in black, which did not suit her luxuriant beauty. He thought she looked positively 'ordinary'.[56]

Having abandoned Oxford, the court left behind a dubious reputation and plenty of scandal. But that was not their only parting gift; as the colleges were cleaned and made ready for the dons to return, they found courtiers had left 'their excrements in every corner, in chimneys, studies, colehouses, cellers'.[57]

Rather than using water closets or going to the loo outside, they had apparently turned any convenient corner into a toilet. Their habits were less than desirable when it came to hygiene or basic decency, even by Restoration standards.

The Dutch regarded the Great Fire of London, which broke out on 2 September 1666, as a divine reckoning for the English raids on unarmed civilians, Sir Robert Holmes having attacked the towns of Vlie and Schelling less than a month before. Many of the English themselves believed that the conflagration was, in one way or another, judgement on the sins of the City of London, and heaped on top of the terrible summer plague, it did seem as though God was determined to do away with the capital. The origins of the fire are both mysterious and not. It started on Pudding Lane, a narrow street named not after delicious after-dinner dessert but unwanted animal entrails or 'pudding', thrown onto the street by medieval slaughterhouses, where they would rot until they were eventually swept into the Thames.[58]

One of the street's Restoration residents, Thomas Farriner, was a baker with a contract making ship's biscuit for the navy. His oven should have been cold when the household went to bed on Saturday 1 September, but at one o'clock the next morning, the family's manservant woke coughing, thick smoke choking him. He called out 'Fire!' as loudly as he could, rousing the house. Most of the family was sleeping upstairs, and by the time the alarm was raised, the flames were too fierce for them to squeeze their way down past the kitchen. They managed to escape across the eaves and in through a neighbour's bedroom window. Only one household maid, either too confused or too afraid of heights to run from roof to roof, was left behind. She burned to death, the first victim of the Great Fire.

Used to the destructive potential of fire on the dry medieval timbers that made up their houses and businesses, Farriner's neighbours hurried to extinguish the blaze. Their job was made more difficult by the extreme dryness of the timber, seasoned after a long, hot summer, combined with a strong wind that whipped the flames higher and fiercer. They used 'whatever came to hand . . . buckets of water; shovelfuls of earth and dung; milk, beer and urine'.[59] But the wind was blowing oxygen into the fire, and the tinder-dry homes were perfect fuel. More serious measures were needed than throwing random materials onto the blaze, and the Lord Mayor was duly summoned from his bed to authorise knocking down buildings, thus creating a gap to stop the fire from spreading from house to house and contain it within Pudding Lane. This was the normal measure Londoners tried when a fire was too big to be quenched with beer. Fire hooks would be manned by teams of people who pulled until the house's timbers tumbled down, hauling them out of the way to create a dead zone, other teams ready with water and earth to smother any stray sparks that bridged the gap.

The Lord Mayor, blinking in the firelight, prevaricated, afraid to be unpopular with business owners for authorising the destruction of their property. Fear of their wrath won over fear of the fire, and he finally declared that it wasn't serious enough for such extreme measures, claiming that 'A woman could piss it out.'[60] He went back to bed. By the morning, it was clear that the fire was more serious than anyone had realised. London was burning, as the diarist John Evelyn vividly recalled: 'the noise and cracking and thunder of the impetuous flames, the shrieking of women and children, the hurry of people, the fall of towers, houses, and churches, was like a hideous storm, and the air all about so hot and inflamed that one was not able to approach it'.[61]

People had been roused from their homes in the middle of the night, confused and horrified by the almighty blaze that was leaping from house to house. It was hard not to see it as a deliberate, malevolent force. Pepys gave personality to the fire; for him it grew 'in a most horrid, malicious bloody flame, not like the fire flame of an ordinary fire'.[62] He huddled on the bank on the opposite side of the Thames, watching with a large crowd as their homes were destroyed.

The great cathedral of St Paul's cracked and shivered, its massive bulk standing over 120 feet taller than St Paul's today. The area was a hub for the book trade, so booksellers had hurriedly stored their stock in the great stone building, believing it would not suffer from the fire. They were wrong, the mass of dry paper only heightening the blaze that overwhelmed the ancient structure on 3 September. All the next day, its stones 'flew like granados, the Lead melting down the streetes in a streame, & the very pavements of them glowing with a firey rednesses, so as nor horse nor man was able to tread on them'. Evelyn watched it burn, describing 'the ruines resembling the picture of Troy. London was, but is no more.'[63] The books burned for another week.

The fire was so huge it was seen and heard as far as Oxford, over fifty miles away. Scholars in the university city watched as the sun was darkened by clouds of smoke, while at night the moon turned red and a noise like waves carried to them on the wind. It was the crackling of fire consuming the city.[64]

The ravaging blaze seemed unstoppable, spreading so fast and so voraciously it tumbled stone. Catherine, in Whitehall Palace, far to the west of the smoking City of London – then not joined into the vast mega-city London is today – began to fear that it would reach her. Reminiscent of their flight from the plague, but in double time, she readied her household to leave for the comparative safety of Hampton Court, a confusion of packing and running servants hellishly lit by the dull red glow of the ever-moving fire.[65] The loud crackle of the flames smothered shouted orders, and everyone raced to save what they could in a palace filled with hundreds of years' worth of valuable paintings, tapestries and silken carpets, not to mention Catherine's dowry of polished lacquerware, jewels and gleaming plate. Orders went out to destroy some of the outer buildings connected to the palace, in the hope that it would stop the fire before it could reach Whitehall proper. The rending of timber and the shouts of teams of men pulling down centuries-old buildings added to the noise and confusion. Eventually, the flames died out before reaching them, helped by gunpowder teams blowing up rows of houses to create a firebreak.

The fire was over, but three days later, the ground burned so hot through his shoes that John Evelyn recorded he could hardly walk on it, and for months new blazes would erupt as people opened cellar doors and ignited the glowing embers with fresh oxygen.

In the aftermath of the Great Fire, a delicate yellow flower, its petals furling outwards, bloomed all over the city. Called London rocket, it was seen again in the aftermath of Second World War air raids, flowering in the ruins. However, London's 1666 population did not linger poetically on the plant. Everyone was quick to point the finger of blame. Was the fire in fact arson? A Dutch reprisal for Holmes's Bonfire? Surgeon Thomas Middleton had climbed a church steeple to watch the fire's progress, and reported that 'These and such like observations begat in me a persuasion that the fire was maintained by design.'[66] The French were also accused of throwing 'fireballs' into houses, stoking the flames further.

Looting of foreign shops occurred, and a mob attacked an unsuspecting Frenchman, hitting him over the head with an iron bar, causing blood to flow from his wound 'in a plentiful stream down to his ancles'.[67] Even the Portuguese were suspected, and a member of the ambassador's household was beaten up after it was claimed he too had thrown a fireball. The man maintained he had merely been walking down the street and found a piece of bread on the ground, picking it up and putting it on a window-sill. The crust of bread was found where he had described it, but he was taken into protective custody and quietly released several days later.[68] Close as she was to the Portuguese ambassador, Catherine would likely have taken an interest in the case. There was no evidence of foreign activity provoking the fire, but in the face of such overwhelming calamity, it seemed easier to blame someone, and fireballs were the favourite accusation of the time. Presumably these were gunpowder concoctions that blew up on contact. It sounds like an unstable item to smuggle under a coat.

The devastation was terrible. Between 70,000 and 80,000 people were made homeless, and the rebuilding would cost around £9 million. Many had lost all their possessions, including the stock they needed for their businesses.[69] On the plus side, there were remarkably few deaths, most likely thanks to the low level of medieval and Tudor buildings. Those trapped in their houses were able, like the Farriner household, to escape over the roof or even jump from a window.

The problems were not confined to London. Farmers could not get their goods into the city, thanks to a chronic shortage of transportation in the chaos succeeding the fire. There was an excess of food in the markets that they were unable to sell. The result? As Anthony Wood recorded succinctly, 'Many fermers broke; clapt up in prison because they cannot pay their rent, corne being so cheap.'[70]

For Charles, the devastation was in some ways a new opportunity. He and his brother had acted quickly and decisively to stop the fire, overruling the Lord Mayor and enabling firebreaks to be created that did eventually stop the blaze. He had not wanted the city to burn, but now that it had, he was excited by the prospect of rebuilding, replacing the cramped medieval streets of old London with a modern city with wide thoroughfares and elegant neoclassical buildings.

Within a fortnight, scientist and architect Sir Christopher Wren had drawn up a plan for the ideal rebuild. Broad streets in straight lines would introduce light and air to the centre of the city, replacing the wooden houses perched precariously atop one another, looming over twisting alleyways, overhanging timbers competing with one another for space. Catherine was involved in the plans, too, Charles meeting another potential architect – the diarist John Evelyn – in her rooms to discuss the rebuild together with her and the Duke of York. All three were extremely pleased by Evelyn's ideas, and 'discoursed on them for near an hour' before the meeting disbanded and Catherine left to take the air, looking extremely fetching in 'her cavalier riding habit, hat and feather'.[71]

However, none of the planners had considered either the amount the new city would cost or the fact that people already lived in London. As soon as the streets were cool enough to walk on again, citizens flocked back into the square mile of the original city, camping out in tents on the plots of their former homes, laying claim to what had once been theirs. It was impossible to align these tiny medieval plots with the new, airy thoroughfares of Wren's master plan. As a result, London was rebuilt largely along its old, higgledy-piggledy lines, and despite modern planning, odd alleyways going nowhere remain today. We are probably quite lucky – the proposed thoroughfares would now be filled with traffic. The only notable exceptions that Wren and Charles managed to impose on the city were two new streets, King's Street and Queen's Street, named after Charles and Catherine respectively. They are still there, running all the way from the Guildhall to the Thames. In a way, they are sisters to Kings County and Queens County in New York, part of a trend for naming adjacent places after Catherine and Charles.

Meanwhile, the final episode of the Anglo-Dutch War was yet to be fought. As the English recovered after the ravages of fire and plague, the Dutch fleet lay in wait not too far from London, ready to avenge the raids on Vlie and Schelling. In March 1667, an unofficial truce had been declared and negotiations had begun. The English were doubly desperate for peace after their year of terrible calamity and lacked the funds to continue a war. They decided to gamble on the Dutch maintaining the unofficial truce, and did not prepare a battle fleet for the next campaign season, instead using small squadrons to defend strategic chinks in their armour.[72]

Although warned by several sources that the Dutch fleet was on its way, the English sat around and did nothing. Indeed, Charles's Secretary of State, Henry Bennet, the Earl of Arlington, believed that the Dutch preparations were merely a 'bravado'.[73] However, with a favourable wind behind them, the Dutch sailed unopposed towards Sheerness Fort on the Isle of Sheppey in Kent, whose defenders were quickly reduced to seven after a rumour went round that there was no surgeon on hand to attend the injured. The seven men were forced to surrender.[74] Suddenly realising that they might need to put up some defence, the English commandeered ships in the Thames estuary to turn into fireships, covering them with tar so that they would burn more easily. Pepys, unimpressed by this manoeuvre, recorded, 'we all down to Deptford, and pitched upon ships and set men to work, but Lord! To see how backwardly things move in this pinch.'[75] A hotchpotch of ships and crew was hastily scratched together, so badly organised that some commanders had a crew but no ship assigned to them, while others with an actual vessel could only find one crew member. Furthermore, the crews had to be guarded or they would run off and desert. No arms were provided, captains making do with anything they could find.[76]

The *Royal Katherine* was one of several English ships that were deliberately sunk in the River Medway in order to try and impede further Dutch progress. This was largely ineffectual, as not enough ships were scuppered to stop the Dutch advance, and they just sailed on past. That obstacle overcome, they then sent two fireships sailing hard at the heavy chain that ran across the river. The first was brought up short, but the second succeeded, breaking the chain and making its way through the English defences. Another fireship set the English ship the *Charles V* ablaze, and thanks to the gunpowder on board it eventually blew up.

The river fast became a criss-cross of burning vessels and flashing muskets, with the occasional splash as men tried to escape their captured ships, the slight sound muted by the cheers of the Dutch and the sound of cannon fire. The demoralised English sailors were few in number and put up little fight. As the Dutch fleet continued further up the Medway, reaching Upnor Castle, morale sank even lower. Most sailors escaped as soon as they could, though Captain Archibald Douglas stayed aboard his ship as it caught fire, and went down with it, 'because it should never be said, a Douglas quitted his post without order'.[77] Much was made of this act of heroism, although some questioned the young man's common sense.

However, the Dutch had used all their fireships in the attack. The commanders decided that they had made their point, and retreated to deeper waters further down the Thames estuary. The English were left to lick their wounds, Pepys recording, 'there is hardly anybody in the Court but do look as if he cried . . . all our hearts do now ake'.[78]

Catherine's world – like that of the rest of the elite – had been shaken by the humiliation of the defeat. The reality of war was more depressing than lively jaunts to launch ships or inspect the fleet. Fearing that the Dutch would take over London, Pepys scattered his possessions and started to carry £300 in gold on his person, in an uncomfortable-sounding girdle that gave him 'some trouble'.[79] He was not entirely delusional; the Dutch fleet was still anchored threateningly in the Thames estuary on 28 June, when John Evelyn went down 'to view not onely what Mischiefe the Dutch had don, but how triumphantly their whole

Fleete lay within the very mouth of the Thames . . . a Dreadful Spectacle as ever any English men saw, and a dishonour never to be wiped off'.[80] Their blockade meant that prices in London rose yet again, fomenting discontent and encouraging the English to make better terms in the peace negotiations that were ongoing at Breda.

Despite the recent and decisive Dutch victory, one diplomatic concession at the talks was made to the English that would change the course of history: New Amsterdam remained New York.*

The *Royal Katherine* was pulled back up from the depths of the Thames and trotted out for the next round of Anglo-Dutch wars. Catherine herself would continue to take great interest in tensions with the Dutch, and in sailing. In 1670, she had her own yacht built, called the HMY *Saudadoes*, or *saudades*, a distinctive Portuguese word that is difficult to translate, meaning profound longing or nostalgia that can bring happiness amid sadness; a sort of pleasurable suffering. For Catherine it expressed her bittersweet yearning for her homeland, easily reachable by ship but perennially too far for her to travel to. She would write in later life of her desperation 'to see my Home land on whose behalf I have been Exil'd from it for six-and-twenty years always longing to be there'.[81] Portugal, for Catherine, had taken on the

---

* For most people, this ends the story of New York and the Dutch. But in 1673, during the third Anglo-Dutch War, the city was recaptured and renamed New Orange. After yet another peace agreement, it was returned to the English and became New York again. If history had gone down a slightly different channel, we would be referring to the Big Orange rather than the Big Apple, and Queens might have taken on a Dutch name. As it is, the city's Dutch history has not been entirely lost. Elements linger in the language today, from the masters once called *baas* – now 'boss' – to the delectable little flat, sweet cakes bakeries and housewives would produce, called *koekjes* – now 'cookies'.

status of a muse, a legend, representing every unfulfilled longing England had failed to provide her with. It was a mystical land, something to work for and to hold in the imagination. The HMY *Saudadoes* was quick and elegant, and she used it to sail along the Thames. It also made the journey to Portugal twice, ferrying news and an outlet for some of her intense, nostalgic longing for her homeland.[82]

She was in sore need of consolation from letters home during the next ten years of her reign, which were to prove some of the most tumultuous both for her personally and for the country. It was not fire and war that were the threats this time, but mob violence, murder and suspicion.

7

Divorce

IN JULY 1658, the twenty-year-old, traditionally minded John Manners, Lord Roos, married his dashing distant cousin, twenty-eight-year-old Lady Anne Pierrepont. Theirs was not a happy marriage, publicly squabbling over jewels, plate and who owed who what money. It became so bad that the whole family got involved. Lady Roos' choleric father, the Marquess of Dorchester, challenged Lord Roos to a duel for ill-treating his daughter, describing Roos as 'a Tippl'd Fool, and a Bragging Coward'. Roos retaliated with the mockery: 'if by your threatning to ramme your Sword down my Throat, you do not mean your Pills, which are a more dangerous weapon, the worst is past, and I am safe enough'.[1] Dorchester was known for self-medicating as much as he was known for fighting, pulling out chunks of his opponent's hair during another public incident.[2]

After the death of their first child, Lady Anne Roos went on a much-needed break to London. There, she became pregnant with a son, whom she named Ignoto – Italian for 'unknown', a rather cruel indication of his mysterious patrimony. The father was never discovered, but the child had certainly not been sired by Lord Roos. She went on to have another illegitimate son, and again, the only fact known about the father was that it was not Lord Roos. Usually, aristocratic ladies were careful to at least give the appearance that the heir was biologically their husband's. Bored, flirtatious and dashing, Lady Roos had flown in the face of all convention.

And she took delight in doing so. She boasted to her lord that regardless of who the child's father was, it would one day succeed to all his possessions and titles. Lord Roos' own biological line would die out, usurped by her illegitimate child. Her elder son was nicknamed 'John', in mimicry of Lord Roos' own Christian name.

In 1663, Lord Roos was granted judicial separation from bed and board, but this was not enough. Poor Ignoto was still his heir. At the time, the Church of England had no other option. Married couples wanting out could pick between separation, death and annulment, but the latter only if it could be proved that the marriage had not been consummated. Lord and Lady Roos had had a child together before Ignoto was born, so Lord Roos brought the case before the House of Lords in 1666, attempting to pronounce his wife's children illegitimate and to petition for divorce. It was a landmark case, and the whole country watched with gleeful expectancy.

The king appeared deeply interested in the progress of the case, frequently attending the House of Lords to listen to the arguments back and forth on whether divorce should be granted, including of course the scurrilous details of Lady Roos' sex life. Courtiers watched anxiously: did his interest mean that Charles approved of divorce in general? Was Catherine to be treated like another woman of her name, Catherine of Aragon, who had failed to produce a satisfactory heir and been summarily dismissed?

Catherine herself was excessively annoyed by Charles's close attention to the case, and said that if she could in all conscience go to a convent, she would do it. However, she felt no vocation for a religious life, and had no desire to cease being queen. She had fought for her position and she loved her husband. Besides, what would happen to Portugal if she simply let go? Their dearly paid-for alliance would be worth nothing without Catherine on the English throne. James, Duke of York, was also terrified by the Roos case: divorce from Catherine meant that Charles would most likely go on to have legitimate children, scuppering James's chance at the throne. Being Charles's only surviving brother, he had long been second in line, and had begun to look upon the crown as his right.

When the Roos case came up before the Commons, debate was tense, some MPs declaring it against the will of God, while others had a more relaxed attitude. Lord Roos' side entertained MPs on a generous scale, plying them with drink at the Dog Tavern before the vote, both to keep them in one place and to ensure they voted in favour of divorce.

Alongside this blatant bribery, there were a few voices of sense: Sir William Coventry petitioned for anyone to be able to divorce their wife on the grounds of adultery, without having to go through Parliament; he argued that he 'knows no reason that a poor man may have a wife as well as a rich man; and therefore if the thing be made an Act, would have it general'.[3] He was ignored, and until 1857, anyone wanting a divorce in England had to go through Parliament to get it, a horrendously lengthy and expensive procedure that meant the poor mostly had to resort to bigamy if they wanted to marry again, or not bother getting legally married in the first place.

On 11 April 1670, Lord Roos was given permission to remarry, spending one shilling and ten pence on wood faggots to light a bonfire in celebration of the divorce – clearly a big bonfire.[4] For the elite, divorce was now possible.

The Roos case marked the first divorce in England since the Reformation, and put fear into Catherine's heart. In the public imagination, her marriage became a cause of furious speculation. Pamphlets were written arguing that 'An incapacity for the ends of marriage, previous to it, makes a Nullity of the marriage upon a subsequent discovery of it.'[5] It seemed like a pointed attack on Catherine's not having produced an heir; her 'incapacity' in fulfilling the main end of marriage, i.e. procreation. They had been married for six years, and she was approaching thirty. Charles's many illegitimate children made the matter worse, placing the blame for infertility squarely at her door (although fertility is also a matter of compatibility between partners, something that wasn't understood at the time). In the seventeenth century, the woman was usually blamed for lack of children – even in Pepys' case, where an operation to remove a bladder stone had sliced him open and rooted around perilously close to his reproductive organs, very likely making him infertile.

Charles made no complaint about putting the royal seal on the document that confirmed the couple's official divorce. Everyone knew that the Roos case was a proxy for the king's own marriage, and Charles approving of it seemed to suggest that he was willing to divorce Catherine.

Here we come to a complicated moment where politics combined with the intertwined familial relationships of the nobility. Anthony Ashley Cooper, later Earl of Shaftesbury, was married to Lord Roos' sister. As a result, he was not in favour of the divorce, since if Roos was allowed to remarry, he would almost certainly have legitimate children and cut Shaftesbury's wife out of the family inheritance. However, once the divorce was a fait accompli, no one spoke more strongly in favour of divorce (and by proxy Catherine's divorce) than rising political star Shaftesbury.

For the next decade, Shaftesbury would be Catherine's nemesis: strongly anti-Catholic, he was always pushing, plotting and gathering support to oust her from the throne. To others, he could be very charming; he was an excellent conversationalist and shrewd politician, with a talent for dominating parties. His portraits show a man with wide eyes, a pointed chin and a look of slight consternation, pressing his lips together either in apprehension or disapproval (or perhaps, like Catherine, he just had bad teeth and did not want to show them). He had long suffered from a debilitating pain in his left side, and when his private secretary, John Locke (yes, the philosopher John Locke), persuaded him to have it operated on, an internal cyst caused by the larval sack of a tapeworm was revealed; this type of sack can release 'daughter cysts' that are transmitted around the body and contribute to weight loss and fatigue. To enable doctors to drain the cyst regularly, Shaftesbury had a silver tube fitted to his side, to which a tap could be attached. It was excellent ammunition for his political opponents, who dubbed the Earl 'Tapski' or 'Potapski', the Polish ending because he was accused of trying to make England an elective monarchy like Poland.[6]

Shaftesbury was much relieved by the operation and eternally grateful to Locke. Despite living with a tube in his side, he managed to continue the hard drinking and flirtations for which he was notorious. As the lawyer and contemporary biographer Roger North put it, he 'was not behindhand, with the Court, in the modish pleasures of the time; and to what excess of libertinism they were commonly grown, is no secret'.[7]

Catherine heartily detested him as much as she detested anyone, for one of his principal schemes was divorcing her from Charles so that the king could remarry and produce a new Protestant heir to the throne. She was not the only one; Poet Laureate John Dryden called him:

> Restless, unfixt in Principle and Place,
> In Power unpleas'd, impatient of Disgrace.[8]

His true threat to Catherine was in his popularity with the people and his ability to shift with the political winds. He was an excellent reader of public opinion, and although real hatred was directed at Charles's bevy of mistresses, as the reign progressed without an heir, poems and pamphlets began to complain about the royal couple's lack of legitimate issue. A popular poem published in 1679 asked:

> Would you once bless the English Nation,
> By changing of Queen Kate's Vocation,
> And find one fit for procreation.[9]

Perhaps the most vicious of the attacks decried Catherine's love of ballets and dancing, claiming:

> Poore Private Balls content ye Fairy Queene,
> You must dance, & dance damn'dly, & be seene,

Ill-natur'd little Goblyn, & design'd
For nothing, but to dance, & vexe mankind.[10]

With such vituperative personal attacks circulating, it was an extremely difficult time for Catherine to be without her husband's support. Charles certainly seemed tempted by the idea of divorce. In 1670, when this poem was written, she was only thirty-five and still technically capable of having children, although no one but the queen herself believed this would ever happen, and the stress connected to her pregnancy and conception increased the difficulty.

Without children, her position would never be assured. Cruelly, the word 'infecund' came to be associated with her. This was not only unpleasant but untrue: the last pregnancy that we know of was only a year before this poem was published, when Catherine was thirty-four, an age at which many women today are only starting to think about having children. In May 1669, Charles wrote obliquely to his beloved sister Henriette-Anne that 'My wife has been a little indisposed some few days, and there is hope that it will prove a disease not displeasing to me.' However, it was not to be. A month later, he wrote, 'My wife, after all our hopes, has miscarried again, without any visible accident. The physicians are divided whether it were a false conception or a good one.'[11] The story goes that a pet fox startled her by jumping onto her bed, inducing a miscarriage on 7 June. There were always odd pets running up and down the corridors at Whitehall, with Charles's beloved spaniels allowed to whelp in his room, the smell of dog a normal accompaniment to the royal presence.

Yet another miscarriage was a devastating blow to Catherine's hopes, and of course was to have important ramifications. As historian K. H. D. Haley has neatly put it, 'Thus a pet fox may have produced one of those dynastic accidents which modify the course of history.'[12]

While divorce was a hot topic during the late 1660s and particularly following the Roos outcome in 1670, in 1671 events took place that made it the pressing question of the hour for Shaftesbury, Catherine, Charles and Parliament. On 31 March of that year, the witty, clever and latterly often unhappy Anne, Duchess of York, had died. She had left behind two daughters, Mary and Anne, both raised Protestant. Catherine had always enjoyed a cordial relationship with her nieces, despite Mary in particular being ill-tempered and rather judgemental. With the two girls next in line to inherit the throne of majority-Protestant England and also that of Scotland, the succession was safe. But following the duchess's death, the Duke of York was keen, with rather unseemly haste, to put his neck into the matrimonial noose once more. And thanks to his own religious convictions, he was planning to marry a Catholic. This would provide a new ally for Catherine as she attempted to persuade the heathen English to embrace her own, true religion. But the threat of James producing a Catholic heir would also intensify calls for divorce. A child born of James and a new Catholic wife would inevitably be brought up Catholic – and if male would also displace James's daughters in the succession.

Rather in the manner of Lord Bristol's journey to Italy to scout out the beauty of the women for his master Charles II, the Earl of Peterborough was appointed Ambassador Extraordinary and sent on a mission to find James a bride. A stout, square-faced man with a tenacity that made up for intelligence, Peterborough had formerly been governor of Tangier and had not prospered in that enterprise. However, on returning to England he become close friends with the Duke of York. Both were flamboyantly unfaithful, and supporters of absolute monarchy. This friendship with James produced better prospects than Tangier had ever done, and Peterborough took his wife-finding mission seriously. James was not over-particular, stipulating only that – besides being a Catholic – his new bride must be beautiful. James had already tried for the lovely seventeen-year-old Lady Bellasys, from a devout Catholic family but not royal herself. Charles had forbidden it, telling him sharply that 'he could not play the fool again at his age'.[13]

Initially Peterborough's plan was to woo Claudia Felicitas of Innsbruck, attracted less by her reputation for intelligence than by her dark-haired beauty. Unfortunately, he received word that the Holy Roman Emperor Leopold I also wanted her hand, and as a matrimonial prize, Leopold blew James out of the water. Peterborough would have to look elsewhere. The French candidate was Madame de Guise, but Peterborough rejected her out of hand, finding 'her low, ill-shaped and of a feeble complexion'.[14] Introduced to Eleonore Magdalene, Princess of Neuburg, he escaped as soon as diplomacy would allow, since she was 'inclining to be Fat'.[15]

A chance conversation in Paris with the Abbé Gaspard Rizzini, the Modenese agent, had revealed both the existence and the perfections of the fourteen-year-old Mary of Modena, daughter of the ruling house of Este. The abbé protested that Mary was not for the duke, since she wished to become a nun, but after traipsing around Europe in an ineffectual search for the perfect wife, Peterborough was willing to grasp at straws and meet the young lady for himself. Seeing her portrait, 'It bore the appearance of a young Creature about Fourteen years of Age; but such a light of Beauty, such Characters of Ingenuity and Goodness, as it surprised the Earl, and fixt upon his Phancy that he had found his Mistress, and the Fortune of England.'[16] He journeyed to Modena post-haste, but was confronted at Lyons with a message that Mary was fixed on being a nun, and would not consent to a marriage. He continued to Modena anyway and, despite Mary's reluctance, the proxy marriage took place on 30 September 1673. She was persuaded partly by the Pope, who wrote to her saying that an English marriage would be a better way of advancing Catholicism than becoming a nun.

Meanwhile, Parliament had heard of the match, and begged Charles to dissolve the proxy marriage and 'stop the princess at Paris'. The next day was Guy Fawkes night, when effigies of the Pope were burned with great glee, amid the normal imprecations against popery. The British envoy at Cologne wrote that, if Mary had arrived into her new country that night, 'she would certainly be martyred'.[17] It was too late, however. Charles refused to dissolve the marriage, and after being wooed and showered with expensive jewellery by Louis XIV in Paris and Versailles, Mary and her party proceeded to England.

As they approached Whitehall, Catherine was waiting at the head of the stairs to meet her new sister, and quickly folded her into an embrace. The duke was delighted with his now fifteen-year-old child bride when they met, but she could not bear to be touched by the jowly forty-year-old roué, flinching every time he came near her and bursting into tears.[18] Eventually, whether from Stockholm syndrome or mere routine, she became 'very fond' of James, though the court pitied her for having such a boring, crass husband, who only talked of hunting and was singularly unskilled at the art of witty badinage.[19]

At first the relationship between Catherine and Mary was a little stormy, dominated by the prickly reaction of Mary's mother, Duchess Laura Martinozzi, Regent of Modena, who had accompanied her daughter to England and was outraged that Catherine should have the grander chapel at St James's Palace while Mary had to make do with a much smaller space for her devotions. The duchess was not aware that Charles had asked Catherine to lay claim to the bigger chapel, thus forcing Mary to pray as quietly as possible so as not to further inflame an angry populace.

Ever tactful, to smooth things over Catherine invited Mary and her mother to dinner at her own apartments. She was careful to arrange every detail, giving the duchess 'an armchair, to which she would be accustomed in her own country', unlike the stools the English normally ate from.[20] However, it was impossible to please everyone. On seeing that the duchess was allowed to sit with the queen – a custom reserved for royalty – many English courtiers took offence and left the room. As a biting riposte, the duchess 'wondered audibly if English ladies would allow her precedence if they knew that in her own country she could raise money without applying to Parliament'.[21] However, she warmed to Catherine after this show of friendship. The two women were very close in age, Catherine just a year older than the duchess, which made her twenty years older than her new sister-in-law.

Despite their age difference, Catherine and Mary quickly developed a close, affectionate relationship, referring to one another as 'sister'. They shared the difficulties of being a foreigner in a frequently hostile country, and would weather the storm of the most difficult period of Catherine's reign together, Mary just as involved in the tumult as Catherine herself.

The rest of the country, however, and certainly Parliament, was not disposed to like this new Catholic royal. As Charles became more absolutist and opaque in his policy, fear of Catholicism grew, especially the fear of secret Catholics pulling the strings of government behind the scenes. This notion of a hidden Catholic conspiracy produced the Test Act of 1673. Its purpose was to remove all Catholics from public office, since it forced anyone holding office to take the sacrament of the Church of England and to renounce the doctrine of transubstantiation (that the bread and wine taken during the Eucharist are literally the body and blood of Christ, rather than a metaphor). By refusing to take the oath and resigning his post as Lord High Admiral, the Duke of York helped to confirm suspicion that there was indeed a secret conspiracy of Catholics acting as the power behind the throne.

Making matters worse, since 1672 James had refused to take Anglican communion, even when pressed by his brother. He openly came out as a Catholic convert in 1673, the same year as his marriage to Mary, amid great popular fear that the next in line to the throne was now openly Catholic, and would impose strict Catholicism on the country if he became king.

Considering Catherine's determination to promote Catholicism in England, she was treated with remarkable leniency, suggesting her public popularity in 1673 at least. Her servants were exempt from having to swear to the conditions of the Test Act, despite technically being public office holders. In a rather poetic reversal, Catherine was allowed to choose which of her ladies of the bedchamber counted as her household staff and were therefore exempt from the Act. She did not include Castle-maine, by now a waning flame and not a lover Charles was going to fight for with the same passion as he had done early in their marriage.

Significantly, unlike Mary of Modena, Catherine was able to worship publicly with no ill-effects. Through her patience and tact over the last ten years, she had earned a degree of leeway that the young duchess had not. She was popular outside of London for her pretty manners and benevolent actions, allowing her subjects to kiss her hand and acting as though they were the focus of her concern, whether such was the truth or not. After a visit to Norwich in 1671, an onlooker reported that 'our whole inhabitants . . . rang and sang of nothing else but her prayses, continual prayers being offered up for all her temporal and eternal blessings'. The populace apparently believed that 'if there was a saint on earth, it was the Queen, since no one had ever heard of more goodness, charity, humility, sweetness, and virtue of all kings than were lodged in her saint-like breast'.[22]

But despite Catherine's popularity, James's marriage was an insurmountable problem for her reign. Any son born to Mary and James would be next in line to the throne, taking prece-dence over his Protestant daughters. For the majority Protestant population of England, this could not be allowed to happen. For some, the only alternative was for Charles either to legitimate his eldest son, the Duke of Monmouth, or to divorce Catherine.

Of course, as Henry VIII had found, it was more difficult to get rid of a wife who was the daughter of a king than one who was the daughter of an aristocrat. If Charles divorced Catherine, a diplomatic incident with Portugal was sure to ensue. Normally her royal-born status afforded her some measure of protection.

However, in 1671, the year of the Duchess of York's death, when Shaftesbury and the Commons began to increasingly agitate for divorce, Portugal was in need of Catherine's diplomatic intervention to preserve the alliance.

As of January 1668, Charles had not been sure whether to recognise the current ruler of Portugal. This was an abrupt turnaround and must have made all Catherine's sacrifices seem as though they had been for nothing. Much had changed in Lisbon since her departure. The new head of the country – Castelo Melhor, ruling on behalf of King Afonso – was a competent administrator, having reorganised the English troops and led Portugal to multiple victories against the Spanish in their war for independence. However, in his organising he had centralised power, and the Cortes, or parliament, had never yet met in Afonso's reign. Whatever his intentions, Castelo Melhor was seen as creating an autocratic, centralised state that undermined noble and parliamentary power.[23]

Now begins the twistiest part of the story, whose tribulations and turns fascinated Catherine.

In order to seal an alliance with France, Castelo Melhor's choice for a bride for Afonso was Louis XIV's cousin, the pretty, graceful twenty-year-old Marie Françoise of Savoy (who, like Charles II, was a grandchild of Henry IV, King of France). Her youthful, chubby-cheeked appearance belied a forceful intellect and an ambitious desire to rule. The marriage was yet another triumph of diplomacy for Portugal on the international stage, uniting the country with the most powerful royal house in Europe.

The pair married in 1666, to days of fireworks and feasting in Lisbon. Initially the marriage seems to have been perfectly cordial, but Afonso 'began to express an extraordinary coldness towards her . . . his Indifferency growing into an utter Aversion'.[24] Much as he had done as a wild teenager, he was happy to brawl on the street and preferred the company of wild companions to courtiers, surrounding himself with friends able to keep up with his hard-partying lifestyle. He loved fighting, although it was seen as beneath his dignity to wrestle or join at 'fisty Cuffs' with his peers. He liked to watch fights too, and when 'the most Blood was shed' it apparently 'pleased the King most'.[25] Rumours made their way through dockside gossip to Pepys, who had reported in 1661 that 'the King is a very rude and simple fellow; and for reviling of someone a little time ago and calling of him cuckold, was run into the cods with a sword and had been killed had he not told them that he was their king'.[26] This sounds extremely uncomfortable, since 'cods' was slang for 'testicles', though the story was likely enlarged upon as it made its way from Lisbon to London.

There was no getting around the fact that Afonso was wild. He frequently 'spent the Night in the most cheap and scandalous Pleasures'.[27] Like his father, he loved hunting, and was a hard rider, but unlike João he was not very interested in holding the reins of government. This he left to Castelo Melhor, a man not willing to share power with the young and ambitious new queen. Marie Françoise was said to have complained that 'she came to *Portugal*, not to be their Queen, but their Slave', and wholeheartedly joined the faction forming around Catherine's younger brother, Pedro.[28] She was popular with the people, careful to cultivate their good opinion with public piety and displays of benevolence. Crucially, the army also loved her.

Within two years of her much-celebrated marriage to Afonso, Marie Françoise and Pedro had begun a scandalous affair. The drama came to a head in 1667. The people feared civil war, a prophecy circulating 'That a Day was coming on, when the Rua Nova (the chief Street in Lisbon) was to be overflown with Humane Blood, so that the Horses should be bemired in Gore'.[29] Pedro and Marie Françoise's faction took over the government and banished Castelo Melhor from Portugal. Marie Françoise herself fled to a convent, demanding the repayment of her dowry from Afonso and claiming that they had never consummated the marriage thanks to Afonso's impotency. Despite tales of his debauchery among 'naughty Women' and 'cheap' pleasures, rumours of Afonso's sexual incapacity had been swirling for some time; whether they were true or not is another question.[30] Perhaps there was something to the stabbing-in-the-testicles story after all. For Marie Françoise, however, these rumours were certainly very convenient, and in December 1667 a court was convened to hear evidence for and against Afonso's impotency, deciding whether their marriage should be annulled.

In dispatches to London, the British emissary, Sir Robert Southwell, reported of Afonso, 'For women he had a kind of seraglio, doting on them (as they themselves affirm) without any effect.' To maintain his power, Castelo Melhor had allegedly invented an illegitimate child of Afonso's, keeping a girl in his house who he claimed was the king's daughter, a bizarre political pawn that he could trot out at any time to prove that Afonso could in fact bear children. Southwell claimed that Marie Françoise had known all about Afonso's impotency before their marriage, 'but being a Lady of boundless ambition, and her desires to govern prevailing over all other passions, the defects of this Prince, and the dissuasions she received against him, were but as so many incentives to warm her in her undertaking'.[31] This is unlikely, since it was Louis XIV who organised the match. Given happy letters home in the early days of the marriage, hoping for children, it is also likely that Marie Françoise and Afonso did have sex. However, in March 1668 the court ruled to annul their marriage on the grounds of Afonso's impotence.

With Marie Françoise already several months pregnant with Pedro's child, the couple were married in the spring of 1668, creating no little sensation in Portugal. Since he was quite clearly the rightful king and therefore a threat to Pedro's power, Afonso was imprisoned. When his presence became a focus for would-be plotters, he was moved from his prison in Lisbon to the Azores islands, then back to the hilltop palace at Sintra. His endless pacing back and forth across the floor like a caged tiger is said to have worn away the tiles.

Pedro became prince regent, refusing the title of king to ostensibly rule in Afonso's name. When Afonso heard the wedding bells from his prison, he is said to have fallen to 'lamenting the Misfortunes of his poor Brother *Pedro*; *Who*, as he said, *would, in a short time, have enough of the* French-*Woman*'.[32] Despite this prediction, the couple seem to have enjoyed a happy marriage, and Pedro relied on Marie Françoise's intelligence and tactical thinking to keep the throne and country together until her death in 1683.

Their daughter and only child, Isabel Luísa, was born in January 1669, inheriting her mother's sweet looks and oval face, although without Marie Françoise's ruthlessness. In a master stroke of diplomatic manoeuvring, Catherine was made godmother, and she took great interest in the child throughout her life. She seems to have been genuinely fascinated by the tribulations of the niece she had never met, writing later in her reign that 'the greatness of this my Affection was the cause of my grief at the report that my beautiful Niece was Sick. Thanks be to God that there comes Better news to relieve me of further Disquiet.'[33] As Isabel Luísa got older, she would act as her father's secretary and write letters for him to Catherine, adding in her own expressions of affection, to which Catherine responded with great pleasure, signing off with sentiments such as 'I pray you give my loving remembrance to your daughter and my niece.'[34]

Her god-daughter was a link for Catherine to her beloved Portugal. Later, she even attempted some diplomatic manoeuvring of her own by suggesting Isabel Luísa marry Louis XIV's son, confusingly also called Louis, after the death of his wife. In 1690, she wrote to Pedro, 'God has opened a door . . . I hope you will consider what a good opportunity this is to dispose of a daughter, a woman of such great talents, and worthy to be among the greatest Queens of Christendom.' Learning that the ship that was to take her letter was not sailing as soon as she had imagined, she took up her pen again, 'to implore you with all possible earnestness to weigh what I say to you on the other page, and maturely to consider that these chances do not come every day, and that if you miss this one, which is the best in the whole world, not only do you lose it, but there may be no other, and you must reckon for that. In fact it is the best chance, because it is the only one, as all the Princes of great name in Europe are already married, and thus you can see clearly that no choice remains to you in such a case.'[35]

Isabel Luísa became known as the *sempre noiva* – the perpetual fiancée – as she was always being engaged to one head of state or another but was never married. Nothing came of Catherine's excited plans for her niece to be 'the most powerful Princess in all Europe', and Isabel Luísa tragically died later that same year, when she was only twenty-one. It was rumoured that she perished of discontent after being pushed out of the succession by the birth of a brother, but this is almost certainly just a rumour.

All this was yet to come. By late 1668, the news had filtered through to England of the changeover of monarchs in Portugal. The then Secretary of State, the Earl of Arlington, wanted to transcribe the news he was receiving from Sandwich, then in Portugal, about the political situation, but Catherine refused to give up Sandwich's letters for diplomatic purposes, busy poring over them in her own quarters and wondering at the upheaval in her home country. Arlington wrote, 'There are other particulars in my Letter, which shall be transcribed for you this Night, if I can get it out of the Queens hands.'[36] He was somewhat doubtful as to whether Catherine would relinquish control of the correspondence, a source of unparalleled fascination for her.

Charles II, like Afonso, had no legitimate heir, presenting a potential constitutional crisis. Also like Afonso, he had a younger brother with ambitions to be king. Despite the long-standing alliance with Portugal, then, advisers asked whether, for his own safety, he should receive the Portuguese ambassador. By condoning Pedro's actions in Portugal, would he not be supporting the idea of a younger brother overthrowing a childless elder one? His Privy Councillors warned him to beware; even if 'the legitimate king of Portugal had no children, that was not a crime deserving imprisonment in the Terceiras' (an island of the Azores archipelago). Subjects 'having barely emerged from the civil wars, it was dangerous to countenance such an example, when England was precisely in the same case, the king not yet having legitimate heirs and the duke being inclined to supply the deficiency'.[37]

Luckily, the Portuguese at this time were becoming less reliant on English support after the difficult years of the Restoration War. After a decisive victory at the Battle of Montes Claros and signing a treaty of friendship with France, Portugal was in a strong position. Spain finally recognised the Braganzas as Portugal's ruling dynasty in 1668.

Although Catherine was undoubtedly overjoyed by these developments, the awkward dynastic situation that accompanied Portuguese victory undermined her position in England. As the discussion of her potential divorce intensified during the autumn of 1671, Charles and his councillors were also debating whether they should receive Catherine's godfather and closest adviser, the astute and ever-ingenious Francisco de Melo, or whether it was best to turn a cold shoulder to the representative of the regime in Portugal and cease any diplomatic discussion. Since he was in such a weak negotiating position, de Melo could not support Catherine in the matter of a possible divorce, but must rely on her intercession on his – and Portugal's – behalf. Pedro and Marie Françoise's joint coup might not have created a diplomatic incident had it not been for the delicate balance of power in England. Possibly through Catherine's agency, considering her close relationship with the ambassador, de Melo was eventually recognised by Charles, Pedro's coup was smoothed over, and the Anglo-Lusitanian alliance continued uninterrupted. Disaster was averted and the new royal couple were left to consolidate their domestic power base.

This they did speedily: Pedro and Marie Françoise were

canny players of the political game. They also deliberately kept Catherine on their side with diplomatic correspondence and sentimental ties like naming her as their daughter's godmother. Although her own position as queen was at its weakest, Catherine was willing to be persuaded to support them; she and Pedro had always been their mother's favourites, and in her letters to Catherine in England, Luisa had taken care to foster their sibling relationship, emphasising that Pedro had wept terribly on her departure from Lisbon. Meanwhile, poor Afonso lived out his days incarcerated. Had Catherine chosen to kick up a fuss and support his right to the throne, the outcome might have been quite different.

While all this was going on in Portugal, France and England, specifically Catherine's household, had been having turbulent times of their own.

Charming, chestnut-haired and flirtatious, Charles II's youngest sister, Henriette-Anne, who was married to Louis XIV's brother, was also penetrating and ruthless. In December 1668, she mooted the idea of a French alliance to her brother, and they thrashed out the details through correspondence in encoded cipher over the next two years. Charles was naturally French-leaning, speaking the language fluently and closely related through his mother and sister to the French ruling house. He was eager, too, for French money, which might finally release him from the tyranny of his own Parliament.

On the French side, only Henriette-Anne and Louis XIV knew about the secret treaty under negotiation. On the English side, the treaty was known only to Charles and 'one person more', that person unspecified since most of his letters were destroyed and it is only through the inefficiencies of English bureaucracy that we have any surviving information about the treaty at all.[38] Considering the evidence, it may well have been Catherine who was the 'one person more' let into this incendiary state secret, which would have been a scandal and perhaps the end of Charles's reign had it been discovered. We know that she was close to Henriette-Anne, the two frequently exchanging letters and professions of love (despite never having met). Charles admired Catherine's piety and also trusted her with the secret of his Catholic leanings. She certainly knew the secret of his Catholicism by the time of his death, urging that a priest be found to administer the Last Rites. Her confessor, Sir Richard Bellings, was used as a messenger to carry secret encoded letters between the king and his sister. We also know that James was not initially privy to the terms of the treaty, so he could not have been the trusted confidante.

Henriette-Anne certainly believed that Catherine was in a position to advise and even exert power over her brother, writing to urge her to persuade Charles to favour France while negotiating the treaty. Terms were eventually agreed, and a visit from Henriette-Anne was arranged to finalise the secret treaty. The agreement was mainly that – in return for a hefty French subsidy – Charles would support Louis' ambitions in Europe, and particularly his claim to the Hapsburg throne.

Another term was that Charles would announce his Catholicism, but this was naturally kept secret.

Luckily, Charles's adviser, the Duke of Buckingham, proposed a French alliance almost immediately after the secret treaty had been finalised, negotiating terms with an ease unparalleled in any treaty negotiations before or since, as he was merely rehashing the secret treaty minus the clause for Charles's Catholicism. The plan was to join with France to finally subjugate the United Provinces, Charles still smarting from the humiliating defeat on the Medway that ended the Second Anglo-Dutch War. Winning a war usually led to an up-swell of popular support, with which he could facilitate his freedom from what he saw as parliamentary tyranny and carry off money and taxes with only a cursory rubber stamp from the Commons. It was an ambitious strategy.

When Henriette-Anne disembarked in England to finalise the secret treaty, she was accompanied by her ladies-in-waiting, including the twenty-one-year-old Louise de Kérouaille (hereafter called the Duchess of Portsmouth, or simply 'Portsmouth', since that was the title she was known by after 1673), to whom Charles was instantly attracted. Considered less beautiful than Castlemaine, Portsmouth had something Castlemaine had never had: excellent manners and a desire to please. She was a brilliant conversationalist and made everything about her seem comfortable and engaging. Portraits show that she had a round face and brown eyes, and was inclined to be plump; Charles affectionately called her 'fubs', meaning a small chubby person. John Evelyn was not very impressed with her looks, describing her as 'that famed beauty (but in my opinion of a childish simple and baby face)'.[39] Charles asked his sister to leave the young lady in England, but Henriette-Anne protested that she had promised Louise's mother she would look after her, and took her back to France.

However, Henriette-Anne's dramatic death a month later would both change Louise's life and threaten to dissolve the secret treaty. In June 1670, she drank some iced chicory water, and immediately afterwards began to complain of a sharp pain in her side.[40] Suspicious of her husband, the Duke of Orléans, she cried out that she had been poisoned. She died the following day. When Charles heard the news, he bitterly decried France and declared that his beloved sister had been assassinated. It was whispered that her husband's lover, the Chevalier de Lorraine, had engineered it so that Henriette-Anne drank out of a poisoned silver goblet.

Louis did all he could to allay suspicion. He quickly ordered an autopsy, at which over a hundred people were present to witness the poor woman being cut open, including one of Catherine's surgeons, Sir Alexander Boscher, who could report back to Catherine and Charles as to the good faith of the proceedings. No trace of poison was discovered. Hearing the news of the autopsy and of the genuine grief of Louis and his court, Charles pulled himself together. The alliance with France held. There were, according to the French ambassador, only three people in the English court who still believed Henriette-Anne had been poisoned: 'Prince Rupert, because he had a natural inclination to believe evil, the Duke of Buckingham, because he was always out to court popularity, and Sir John Trevor, because he was Dutch at heart and consequently an enemy of the French.'[41] Catherine seemed to be satisfied by the testimony of her physician, tragic as the death of Henriette-Anne was and despite her own tendency to cry 'poison' at the slightest glimmer of suspicion.

With the loss of her protector, the lovely Louise joined Catherine's household instead, along with others of Henriette-Anne's entourage. Knowing Charles's preference for the baby-faced Breton, 'fubs' had been purposefully sent to England by the canny Louis XIV as a honey-trap. He wanted her to become

Charles's mistress, access confidential information and report back to Louis, as well as petition generally for French interests. Louis was ever interested in the backstairs gossip from England, and always looking for ways to influence Charles.

However, Louise was reluctant at first to accept Charles's advances, despite his showering her with gifts and granting her a suite of rooms in Whitehall. She was appointed as one of Catherine's maids-of-honour, and was eventually swayed to get into bed with Charles because it was argued that the queen wished it, suggesting a level of friendship and respect between a wife and a mistress that comes across as rather odd to modern eyes. She finally became Charles's principal mistress in October 1671, when they were staying at the Earl of Arlington's country estate, near the races at Newmarket.

It was a fun-filled party, with hunting and hawking in the morning, followed by cards, dice, reading or taking the air, according to each guest's inclination. In the evening they would feast mightily; John Evelyn declared that 'there was such a furnished table, as I have seldom seen, nor anything more splendid and free'. Portsmouth had taken to lounging around 'for the most part in her undress all day', and from Charles 'there was fondness and toying with that young wanton'.[42] It was unsurprising, in this hedonistic atmosphere, and under the eye of Arlington, who wanted the king to have a French mistress and so continue his pro-French foreign policy, that Portsmouth finally gave in. There may even have been a kind of mock marriage ceremony between the couple in order to grant Louise recognition as *maîtresse-en-titre*. There was certainly a bedding ceremony, in the manner of a marriage, with 'the stocking flung'.[43] Louise and Catherine continued to get on as well as could be expected.

When the Test Act was passed in 1673, Catherine included Portsmouth in her list of household staff, allowing her to remain in the country despite her religion.

During the 1670s, as talk of divorce rumbled on and no heir came forth, Catherine felt increasingly under siege. In February 1673, she was seriously ill, and believed that she may have been poisoned by anti-Catholic sympathisers who wanted her out of the way so that Charles would be free to marry a Protestant. Even her sometime friend Portsmouth was delighted by the idea that she might die. A year earlier, as Portsmouth made merry, the French ambassador feared she 'might be taken up by all these parties, and all the more so because she does not keep her head sober, since she has got the notion that it is possible she may yet be Queen of England. She talks from morning till night of the Queen's ailments as if they were mortal.'[44] Portsmouth was – quite frankly – delusional. There was no way Charles would have been allowed to marry his Catholic mistress if Catherine died.

Charles was by now increasingly suspicious of Shaftesbury's loyalty, in large part because of his vocal support for divorce from Catherine and his antipathy towards the Duke of York. Shaftesbury was sacked as Lord Chancellor in November 1673. In response, he said, 'It is only laying down my gown, and putting on my sword.'[45] He then spent the 1673–4 parliamentary session campaigning for Charles to divorce Catherine and marry a Protestant. He was by now working with the opposition, or 'country' faction, in Parliament (later forming into the Whig party). However, he promised to remove his opposition and begin working with Charles again if only the king would agree to 'repudiate the queen and make a second marriage, so as to exclude by his own offspring the suspected progeny of the duke of York'.[46]

As discussion of divorce continued, Catherine continued to fear for her life, suspecting further poisoning attempts to get her out of the way. It would have been considerably easier for her to return to Portugal or enter a convent, but she was firm in her purpose to survive as queen consort. She had carved out a life for herself and maintained the alliance with Portugal despite her brother Pedro's best efforts to jeopardise it, and no one was going to take that away from her.

In the summer of 1674, Louise and Catherine went to Bath together to treat one of Catherine's many minor ailments – probably depression and anxiety rather than any particular illness. They bathed in the surprisingly public Queen's Bath, which a contemporary engraving shows ringed about by houses and balconies. Faces peer down from every window, while spectators lean over the rails to get a better look at the bathers. The scene is chaotic, women splashing about while naked boys try to jump into another, more public pool. Catherine – like every other bather – would have been clad in a cap and loose smock, the wet material clinging to every contour in the water.[47] She enjoyed these escapes from the court and from her husband when she could indulge in them.[48]

That autumn, the Venetian ambassador reported that 'Contrary to her usual custom, stifling the pangs of jealousy by which she is tormented, her Majesty made an effort to amuse herself during the whole of this last season with hunting and dancing.'[49] She was also an excellent archer, and enjoyed fishing; Charles had been known to get up at five a.m. to join her fishing at

Hampton Court.[50] In the winter, she returned 'unwillingly to London where the customary freedoms of the king and even more the flaunting of his mistresses dispirit her and render her incapable of disguising her sorrows'.[51]

Around this time, Charles excused himself from attending Catherine with a message that he was ill. Concerned for his health, she appeared in his bedchamber to see if she could do anything for him. He was in bed with Nell Gwyn, who quickly whisked behind a window curtain but, like Cinderella, left a slipper plainly visible on the floor behind her. Catching sight of it, Catherine trembled with suppressed anger, declaring that she herself would leave before whichever fool owned it fell ill from being in the cold.

In March 1675, Catherine once more became seriously unwell. Her doctors thought this was mental as much as physical, caused partly by the talk of divorce.[52] Charles was hardly playing the part of supportive husband. However, likely as a way to broadcast that he was not intending to split from her, he did allow her to appoint her favourite, Francisco de Melo, as her lord chamberlain. It was a controversial choice, and de Melo only lasted a year in the post, since he was discovered to have printed a Catholic book.[53]

It was Catherine's sufferings during the 1670s that seem to have inspired the Poet Laureate John Dryden's play *All For Love* (1677). Ponderous in person and middle class in his tastes, Dryden was sensitive to the queen's ill-usage by her husband. In the play, he imagined her anguish through a retelling of Shakespeare's *Antony and Cleopatra*. The only major change he made to the original (besides a lot of rhyming couplets) was to introduce Antony's long-suffering wife Octavia as a main character.

Octavia, performing as a ventriloquist's dummy for Catherine, describes herself to her husband as 'your much injur'd Wife'.[54] Octavia and Cleopatra then go on to have a historically inaccurate but highly entertaining catfight, Cleopatra calling her rival a 'Household-Clog', while Octavia hotly ripostes with the insult 'Shame of our Sex', declaring that Cleopatra has 'ruin'd my dear Lord'.[55] The allusion to the ruination of a formerly great king by his mistress was a common cry in any part of the kingdom, with much of the blame for anything that went wrong with Charles's government, as well as his spending habits, laid unfairly at their door. In the 1670s, Charles was particularly unpopular thanks to the expensive and unproductive Dutch wars.

Although she did not feel very lucky, as a Catholic queen without issue living in a time of upheaval and suspicion, Catherine was in fact rather fortunate to have the mistresses as a scapegoat. Charles I's wife, Henrietta Maria, whose spouse had been ostentatiously uxorious, had taken much of the popular blame for his government.

While Catherine managed to hang onto popular support, this was a dicey time for her. Without children, she would always have to cling tenaciously to her position, and divorce and disgrace would forever be a possibility. And as anti-Catholic sentiment in England increased, her position would become ever less secure. The next years of her reign would undoubtedly be the most dangerous, bringing her close to losing her throne.

8

Plots True and False

O N THURSDAY 17 October 1678, magistrate Sir Edmund Berry Godfrey was found lying face-down in a ditch at the bottom of Primrose Hill in north London. He had been pierced right through his body, from the left breast to the right shoulder, by his own sword, his coat thrown up over his head. There were signs of a struggle: his hat and periwig were strewn over nearby bushes, while strangulation marks were discovered marring his neck. He had last been seen alive five days earlier, at three in the afternoon. The discovery of the body would trigger perhaps the most difficult episode of Catherine's life, putting not only her place on the throne but her personal safety at risk.

In life, Sir Edmund had been a difficult and querulous man. He had become increasingly eccentric in later years, and growing deafness may have rendered him less sociable, finding being in crowds uncomfortable. Roger North described him as being 'black, hard favoured, tall, stooping . . . commonly wiping his mouth and looking [up]on the ground'.[1] Godfrey was a shrewd businessman and keenly prosecuted anyone who owed him a debt. He loved going to law, and was wrapped up with multiple lawsuits in life, notably with his nephew. He even tried to have

Charles II's physician arrested for an outstanding debt. Born to a gentry family in Kent in 1621, he also had what we would think of today as good points: his social equals were shocked by his friendship with footmen and 'ordinary' people.

However, there was plenty of bad blood in Godfrey's familial and business relationships, mainly caused by his passion for taking people to court. Added to the list of suspects for his death were the criminals he prosecuted as a magistrate. He was increasingly gaining a reputation as a severe judge. As a result, in 1660 he was cornered in an alleyway and threatened with a cudgel. Drawing his sword, he fought his assailant off while crying for help. Despite this near-death experience, Godfrey did not seem to be deterred, and his sentencing remained harsh. The 'sense of duty he possessed was thought by some to be almost maniacal in its intensity; in 1665 he was reported as having followed an absconding criminal into a plague house in order to seize the felon'.[2] Fancying himself a super-sleuth, Godfrey would spend his night hours peering down back alleys in search of miscreants he could bring to justice.

During the 1670s, he was increasingly drawn into Sir Robert Peyton's 'gang', a group hostile to the policies of Charles and his chief minister, the Earl of Danby. The gang was afraid of a French alliance, believing that that way led to popery and loss of liberty – a common theme in English politics that would eventually result in the Glorious Revolution of 1688, overthrowing the Stuart monarchy and putting parliamentary democracy firmly in the top spot.[3] Like many others, they despised Charles's mistresses, who stood for the lavishness and perceived immorality of court life.

The early 1670s was a time of rising dissent more generally

against the king, doubters discussing in coffee houses whether they should have invited him back to power in the first place. His morals did not accord with those of the population, and successive losses to the Dutch were humiliating. To make matters worse, Charles tried as much as possible to ignore Parliament, leading to accusations of tyranny. In 1674, poet Andrew Marvell cried:

> Of Kings curs'd be the power and name,
> Let all the earth henceforth abhor 'em.[4]

A 'country' (Whig) and 'city' (Tory) divide was developing apace, the 'country' party rejecting absolute monarchy entirely and allying the idea with tyranny and loss of individual freedom.

The identity of Godfrey's killer remains a mystery to this day. Possibly the most believable theory is that put forward by pamphleteer Sir Roger L'Estrange, who collected the evidence of forty witnesses and argued that Godfrey – who had been moody and depressed in the weeks leading up to his death – had committed suicide. Commenting on the positioning of the body, knees close together and under him, belly and breast supported by a bank, L'Estrange stated, 'No *Painter* could have drawn a Man that had Cast himself in a *Ditch* upon his own *Sword*, more according to *Nature*, than the *Publisher* of *This Description* has done.'[5] Godfrey's two brothers, L'Estrange continued, had covered this up to stop their elder brother's estate from going out of their hands, since by law the property of a person who had killed themselves could be seized by the Crown. There was certainly something very odd about the case – Godfrey seems to have been both strangled and stabbed, and his body was almost certainly moved post-mortem.

Despite Godfrey's support of the 'country' party and his rather puritanical leanings, when Catholics and religious dissenters came before him in court, he would generally bend the law as much as possible to release or give them a lenient sentence. He was religiously, if not morally, tolerant. After his death, however, his tolerance towards Catholics was not remembered. All that mattered was that a Protestant magistrate had been murdered in mysterious circumstances. Popular hysteria decided that he had been killed by Catholics, the first victim of an octopus-like popish plot, gripping the nation in its malicious tentacles.

Since the Reformation, England had delighted in fearing Catholics; they were compared with atheists, Jezebel and the Antichrist. Rome was the root of vice and corruption in the world. Pope-burning processions had been popular since at least 1673, where an effigy was carried through the streets before being ritually burned.[6] The Accession Day of Elizabeth I was also increasingly celebrated on the streets, sometimes with another Pope-burning, representing Protestant patriotism in the face of Stuart Catholic sympathies. Some citizens, like Godfrey, were tolerant of religious dissent, but mob hysteria has always been easier to produce than rational judgement. The country was ready to release its fear and rage, and a man called Titus Oates was shockingly well-equipped to capitalise on its darkest fears.

A contemporary description suggests that Oates had a very odd appearance: 'his face a Rainbow colour, and the rest of his body black . . . His mouth is in the middle of his face, exactly between the upper part of his forehead and the lower part of his chin';[7] his 'brow was low, his eyes small and sunk deep in his head; his face was flat, compressed in the middle so as to look like a dish or discus . . . His head scarcely protruded from his body, and was bowed towards his chest.' Portraits, even ones designed to flatter, support these rather odd proportions: 'his chin was almost equal in size to the rest of his face'. Oates was 'very remarkable for a Canting fanatical way', embellishing his discourse with theatrical flourishes.[8] He had 'the speech of the gutter, and a strident and sing-song voice, so that he seemed to wail rather than to speak'.[9] However, his delivery was never backed by much substance, and he scraped through life as an ecclesiastical con man of sorts.

By faking a degree, Oates had managed to get hired as an Anglican preacher in the navy. In 1675, he set sail for Tangier on the *Adventure*, and it was here that he claimed to have heard the first whisperings of a popish plot. Since part of Catherine's marriage treaty had included freedom of worship for the Portuguese Catholics already living in Tangier, Oates would have for the first time (other than in the queen's household) seen Catholics worshipping openly, living alongside Protestants and Jews. Initially he seems to have been attracted by this form of worship, and, after being thrown out of the navy for homosexuality, in 1677 he converted to Catholicism.

He was sent to a Jesuit training college, but was not exactly popular there. He did not speak any Latin, more than a slight problem for an aspiring Catholic divine, and nor did he manage to make many friends; one fellow student 'broke a pan about his head for recreation'.[10] He did, however, return to London with a fake doctorate to embellish his phony BA, and became known as the 'Doctor of Salamanca'. After failing to make it as a Catholic preacher, he became embittered against all Catholics, who he saw as having blocked his path to glory as a priest. The pan incident probably did not help. In July 1678, he met up with rabidly anti-Catholic Israel Tonge, an old acquaintance from his time in Tangier, and vented his anger and disappointment by fabricating the story of the Popish Plot, a vast web of conspiracy that would embroil many prominent Catholics, including Catherine, in its network of lies.

The Catholics, according to Oates, believed that the oath of allegiance to Charles II was 'Heretical, Antichristian and Devilish, and that *Charles Stuart* the King of *England* is no lawful King, but comes of a spurious Race, and that his Father was a *Black* Scotch-man, and not King *Charles* the first'.[11] He claimed that the plotters aimed to ignite rebellion in Scotland, 'now that the King was so addicted to his pleasures' he 'could take but little care in that concern'.[12] As usual, Charles's preoccupation with his mistresses was the rallying cry of all opposition to the king.

Tonge revelled in these tales, which had the seductive advantage of confirming everything he already thought about Catholics. Indeed, many of Oates's allegations were a mishmash of tales already circulating about Machiavellian Catholic schemes, such as the idea that the Great Fire was laid by Catholic arsonists, a rumour that never really died, despite the government's best efforts. In 1674, another virulent rumour had spread that there was a second gunpowder plot about to blow up the Houses of Parliament. Despite a tense moment of hysteria, no evidence of such a plot was discovered.[13] Oates combined these fears with random pieces of gossip and his own set of personal vendettas; for example, as a principal plotter he named an unfortunate Benedictine monk who had refused to give him money.[14] Full of fervour at this dastardly conspiracy, the excitable Tonge decided to try and interest Charles in Oates's wild accusations. It was never wise for a king to ignore warnings of an assassination attempt. He and Oates went to Whitehall by river, mounting the Privy Stairs to come face to face with their king. Charles heard enough to pass the matter on to his chief minister, the Earl of Danby.

Despite this interview with the king, Tonge felt that the whole business was not being taken seriously enough. He wanted proper recognition of the danger engulfing the country. On 6 September 1678, he got Oates to swear to his story under oath to Sir Edmund Berry Godfrey (they had originally tried another magistrate, who refused to cooperate, since he thought Tonge was mad). Between 28 and 29 September, Tonge and Oates appeared before the Privy Council, implicating prominent individuals far and wide. They claimed that all Charles's problems and the Civil War had been masterminded by 'these everlasting holy Cut-throats', the dastardly Catholics.[15] Oates reported multiple chilling assassination attempts that had been tried and failed, one thanks to the loose flint mechanism of a pistol, another due to the assassin's faint-heartedness. The Catholics were apparently very organised and determined, but ineffective.

Grasping at a stray hint dropped by the Earl of Danby, one of the people Oates implicated was the Duchess of York's secretary, Edward Coleman, who was a prominent Catholic. Although Oates failed to recognise him in person, the fact that Coleman was in contact with Louis XIV, via the King of France's confessor (as Oates claimed, making a wild stab in the dark), served to give credence to his allegations. The silver-tongued politician Sir Henry Coventry, watching Oates give evidence, was disturbed by what he saw: 'If he be a liar, he is the greatest and adroitest I ever saw, and yet it is a stupendous thing to think what vast concerns are like to depend upon the evidence of one young man who hath twice changed his religion.'[16] Oates's experience preaching as both an Anglican and a Catholic was coming in handy. But his theatrically delivered tales would have been given far less air time if not for the apparent confirmation of his wild theories: the sudden death of Sir Edmund Berry Godfrey, so dramatically found both stabbed and strangled.

The discovery of Godfrey's body was like a match to dry tinder. It began a witch-hunt remembered as 'Godfrey's Autumn' although in reality the persecution went on for three years. Up until now, the Popish Plot had been investigated by Charles's chief ministers and Privy Council. Disturbed by the rumours they had been hearing about Catholic plotting, in October 1678 the Commons sent for Oates in an attempt to get to the bottom of the matter themselves. Here he added another detail of the plot, naming a number of known Catholic noblemen as future heads of a 'Papist army'. It was a time of terror and uncertainty for many Catholics as Oates traipsed hither and thither about the city, accusing them of conspiracy, his words enforced by soldiers. Catherine kept her chapel in Somerset House open, candlelight glimmering on her silver plate, the air filled with incense and the sound of her choir, proud of having a free space where Catholics could worship. But all her work in trying to assure freedom for Catholics and to promote Catholicism in England was crumbling.

And things were heating up for the queen personally. London was swept up in anti-Catholic feeling, the Commons initially impressed by Oates's confident and charismatic delivery, full of flourish and invective. Would-be detective Sir Roger L'Estrange described the collective hallucination well: 'Men have got the

Trick of *Trouping One* after *Another*, in Flocks, like *Sheep*; They follow the *Bell*, and if the *Formost Leaps* the *Bridge*, the *Rest* Drown for *Company*.'[17] Mass hysteria has always been a 'trick' that humans – of all the animals – are very good at catching. Paranoia reached new heights when orders were given to search the coffins of all funeral processions for proof of secretly stashed firearms. The cellars under Parliament were investigated in real fear over another yet another would-be gunpowder plot, and great was the hysteria when a French Catholic was found operating near the building, in possession of gunpowder. It didn't much matter that he turned out to be the king's firework maker.

James, Duke of York, was implicated in the plot, partly through Coleman, his wife's ambitious Catholic secretary. Unfortunately for James, Coleman had been highly indiscreet in his correspondence, freely sharing hopes that the duke would convert England and Scotland to Catholicism, and that 'the Protestant party' would be ruined.[18] The Commons clamoured to disinherit James from his position as heir presumptive to the throne. Concerned, Charles gave a speech in Parliament promising that he would fall in with any proposed law 'to make you safe in the reign of my successor, so as they tend not to impeach the right of succession, nor the descent of the Crown in the true line'.[19] The purport of his speech was transmitted through the city, so garbled as it travelled from ear to ear that people on the streets rejoiced in the belief that Charles had decided to legitimise the Protestant James Crofts, Duke of Monmouth, his eldest illegitimate son. People let off guns and opened casks of ale in celebration, drinking 'healths to the King, the Duke of Monmouth and the Earl of Shaftesbury, as the only true pillars of our safety'.[20]

With the popularity of Catherine's inveterate enemy Shaftesbury on the rise, and the implication of her allies James and Mary in the Popish Plot, the situation was becoming dicey. It was made even worse by Oates and Tonge naming her Catholic physician, Sir George Wakeman, as a would-be assassin. They claimed that Wakeman had initially been offered £10,000 to kill Charles and had refused. However, he could not pass up the offer of £15,000 and finally agreed to assassinate the king, possibly through Catherine. They were not very clear on the details at this stage.

Wakeman's reputation as a 'worthy gentleman' had so far protected him from prosecution, and Catherine from close embroilment in the plot.[21] Things had not yet reached boiling point for the queen. James was another matter: whether as a Catholic he should be banished from the House of Lords led to impassioned debate in both houses of Parliament, the Cornish MP and staunch Royalist Sir Jonathan Trelawney sent to the Tower for hitting another MP in the lobby of Parliament.[22] Despite these dramatic happenings, so far the plot was a load of hot air. There was only Oates's testimony and Coleman's letters to substantiate it. In a court of law, two witnesses were needed to hang a man. Oates had whipped up enough hysteria that the Commons and the law courts were more than willing to kill a few Catholics, but they needed a little more evidence.

Enter William Bedloe. Fraudster, horse thief and all-out rogue, Bedloe had actually robbed Oates while the two were staying in Valladolid, north-west Spain. With a practised eye for any opportunity that might be of financial benefit to himself, he now emerged to add his testimony to the general conflagration, claiming that he knew the two Jesuits who had killed Godfrey, and moreover that they had done the dark deed in Catherine's principal residence, Somerset House. He claimed that he had been asked to help move the body by two of Catherine's servants, but had fled after seeing it at her house. The plotters, he claimed, had then carried Godfrey's corpse to Primrose Hill in a sedan chair and stabbed him with his own sword.

This was a dangerous moment for Catherine, implicating her and those close to her unequivocally in the plot. She asked for Somerset House to be searched and, unsurprisingly, no evidence was found to corroborate Bedloe's testimony. He also reported that Godfrey had been smothered, when he had in fact been strangled, then stabbed. This did not stop the Commons from believing him and, in October 1678, Wakeman was thrown in the Tower. Among the public, there were dissenting voices. The forthright Marchioness of Worcester wrote to her husband, 'I cannot but lament the unhappy age we live in, where a man whose whole life hath been nothing but villainy and pageantry, and whose word would not have been taken for sixpence, shall now have it in his power to ruin any man.'[23]

On 14 November, another magistrate involved in the case went missing: a highly strung man named John Powell. It was instantly assumed that he had been murdered by Catholics because he knew too much about their evil schemes. Trained bands were ordered to patrol the City of London at night, and in the daytime a twenty-minute walk was like wading through treacle, taking an hour thanks to all the guards investigating passers-by for popery and plotting.[24]

Now deeply concerned about Catherine's safety, the king sent for Oates and questioned him closely about her alleged role in the plot. This may have set Oates off; Charles certainly believed that he had accidentally given him the impression that he wanted her to be implicated, in order to be rid of her and marry elsewhere.[25] It would be divorce by another name. Prompted by this apparent encouragement, Oates claimed that he had been at Somerset House and overheard a woman 'say that she would not take these affronts any longer that had been done unto her, but would revenge the violation of her bed'.[26] It sounds like the plot of a revenge play from earlier in the century.

He was cross-questioned and taken to Somerset House to point out the room in which this had all taken place, but despite having the run of the place, he could not find a room that matched his earlier description, much to his chagrin.[27] The Privy Council were not convinced, and Charles was furiously angry. He remarked that, although Catherine 'had some disagreeable humours', she 'was not capable of a wicked thing; and considering his faultiness towards her in other things he thought it a horrid thing to abandon her'.[28] With a desire to push the lie to its limit, Oates's attempt to implicate Catherine marked the moment at which his tales started to unravel. He was confined to lodgings and his private papers seized by the government.

However, such was his rising star that to deny him was to be complicit in the plot. Even the king could not control the rising tide of panic and suspicion, although he now tried to limit the damage. Throughout the time of the Popish Plot, the atmosphere of mob violence and groupthink was enhanced by a fear of not saying the right thing and being accused of Catholicism oneself. Lawyer and biographer Roger North remarked, 'It was not safe for anyone to show scepticism. For upon the least occasion of that sort, What, replied they, don't you believe in the Plot? (As if the Plot were turned into a creed.)'[29] The Popish Plot had become its own religion, and the tide of popular opinion must run its course.

After Oates gave testimony to the Commons, repeating the story about a woman complaining of her husband's infidelities and vowing revenge, the House asked Charles to banish Catherine from London. But the Lords, many of whom knew and liked the queen, refused to pass the resolution. Instead, 'such of them as took but time to deliberate and to consider how the Queen hath lived, found motives to reject the complaint, and instead of favouring the accusation the time was only spent in magnifying her virtues'.[30] There was not only 'a recognizable "Queen's party", but she had the general support of the House'.[31] Everyone was willing to be believe in an underground Catholic menace, subversive and invisible, like a Bond villain dwelling in an underground lair, but few seriously believed that the queen – whom they had all seen dine publicly, and who always appeared to be devoted to the king, despite his bad treatment of her – was really plotting to poison her husband. Catherine was godmother to half the aristocracy's children, and took care to write notes of condolence and congratulation. Most of the Lords had lost or won money from her playing at cards, while she smiled too widely in delight at the game, showing off her protruding teeth. This did not fit with Oates's testimony of an embittered woman obsessed with her wrongs. Catherine's innocence was such an obvious and even boring conclusion that many of the Lords left before the end of the debate. Only five voted to exile her from London. Of course, the Earl of Shaftesbury was one of them.

It is possible that the Commons had already thought better of its decision to exile Catherine after a more sober consideration of Oates's evidence, since the House of Lords' decision did not meet with much dissent. Charles wrote to Pedro, 'We doubt not that your Highness hath already heard of the unhappy reflection that hath been lately raised against our dear consort the Queen, and do believe your Highness hath taken a sensible part with us in that indignation wherewith we have resented the issue.'[32] However worried he might be about potential plots and assassinations, Charles never countenanced the idea that Catherine was plotting to poison him, and stated of her defenders in the Lords, 'We have already fixed the Marks of Our Grace and Favour on those of Our subjects who appeared most zealous in this vindication.'[33] Charles was doing everything he could to signal his loyalty to his wife, and the way he wanted the plot to be treated.

For her part, Catherine found consolation in the very religion that had brought her all this trouble in the first place. She wrote, 'my trust is that the Almighty will establish the Truth, 'tis to his Hands I commend myself, desiring nothing save to conform to His Will'.[34] She asked Pedro to speak special prayers for her preservation in Portugal, and undoubtedly did the same in her chapel in England. Meanwhile, many of her servants were forced to leave the country, including her faithful secretary, Sir Richard Bellings, who had carried her diplomatic correspondence and helped negotiate Charles's secret treaty with France.

Despite Charles's displeasure and a lack of evidence, the rainbow-complexioned Oates was soon released from house arrest and free to cause trouble again. The Commons actually gave him the enormous pension of £1,200 a year (around £200,000 today), and an apartment in Whitehall. After a life of scraping together pennies, Oates luxuriated in his fame and privilege, later recalling these halcyon days: 'I had my guard of Beefeaters to protect me from being insulted or assassinated, my ten pounds a week duly paid without deductions, Venison Pasties and Westphalian Hams flew to my table without sending for, I was as much stared at, at the Amsterdam Coffee House and at Dick's as a Foreign Ambassador, when he makes his entry through Fleet Street.'[35]

Oates had his first star turn as chief witness in the trial of William Staley, a Catholic banker who had been overheard verbally threatening to kill the king (the charge was genuine, but Staley probably would not have been prosecuted if not for the atmosphere of the time; he had exaggerated a little while drunk at the pub).[36] The trials continued apace after this first case, the defendants appearing almost universally with even more inadequate grounds for conviction. The problem for them was that it was almost impossible to defend against stories that were entirely fabricated: what was there to disprove? Democracy – in the form of the Commons – had already failed to adequately assess the evidence and stem the tide of mob justice. Now it was down to the judicial arm of government. But the legal system, staffed by judges keen to see Catholic conspiracy everywhere, also failed. Oates's testimony was often demonstrably contradictory, but when holes were poked in his story he got away with it by claiming failing eyesight or headaches. Personal grudges were avenged as more and more informers came forward, pointing their fingers at alleged conspirators. Oates was responsible, either directly or indirectly, for the deaths of thirty-five men.[37]

Catherine watched the popular mania with dismay, referring to the Popish Plot as her time of 'Troubles'.[38] Both her ideology and her personal safety were threatened. Her physician was in the Tower, and if someone so close to her were found guilty, she was likely to be next.

Watching mob suspicion take over the streets and plunge the country into a finger-pointing mess of anarchy and suspicion, supported by the House of Commons, probably further bolstered Catherine's belief in absolute monarchy. It made a benevolent and all-powerful king or queen seem a far more sensible option than an elected institution.

Soon the mania of the Popish Plot had spread well beyond London. 'Night riders' were seen and heard all over the country, from Whitby to Wiltshire to Gloucestershire. These were alleged Catholic plotters carrying out their dastardly deeds under the deep cover of dark, their horses' hooves ringing through the streets in the small hours of the morning. No such riders existed: the phenomenon was a national hallucination.[39]

Fears of armed Catholics taking over the country by force, burning Protestants, reached a climax with the Purbeck invasion scare of December 1678. Two months after the discovery of Godfrey's body at the foot of Primrose Hill, a great force of armed men was seen in Purbeck, a peninsula on the Dorset coast with an enormous sweeping bay ringed by chalk cliffs. Hearing of this 'invasion', the Bristol militia was called out in alarm, and rumour swept on winged feet to London and throughout the country as far as Yorkshire.[40] This frenzied pitch of paranoia was brief. When the missing magistrate John Powell appeared (having suffered from a nervous breakdown rather than a murder attempt) and no invasion force appeared to substantiate the Dorset rumours, the country effectively transitioned from red alert to amber. Looked at historically, this moment of collective hallucination is fascinating. At the time, it was terrifying for any Catholic, including Catherine.

While the country's hysteria may have subsided, Catherine's

situation remained extremely perilous, and she knew it. When it came to the power of rumour and political alliances, she understood her own position, balanced on a knife edge, all too well. She wrote, 'In that which concerns me I am most sure of my Innocence of all those things which Malicious Reports do impugne against me; likewise I am sure the King alsoe doth hold me innocent of them, and all those who are fair-minded: but for the Evil-minded there be no greater crime than Innocence.'[41] The truth of events did not matter. Pedro, afraid for his sister's life, suggested that Catherine return to Portugal and wait out the storm there. She refused.

Regardless of the personal danger she stood in, if she had left for Portugal, she would have cut off all influence over her husband, leaving him to the persuasions of Shaftesbury, the royal mistresses, and anyone who thought they might benefit from a new queen. It had become clear that Catherine was never going to bear a legitimate heir to the throne, and the Duke of York's marriage to the Catholic Mary of Modena had presented a grave problem in terms of a Protestant succession. Catherine might have been well liked by the English elite, but absence does not always make the heart grow fonder; it also makes the heart forget. She told Pedro, 'News from this Country shall be left to those who can better Relate it. You will hear such as shall seem like to every kind of Novels & Comedies, whereas my own must appear but Tragedies, all my efforts to satisfy Everybody being Unavailing.'[42]

She had spent the last seventeen years carving out a place for herself at court, sacrificing her own happiness and dignity to be on good terms with everyone, devising entertainments, writing notes, smiling when she felt like crying. She could do nothing for

Portugal without these strong personal relationships. Both the former Lord Chancellor, Clarendon, and Henrietta Maria – who had loathed one another with a gleeful passion – had liked her. Castlemaine had had her own portrait painted as St Catherine as a compliment to the queen. Yet despite everything, Catherine was under attack, threatened with disgrace and divorce.

When it reached Portugal, the news set off a storm, people believing that the accusations against Catherine were a deliberate plot to enable Charles to divorce her and so secure the succession.[43] The citizens of Lisbon were so angry it was feared they would do violence to the English inhabitants of the city in reparation for Catherine's treatment. In Lisbon at least she was always loved, as the saviour of the country in its war for independence against Spain. Before any violence could occur, however, a ship from Plymouth docked with the news that Catherine had been seen driving out with Charles, and the Lords had overturned the slander against her. The news 'changed the faces' of the would-be mob, which was just as well, 'It being impossible that all the proofs in the world should ever persuade them that Her Majesty could entertain a thought against the King's life.'[44]

Concerned at the increasing hostility in England, Pedro appointed a new ambassador to London to act as protector and support for Catherine, settling on the Marquez de Arroches. She was excited to receive such a prestigious personage, responding, 'This Court be in such state of Turmoil I fear lest he be not receiv'd with that Acclaim I could desire. Yet we will doe all we can.'[45] Unfortunately, she and de Arroches did not get along, in contrast with the close relationship she had enjoyed with the clever former ambassador Francisco de Melo. De Arroches was annoyed by her refusal to return to Portugal at his urging. He overstepped his bounds as ambassador and made a scene, mortifying Catherine, who wrote to Pedro that 'your Ambassador takes it upon himself, before the chief notables of the Court in my Reception room, to acte with such great Discourtesies as to Scandalize all Present, the King himself being much offend'd thereby & expressing himself to me in Blunt Terms against the Marquez'. She took his behaviour personally, aware that it made her look ridiculous through association and could not help her at a time when her position was so perilous.[46]

While Catherine had spent over twenty years accustoming herself to English norms, de Arroches immediately made enemies with his high-handed behaviour. She complained that 'it seeming to me sufficient all I suffer from the English . . . it is hard & new indeed for me that no Portuguese hath part in my Disconsolations'. She wrote sniffily to Pedro that she had 'Hop'd you should choose someone with greater Talents'.[47] However, this was as close as she came to actually blaming her brother; with the tact of a born political survivor, she was always careful not to antagonise Pedro too far, adding, 'I beseech you to effect a Remedy to all this in that I fear the Marquez shall proclaim my grievances have no Mending & shall soe misrepresent me to your eyes as to make my sorrow Everlasting.'[48] She knew the power of rumour and representation, and was careful to tell her own version of the story to Pedro as quickly as possible, and to undermine the ambassador.

The year 1679 began in darkness. It was an ill omen. On 12 February, candles had to be lit in churches, and the air was misty and soup-like. The accusations and trials of the Popish

Plot continued apace, rumours swirling around Catherine despite Charles's best efforts to quell them. His continued efforts to signal support for his wife, including driving out and dining together, only increased the House of Commons' fears of a Catholic successor. It seemed that Charles would never divorce Catherine, and in May, the Commons passed a bill excluding the Catholic Duke of York from succeeding to the throne.

While the Commons feared the tyranny of absolute monarchy, Charles feared the tyranny of the majority. From his perspective, Parliament had been responsible for killing his father, and had almost managed to dispose of both his brother and his wife. He quickly prorogued Parliament before the bill could pass through to the Lords, blocking it from becoming law. However, he felt forced by the tide of popular anti-Catholic sentiment to send James away to France. While he assured his brother that this was not permanent, and that he would send for him again when the furore died down, Catherine was less politically flexible than her husband. She wrote to her own brother that 'This was not Expected, it being held indeed that the King wd. always Uphold him, there being such manifest reasons, he being a Prince of notability, and having serv'd him with great Fidelity and Competence; but the King fearing the Fury of Parliament hath seemingly clos'd his Eyes to all this and taken a Step soe contrary to the affection he bears towards this Brother to whom he owes soe much. Such Decision evokes alarm that were others to support his attitudes they must suffer the same Fate.'[49] Clearly, James's exile worried her: if Charles was morally flexible enough to send his brother away from him, what might he do with an inconvenient wife?

Catherine's troubles were far from over. More and more

innocent people were brought to trial and executed. Hysteria still reigned: any fire was blamed on Catholic conspiracy, when in reality most of London's wooden buildings were a fire hazard only needing a spark to set them ablaze. The Popish Plot kept skirting uncomfortably back to the queen. Manacles were found at Somerset House, suggestive of some nebulously dark scheme. On 21 December 1678, Catherine's former servant and silversmith, Miles Prance, had been arrested. Bedloe had accused him of being one of the conspirators he had seen near Godfrey's body at Somerset House. He was chained, threatened with the rack, a torture device that had been illegal for fifty years, and finally stowed in the ironically named cell 'Little Ease' in Newgate Prison. Terrified and desperate to save his own life, the silversmith eventually broke down and made a false confession in exchange for a pardon.

Prance's experience with the law was something of a rollercoaster ride. Asking to see Charles in private, he threw himself on the king's mercy and confessed that his testimony had been false. However, he was sent back to Newgate, where he almost froze to death in the harsh winter conditions of Europe's 'Little Ice Age'.[50] Presumably thinking (and with good reason) that he would die otherwise, he falsely confessed again at the beginning of 1679, implicating Catherine's chaplain Thomas Godden among others in Godfrey's death, and saying that the conspirators had strangled the magistrate while he himself kept watch, hiding the body in Somerset House. Catherine had brought Godden to England with her when she was first married, and he was one of her close supporters.

The 'evidence' increasingly converged on Catherine's servants and her private residence. With everything seemingly stacked against her, she herself referred to these years as 'this time of Cruel afflictions'.[51] It shows something of her generosity that she later intervened to save Prance's life after it had been found that he had borne false witness, despite all the fear and trouble he had caused her. Godden's lodgings in Somerset House were searched – this time without Catherine offering access first. Charles was furious, telling Secretary Williamson, who had given the order, 'in great anger, that he marvelled at his effrontery in ordering his own house to be searched, that his head was turning, and he did not wish to be served by a man who feared anyone else but him'.[52]

The Lords and the Privy Council were increasingly unconvinced by the plot, but in the City of London, Oates remained as popular as ever. He was in high demand as a preacher, congregations listening with rapture to his sing-song theatricality. Catherine's physician, Sir George Wakeman, had been languishing in the Tower since October 1678, but in July 1679, on a tide of popular support, Oates finally managed to have him indicted for high treason. This was a perilous moment for Catherine. If the trial went badly for Wakeman, or if, like Prance, he broke down and made a false confession, she herself might be irrevocably implicated in the plot, rather than just being placed dangerously on the periphery as she had been up until this point. English queens had been tried and beheaded before. Catherine had long presented an uncomfortable problem for the Commons, and getting rid of her would mean that the king would be free to marry again (a confirmed Protestant this time) and sire a legitimate heir, brought up in the Church of England.

Afraid that Oates and his fellow witnesses would implicate Catherine, Charles sent for them privately prior to Wakeman's trial to hear what evidence they had against her. There was nothing that could directly implicate her, only hearsay (though that had been more than enough to hang Catholics less well connected). He consulted law officers, who assured him that a case could not be made up against the queen from what Oates and his fellows had said, putting Charles 'much at his ease'.[53] However, popular opinion around the trial would still prove important for Catherine. The witnesses involved were prone to conjuring last-minute accusations out of thin air, and had not hesitated to fabricate evidence in any other trial. She was far from safe yet.

Wakeman came up before Lord Chief Justice Scroggs, who in similar past cases had accepted Oates's testimony immediately, issuing warrants and hotly airing his anti-Catholic beliefs in court. Between November 1678 and June 1679, Scroggs personally sent fourteen men to their deaths, including Edward Coleman, the Duchess of York's secretary. He was a fluent speaker, admired for his wit and skill in debate, but was intolerant and without nuance; biographer Roger North wrote, 'If he did ill, it was extremely so, and if he did well, in extreme also.'[54] Scroggs was frankly sceptical that anyone 'of understanding' could possibly be Catholic, and declared in one trial, 'They eat their God, they kill their king and saint the murderer.'[55] In his defence, people really were afraid, and he does genuinely seem to have believed that there was a conspiracy. At Coleman's trial, Scroggs told him, 'You shall find we will not do to you as you do to us, blow up at adventure, kill people because they are not of your persuasion ... We seek no man's blood, but our own safety.'[56] In retrospect, this speech is rich with dark irony, as the hounds of the state were baying for innocent blood. Things did not look good for Catherine.

The trial was a serious one, both sides aware of the high stakes they were playing for. Would the queen fall, or would she survive to reign another day? Charles made very public the way he wanted proceedings to go, showering Catherine with more attention than she had seen through her whole marriage. The Countess of Sutherland wrote privately that the queen was 'now a mistress, the passion her spouse has for her is so great'.[57] Charles spent more time with her than ever, publicly and ostentatiously granting her favours and laying on displays of affection. Later in the year, Catherine wrote to Pedro praising 'the loving kindness with which your brother-in-law treats me, and how he doth take to himself in person everything that hath relation to me & my affairs soe that he may thereby Protect my Interests'.[58] She was scared by the potentially dangerous implications of the plot, but Charles was an effective support and for the first time in their married life an exemplary husband. They presented every appearance of unity, Catherine even drinking wine for the first time in many years to publicly pledge her husband's health.

Wakeman defended himself ably at his trial, bringing up his family's history of Royalist support, and asking why Oates had not recognised him when he first saw him, and also why he had not had him arrested immediately if he really did believe that he intended to assassinate the king. Oates had no response. In his summing-up to the jury, Scroggs cast doubt on the likelihood of Wakeman's being an assassin, telling them, 'We would not, to prevent all their plots (let them be as big as they can make them) shed one drop of innocent blood; therefore I would have you, in all these gentlemen's cases [Wakeman was on trial with three others], consider seriously and weigh truly the circumstances and the probability of things charged upon them.'[59]

Oates did not make a generally favourable impression at the trial, which was watched by many. John Evelyn, who attended to find out whether there was any truth in the plot, reported, 'For my part I do look upon Oates as a vain, insolent man, puffed up with the favour of the Commons . . . That he was trusted with these great secrets he pretended, or had any solid ground for what he accused divers noblemen of, I have many reasons to induce my contrary belief.'[60]

After long deliberation, Wakeman was found not guilty by the jury. This was a huge relief for Catherine; the witnesses had revealed no further evidence against her. Knowing full well what a guilty verdict would have meant for his wife, Charles wept with joy at the outcome.[61] However, the public was far from convinced of Wakeman's innocence and furious at Scroggs for pronouncing the verdict. Catherine's detested new ambassador, the Marquez de Arroches, made the situation worse for everyone by paying him a call of thanks the day after the trial, leading to outcry that Scroggs was being bribed by the Portuguese regime. Popular satires accused him of acquitting Wakeman for £10,000. A dead dog was thrown into his coach and mobs threatened him wherever he went, while Oates accused him of deliberately undermining evidence. Scroggs protested 'that he had acquitted Coleman against the will of the Court, that he had acquitted Wakeman against the will of the City, and that he would keep his office against the will of the Devil'.[62] The jury, meanwhile, 'had to flee from their homes in fear of the mob'.[63]

Popular feeling was still running hot against Catholics in London (increasingly in the provinces juries were reluctant to convict on such tenuous evidence), and although Wakeman's acquittal was an enormous relief, removing Catherine from immediate danger, her trials were not over yet. The Duke of Monmouth's cook suddenly came out with fresh 'evidence' against her, alleging that while at Windsor he had overheard two of the queen's servants plotting Charles's death, with four Irishmen as the assassins. The cook's evidence was at first discarded, but when it was submitted again, Catherine's confessor's servant was arrested.[64]

Thankfully, this was only talk. By August 1680, things finally seemed to be turning Catherine's way. Infamous con man and informer William Bedloe died in Bristol of 'extreme looseness' (presumably of the bowels) and vomiting.[65] This was a windfall for the queen, since with his dying breath he pronounced her totally innocent of any complicity in the plot. Great semi-mystical weight was attached to the words of the dying, stepping as they were towards the other side. His testimony helped shore up Catherine's shaky position.

A final chapter in the saga of plotting came from the dogged Earl of Shaftesbury, unable to let go of his plans for a Protestant succession by way of a divorce. On 17 November 1680, he introduced a divorce bill to the House of Lords, arguing that it was the country's last chance of liberty, protecting England from a Catholic succession. Like previous attempts to turn the Lords against Catherine, it found few supporters, and Shaftesbury was forced to drop the bill. Charles had agitated against it, and 'on leaving the House of Lords he went straight to the queen, and to give a proof of his extraordinary affection for her he seated himself after dinner in her apartment, and slept there a long time, which he had been in the habit of doing only in the Duchess of Portsmouth's chamber'.[66] Sleeping in Catherine's room – how privileged she must have felt! At least, with the clear unpopularity of Shaftesbury's bill, divorce was finally off the table.

Anti-Catholic feeling was still high, but the plot had finally run its course. And just as the mob had been keen to punish the Catholics, they were keen to punish Oates and his crew. The revolution always kills its children. Oates was quickly arrested for sedition and derided up and down the country. He was later sentenced to be whipped through the streets of London for five days a year for the rest of his life. A contemporary poem narrates the downward turn of his life:

> . . . at the wheels of Fortune let him Dance
> A Jigg of Pennance that can make him *Prance*;
> . . . put him to the touch, make *Titus* rore,
> The Chase is turn'd, now he's *Son of a W*—
> Then conjure him with Eggs and Kennel Dirt;
> And Contradictions that his Mouth did squirt.[67]

One of the accompanying images shows Oates locked into the pillory, ready for onions and rotten vegetables to be thrown at him, hands and face sticking out awkwardly from the wooden cross-beam, while the legend 'PERJURY PERJURY' clearly states his crimes above him. In another image he is tied to the back of a cart, looking back at his tormentors, who stand, hands raised, ready to whip his back. After scapegoating so many innocent Catholics, Oates had become the scapegoat himself, a victim of the crowd he had incited.

At the end of 1681, Catherine was more secure as queen than she had been since the Roos divorce case in 1670. But the ordeal had left its scars: she remained fretful, periodically depressed and ill. There was, of course, another side: she and Charles had reached a new accord. She had always been devoted to her husband, but she was forever grateful for his support during the greatest challenge of her reign. He had shown that, however he might humiliate her in private, he would never let anyone else do so in public.

The plot, if anything, confirmed Catherine's faith – like her namesake, Catherine of Alexandria, she had suffered for her religion. Far from hiding her beliefs, she continued her project of beautifying her chapels in both Somerset House and St James's Palace, fostering Catholic worship. In 1683, she commissioned her favourite painter, Jacob Huysmans, to paint an altar and cupola for her chapel in St James's Palace. The imagery has since been replaced with windows, but a 1688 sketch hints tantalisingly at florid shapes of angels and a kneeling figure. There were no pews in the chapel, and women knelt with their hoods covering their hair, contemplating Huysmans' altar.

In surviving the plot and steadfastly refusing to leave the country, Catherine had made it through the most dangerous and difficult years of her reign. She and Louise continued their odd friendship, living in close proximity and outwardly respectful towards one another, if the occasional tension persisted. Catherine's power and political importance was increased by allying with Mary Beatrice and James, united by the shared political aim of avoiding divorce from Charles. Their alliance would only strengthen during the final years of Catherine's time in England.

9

The Queen Dowager

O N 30 JANUARY 1685, John Evelyn watched the scene at Whitehall Palace with disgust. He described the court's 'inexpressible luxury, profaneness, gaming, and all dissoluteness, and as it were total forgetfulness of God'.[1] However much he interacted with society's elite, Evelyn never became inured to their ways, somehow managing to be forever shocked. It was a quite remarkable facet of his character.

As Evelyn looked on disapprovingly, Charles sat making merry with three duchesses: Portsmouth, Mazarin and Cleveland (formerly the Countess of Castlemaine). After several tumultuous affairs, Castlemaine had recently returned from France (always known for her excessive spending, she had left England in order to economise). They were entertained by a French boy, singing love songs in his fine, 'delicate voice'. On the other side of the room, around twenty courtiers joined 'other dissolute persons' in a round of basset, a card game only played by the elite because of the huge gains and losses involved. Fortunes changed hands at every deal, and the bank always won in the end, so much so that in France only the sons of noblemen could be the banker, in order to keep wealth within the nobility rather than promoting an upstart. The group at Whitehall, assembled for an ordinary evening, played with a bank of £2,000 (just under half a million today). Evelyn was suitably scandalised by the vastness of the amount, and to make matters worse, it was a Sunday, supposedly a day for prayer and reflection. Rather morbidly, he managed to find a moral in the scene: 'Six days after was all in the dust!'[2] Merrymaking and gambling was ended. Charles II had died.

His leg had been troubling him for some time, and he had probably weakened himself by self-medicating, one of his many quasi-scientific passions. He liked to make up concoctions in his own laboratory, being particularly fond of 'King's Drops', which were based on a recipe by the famous physician Dr Jonathan Goddard, for which Charles was said to have paid £1,500. They contained, among other ingredients, human skulls (from victims of violent death) and dried vipers. Even these drops, however, had not improved Charles's condition, and he had found moving difficult for some time, a trial for someone so physically active throughout his life. It has been speculated that he was suffering from a stroke or from kidney disease, but it may also have been infection and complications from an ulcer on his leg caused by gout – essentially an open wound that was left to get infected.

On 1 February, feeling the pain in his leg, Charles was driven out rather than taking his usual walk. He ate a hearty meal involving goose eggs, the unusual food later suspected of having something to do with his death. His attendant, Thomas Lord Bruce, conducted him to bed, the candle blowing out as they made their way through Whitehall's labyrinthine corridors. Bruce took this as a bad omen. No matter that the building was ancient and draughty. Charles passed a restless night, unusual for a normally deep sleeper, muttering and tossing back and forth. As soon as he woke, his attendants knew something was seriously wrong. His 'black' or olive complexion was an unhealthy white, and when Robert Howard, one of the grooms of the bedchamber, exclaimed, 'Sir, how do you do?', Charles's only response was to puff out his cheeks, as he habitually did when he was annoyed at something.

He staggered off to the loo, but seemed to get stuck. Keeper of the Privy Closet William Chiffinch was the only one with the authority to enter, and finally did so, perturbed by Charles's inability to properly form words. He could only say disjointed sounds, and at one point began to mutter in French, returning to the language of his youth. His servants, too scared to do anything, continued in a state of terrified denial. They delicately tried to dress and shave their unresponsive master, but before the razor could scrape off a night's worth of bristles, Charles gave 'the dreadfulest shriek', as though of a dying man, and doctors were finally called to intervene. Sir Edmund King immediately began bleeding him, while his attendants sent urgently for his brother, James, Duke of York, and the Privy Council.[3]

James, tumbling from his chambers, was so distressed by the urgent summons that he arrived with one shoe and one slipper on his feet, not noticing his own disarray. Catherine watched the bloodlettings and Charles's semi-unconscious state with increasing alarm. Finally, she turned to her sister-in-law, Mary of Modena, telling her, 'My sister, I beseech you to tell the duke, who knows the king's religion as well as I do, to endeavour to take advantage of some good moments.' Overcome by stress and the realisation that she was attending her husband's death, she then collapsed into a swoon, and had to be carried from the room. When Mary whispered Catherine's message to James, he replied weightily, 'I know it. I think of nothing else.'

Finally, two hours after his first collapse, as his servants tried to attach his shaving bib, Charles regained consciousness. His first thought was to ask for Catherine. Still unable to rouse herself, Catherine sent the reply that she would come as soon as she could, and asked his pardon if she had ever offended him. Charles's reply was a poignant summary of their marriage: 'Alas! poor lady, she begs my pardon! I beg hers with all my heart.' Many historians assume that this was their last interaction; however, despite her swoonings, Catherine was near-constantly with Charles as he slowly sank into death over the next five days, only absenting herself to be bled to cope with the pressure, a procedure that ironically probably contributed to more swoonings.

With a flash of his characteristic humour, the king apologised for being 'an unconscionable time a-dying'. His physicians, alarmed at his serious condition, tried everything they knew to keep him alive. They bled him multiple times, trying every remedy from Peruvian bark to powdered pearls to melon seeds and tincture of human skull. Another desperate measure was blistering: cantharides, or the powder of the poisonous Spanish fly, was applied, raising blisters on Charles's skin, which were then pricked and drained to remove the noxious humours contributing to disease. Nothing worked; in fact all these treatments merely hastened the end.

In a lucid moment, Charles exclaimed, 'I would give anything in the world to have a priest!', to which James replied, 'I will bring you one.' 'For God's sake, brother, do. But will you not expose yourself to danger by doing it?' Charles asked. 'Sir, though it were to cost me my life, I will get you one.' Their language here seems rather highfalutin, but something more or less along these lines did take place. It proved difficult to smuggle someone into the room, and eventually one of Catherine's priests, Father John Huddleston, disguised in an Anglican cassock and wig, was brought in by the secret entrance next to Charles's bed that had often been used to smuggle his mistresses into the room. Huddleston had hidden Charles after his escape from the Battle of Worcester in 1651, and James announced, 'Sir, I bring you a man who once saved your life; he now comes to save your soul.' However, Huddleston had forgotten to bring the sacrament with him, and one of Catherine's Portuguese priests had to make up the deficiency.

At six o'clock on his last morning, Charles asked for the curtains to be drawn and the windows opened, 'that I may behold the light of the sun for the last time!'[4] He died in great pain, his suffering increased immeasurably by his tortuous treatments, around noon on 6 February 1685. Catherine was a widow, and queen dowager where she had once been queen consort. She lay mute and grieving terribly in her candlelit apartments, surrounded by heavy black velvet drapes, as though she too had died and was lying in state.[5] Her personal priest, Padre Manuel Dias, wrote a touching account of her days of intense grief: 'nothing . . . is sufficient to console her in such great affliction; I and the other of her servants have attended her all this time by day and by night, and console her as much as is possible; but when we see her now in this solitude, all dressed in mourning, weeping such tears, we cannot indeed restrain our own; and thus all is grief and tears which shall last until God shall mitigate so great a grief'.[6]

Dias was amazed by the respect James was careful to always display to his bereaved sister-in-law during this time. Even though he was now king and the highest-ranking person in the land, he knelt rather than sat when in Catherine's presence. It did little to penetrate her thick wall of despair, so absorbed was she in mourning her husband. Depression always upset her stomach and ruined her appetite, and she was unable to eat for days.

When she did revive somewhat, she had a flamboyant marble bust of Charles commissioned, a shroud around his head, complete with a weeping Cupid, crowns and sceptres. It is a shame this orgy of symbolism does not seem to have survived to us today. The model for the bust was Charles's death mask, a wax impression of his face taken immediately after his last breath. Seeing the mask – confronted with his face as it was in life and the reality of his passing – she sank again. Dias recalled, 'she has since been very much pulled down'. There was great consternation at her insistence that she be shown such a morbid relic in the first place; the sculptor claimed he would 'sooner be hung-by-the-neck' than show it.[7]

Her entourage enjoyed the melodrama of the situation, and also tried to persuade her not to see Charles's face again. But perhaps the whole experience was cathartic. After many tearful scenes at her bedside, surrounded by oppressive drapery, Catherine finally acknowledged the handover of power from queen to queen on 7 April 1685, almost three months after Charles's death, when she paid her first formal call on the new queen, Mary Beatrice of Modena. Handing over the chapel at St James that she had so recently and magnificently renovated, she retired with her entourage of priests and ladies to Somerset House, also giving up her apartments at Whitehall to Mary Beatrice.[8]

As usual after any death or illness in Restoration court life, there were rumours that Charles had been poisoned, although by this time Catherine was so firmly entrenched in the popular imagination as a good, pious and hard-done-by wife that James or other unnamed Catholics were blamed as the potential plotters. She also had nothing to gain from his death, in fact losing power by becoming queen dowager. However, even these accusations against James did not have much vigour behind them, and his accession as King James II was surprisingly trouble-free. Worried that the populace might revolt, he made sure that he was protected by 'four or five thousand men-at-arms', but they were not called for.[9]

Charles was much mourned, with poems such as 'The Mournful Mite Or The True Subject's Sigh' being penned. However, the transition between brothers, and the return of a Catholic monarchy, was smoother than anyone could have predicted, especially in the heady days of the Popish Plot. The irascible Oxford don Anthony Wood commented that five years ago, James had been 'written against by every scribbler; vilified and abused and scandalised', but 'was now proclaimed generally with great applause and settled in his throne without a bloody nose. Such is the world's career.'[10]

The calm, however, would not last for long, and Catherine – as the third-highest-status person in the kingdom – was to be instrumental in James's short reign. In a potentially apocryphal but telling quote, Charles was said to have pronounced before his death that 'My brother will lose his kingdom by his bigotry and his soul for a lot of ugly trollops.'[11] A popular prince in his youth, James had never possessed his brother's moral flexibility or quick intelligence. He was solid, dependable and slow to new ideas, but once he had taken them on, he would cling to them doggedly, regardless of how circumstances changed. Despite all evidence to the contrary, including the mass hysteria of the Popish Plot, he had the idea that on his accession to the throne, the kingdom could be made more tolerant and more Catholic. At first, Catherine was united with James and Mary Beatrice in this joint delusion, having always promoted Catholicism in England, and in her zeal was confident that the ignorant must see the light of the one true faith.

Charles's eldest illegitimate son, the Protestant Duke of Monmouth, was the first fracture in James's rule. He had always been a potential threat, with Parliament attempting throughout Charles's later reign to legitimise him and make him heir. Inconveniently, his first name was also James, making him – in his followers' eyes – another James II. They got over this difficulty by titling him King Monmouth. He and the Duke of Argyll planned two simultaneous rebellions, Argyll stirring up trouble in Scotland and Monmouth in England. Despite warnings of bad timing, and 'a great backwardness in the gentlemen' who were supposed to support the rebellion, Monmouth pressed ahead with their plan.[12] Argyll was quickly repulsed, and Monmouth's ill-prepared rebels fared little better. Both plotters were sentenced to death.

Monmouth wrote to his stepmother, Catherine, begging her to help save his life. He told her that he had 'none left but your majesty that I think may have some compassion of me', asking her to intercede with James 'for the last Kings sake'.[13] Catherine, affectionate towards Monmouth and often having driven out with him or whiled away an evening together, duly begged James for his life. Close as she was to both James and his nephew, she was said to be present at their final interview together.[14] However, her pleading was to no avail. Monmouth was too dangerous to be allowed to live.

His death at the Tower of London on 15 July was a horrifically slow and painful one, since it took his executioner five strokes of the axe to sever his head. An angry mob had to be restrained from tearing the executioner to pieces amidst this blundering performance.[15] Despite so many people having witnessed Monmouth's death, rumours soon cropped up, born from desire rather than fact, that he had not died. It was alleged that 'an old man with a Beard' had been killed in his place and Monmouth was still going 'about in womans Cloaths in Bristoll and Summersettsheer'.[16] Unfortunately for his supporters, however, he was definitely dead.

The Monmouth and Argyll rebellions successfully suppressed, James continued to push for increased religious tolerance. His only real fault was being Catholic, and his tolerant attitude is more acceptable to us today than the zealous anti-Catholic vitriol spat by his detractors. In the summer of 1687, he went on a speaking tour of the west of England in a bid to promote his policies of toleration and his recently issued Declaration of Indulgence, which was supported by William Penn, a Quaker and the founder of Pennsylvania. The declaration granted religious freedom to everyone, reversed the penal laws, and allowed people to worship at home however they wished.

He was certainly not trying to make everyone convert to Catholicism, recognising that this would be impossible. On his speaking tour, he speculated, 'suppose . . . there should be a law made that all black men should be imprisoned, it would be unreasonable and we had as little reason to quarrel with other men for being of different opinions as for being of different complexions'.[17] These sentiments were enlightened, considering the religious zealotry espoused at the time. They were not shared by much of the population. When the Archbishop of Canterbury and six other bishops refused to read out the declaration, they were sentenced to the Tower. This measure had the opposite effect to James's intentions: as the bishops were rowed from Whitehall to the Tower, their cheering supporters lined the banks of the Thames.

Meanwhile, Catherine was pursuing her own pro-Catholic agenda and ensuring that the community of nuns she had set up in London would survive uncertain political times. During Charles's reign, she had invited a community of English nuns over from Munich and settled them at a house in St Martin's Lane, conveniently located between the City and Whitehall. After his death, she helped the convent find a new residence, settling on the largest house in Hammersmith, much further from the Protestant City. Although not suited for a convent life herself, she had a passion for visiting religious establishments, and the convent was conveniently near her summer palace. It was run on Benedictine lines, with a focus on communal living and a strict timetable.

Catherine was most likely safeguarding the future of the convent because she knew she would not be able to keep it under her protection for much longer. She announced to James, via his confessor, Father Warner, 'that she intended to go into her own country; that she had acquainted her brother with it, and that an ambassador would speedily come for her'. James was rather miffed at this and felt that she should have told him of her intentions before writing to her brother. Considering that he had 'used her with the same respect, as when the late king was living', he thought 'he deserved to be better treated by her'.[18] It was one of the moments of rupture in their relationship that contributed to cooler relations on both sides, with Catherine feeling that James had not supported her interests enough. However, they made up, and James went down to Portsmouth to look at ships for her imminent departure. Unfortunately for Catherine, she was either too ill to travel or circumstances were not quite right, and it would be years before she made it back to Portugal.

Only forty-eight, she was often ill, referring to herself as 'very indisposed and under physic, as I have always been since the King left me'.[19] At times, she had difficulty using a pen; whether suffering from gout or paralysis the doctors did not know. Considering that one of her pet hobbies was to be ill, and she had been doctored very frequently during Charles's reign, it is difficult to disentangle when there was a physical complaint, and when she was depressed. But body and mind are related, so perhaps she suffered both at once. She devoutly believed that the only possible cure for her ailments was to return to Portugal. She longed to meet her god-daughter and niece Isabel Luísa, and the two kept up a regular affectionate correspondence. Isabel Luísa continued to act as her father's scribe, maintaining the family tradition in which the womenfolk were considerably more able with the pen than the menfolk. Catherine yearned to see her homeland, and to be reunited with her brother after so long.

By far the majority of the surviving letters we have from Catherine date from around this time, begging her brother to allow her to return to Portugal. She wrote consistently for years asking to return, trying her hand at self-effacement, pointing out the difficulties of her staying as a Catholic in England, and pulling on Pedro's heartstrings. He continued to ignore her pleas, causing her finally to cry, 'my ease is already at an end, when I consider that my joys have no foundation, since I understand that you do not wish to see me, while I perpetually long to see you'.[20] After the death of Pedro's first wife, Marie Françoise, Catherine thought she might travel with his new German queen, Maria Sophia of Neuburg, who actually sailed to Portugal in an English ship in 1687. But he ignored the request, not quite so eager to see his sister, or to pay for her maintenance. Finally, in 1688, he began moving towards the idea that she might return home, and sent an ambassador to Paris to help with her journey. Unfortunately, Catherine was so ill at the time that she was unable to travel. Circumstances conspired so that she would outstay both James and Mary Beatrice in England.

Besides illness, her departure was complicated by money matters. She had found herself embroiled in a legal dispute with her former favourite and Lord Chamberlain, Henry Hyde, the second Earl of Clarendon. The young earl had soulful dark eyes and a flared nose that gives his portrait a slightly disdainful expression, but contemporaries described him as fanatically faithful and dependably discreet, if unlikely to set the world on fire with his brilliance.[21] As Clarendon himself acknowledged, despite being the elder of the two Hyde brothers, he was the less politically talented, and also less skilled in money matters; unable to maintain the family seat, he had sold it to his younger brother, Laurence, in secret so as to avoid embarrassment. It helped, of course, that Laurence had married an Irish heiress.

When Catherine claimed that he owed her payments from his time serving her, Clarendon refused to pay. In response, she

sued him, an almost unheard-of act for royalty that was rather
an embarrassment in court circles, thought to be beneath her
dignity. James privately confessed to Clarendon that 'he was
ashamed at the queen dowager's prosecuting me in this manner',
but felt obligated to back her up in public, so that royal power
in general was not undermined.[22] Clarendon offered to submit
the whole matter to the king and let him be the judge of their
dispute, but James 'answered, he could not meddle; the queen
dowager was a hard woman to have to do with, and she knew
his mind in this matter already'.[23] Although popular, thoughtful
and sweet-tempered to her friends, Catherine was hard-nosed
in matters of business, and not willing to roll over, no matter
James's advice or the possible knock to her reputation at being
seen to wrangle so openly. It is far from the British monarchy's
policy today of 'never complain, never explain', and certainly
never to air dirty laundry in public.

Luckily, Clarendon kept a diary, so we have a fairly comprehensive account of their dispute. In among the narrative of his
daily life – undergoing bloodletting, a murdered body being
found on a dung heap, and sipping tea from China with a
Chinese visitor – he describes how their legal wrangling went
back and forth over months, costing money in legal fees that
he could ill afford.[24] In his account, neither he nor Catherine
comes off particularly well, although who does while arguing
over money? It is difficult to tell who was in the right, if either
of them were. For Clarendon, it was something of a David and
Goliath situation. For her legal team, Catherine had retained
almost the entire king's council. One of the lawyers serving on
the council refused her fee and advised Clarendon privately,
perhaps as a matter of conscience, but Clarendon's legal defence

was nonetheless a poor showing compared with Catherine's. Since it was a lawsuit involving royalty, the principal of the king's prerogative was thought to be involved, and Clarendon despaired of winning the suit or maintaining his reputation. On 7 February, he wrote, 'I am thought to be in disgrace, and am to be ruined by a high hand.'²⁵ James was uncomfortably caught between the disputants, importuned and made to feel guilty by Clarendon at parties, while Mary Beatrice took Catherine's side. Eventually a compromise was settled upon.

Despite their dispute, Catherine and Clarendon maintained an odd sort of affection for one another: he defended her against her detractors, while one of her supporters assured him that 'she was well disposed to be kind to me'.²⁶ They would later become friends again, drawn together by their loyalties and the tectonic events that would soon change the British political landscape.

James's tolerant religious policies were uneasily accepted by the people and by Parliament, who accepted the new king's rule on the proviso that his heir – his elder daughter Mary, a committed Protestant married to her equally Protestant cousin William of Orange (James's fractious sister Mary's son) – would inherit. Mary Beatrice and James had, after all, been married for over a decade with no living children.

This all changed on 10 June 1688, when Queen Mary Beatrice gave birth to a son. He would inevitably be raised a Catholic by his parents, and as a boy his claim to the throne superseded that of his elder half-sister. Catherine, close to Mary Beatrice, would once more have a pivotal role to play in English politics. She arrived during the queen's labour, at 9.15 a.m., and sat on a stool, surrounded by her ladies, to watch, with the Lord Chancellor and a host of other witnesses, as Mary Beatrice gave birth, a tiny amount of privacy afforded by a thin screen. It was a horribly public ordeal for the thirty-year-old queen; her husband would later say proudly, 'scarce any Prince was ever Born where there were so many Persons present'.[27] Mary Beatrice was embarrassed to have so many men looking at her, and asked James to hide her face with his head and wig.[28] Catherine was thrilled by the birth, writing of the newborn, 'I pray God may preserve him for the increase of this Young Christianity which the Gospel here continues to sow.' She added in a hurried postscript to her brother, 'I forgot to tell you that the Pope is godfather.'[29] Momentous news indeed.

Despite James and Mary Beatrice's precautions in calling witnesses, not one person in a thousand believed their son was legitimate. Speculation had begun early, Clarendon recalling in his diary that when he went to church for the thanksgiving ceremony to celebrate the queen's being with child, there 'were not above two or three in the church, who brought the form of prayer with them: it is strange to see, how the queen's great belly is everywhere ridiculed, as if scarce anybody believed it to be true'. Aware of the potential for unrest, and afraid of another cataclysm like the Civil War, still in living memory, he added, 'Good god help us.'[30] There was widespread scepticism about whether Mary Beatrice was even pregnant, or if her stomach was just a cushion pushed under her dress. Other stories claimed that she *was* pregnant, but with the illegitimate product of an affair. Her decision to give birth in St James's Palace (her principal residence) was instantly seen as suspicious, as the Great Bedchamber there had four doors, the perfect set-up to smuggle a changeling child, born of some poor servant, into the room. The rumours, kept at a low simmer throughout the queen's pregnancy, burst into flame when a son called James Francis Edward Stuart, legitimate heir to the throne, was announced.

Something had to be done.

To prove that Mary Beatrice really had given birth to a baby boy, James called an extraordinary council and had the account printed as propaganda in his war to keep a hold on power. Catherine was a central part of this drama, her name first and most prominent on the title page as the most important attendee of the meeting. She sat in a chair placed on James's right hand, a visible support to his story and a named witness to the birth. The room was packed with both Mary Beatrice and Catherine's friends and supporters, including Frances, née Stuart, now Duchess of Richmond and Lennox; Catherine's Lord Chamberlain; and her ladies of the bedchamber, who had stood in the Great Bedchamber with her to witness the birth. Catherine herself gave a succinct testimony, 'That when the King sent for her to the Queens Labour, she came as soon as she could, and never stirred from her till she was Delivered of the Prince of Wales', signing herself 'Catherina R'.

Mrs Mary Crane, one of Catherine's ladies, gave a very similar testimony: that 'she went with the Queen Dowager to the Queens Labour on the Tenth of *June* last, and never stirred out of the Room till the Queen was Delivered'. The Duchess of Richmond and Lennox was an important witness in testifying that Mary Beatrice really had been pregnant, with all the physical changes in a woman's body that pregnancy entails. When she visited the queen before the birth, the two women had a discussion about Mary Beatrice's fear of miscarriage. As the duchess 'stood by her Bedside, her Majesty said to her, *My milk is now very troublesome, it runs out so much.'* Mary Beatrice then threw 'down the Bed clothes to the middle of her Stomach, and shewing her Smock upon her Breast to the said Deponent, which was very wet with her Milk'.[31] Others testified to witnessing the birth; the midwife apparently held up the afterbirth and showed it off to the busy room full of spectators. It was extremely intrusive and public by today's standards, but these facts of life were presented straight, everyone aware of the normal processes of childbirth.

These were important testimonies, but a throwaway comment from Mrs Margaret Dawson, one of Mary Beatrice's ladies of the bedchamber, produced a new and scandalous conspiracy theory that quickly grew legs and ran around the country. As a witness to the birth, Mrs Dawson testified that 'she saw fire carried into the Queen's Room in a Warming-Pan, to warm the Bed, after which the Queen went into her Bed'.[32] After this, Dawson had not stirred from her spot as witness until Mary Beatrice delivered a son, a testimony designed to support the idea that the queen really had given birth under the watchful eyes of her ladies and of Queen Dowager Catherine, seated on a stool throughout the whole ordeal. But the statement was quickly seized upon as evidence of deception. This, cried the gossips, must have been how the trick was carried out under so many watchful eyes. The warming pan had held not hot coals to warm the bed, but a baby who was planted under the covers and then produced by Mary Beatrice after she demonstrated some very effective acting, crying out in pretend labour. How the afterbirth was faked or the child kept silent while in the warming pan the story did not bother to explain.

Catherine was a central player in the royal couple's attempts to prop up their power and prove the legitimacy of James Francis

Edward. After serving as an unimpeachable witness to the new heir's highly contentious birth, she was one of the high-profile figures in attendance at the lavish firework show to commemorate the occasion, as James tried to quell the gossips with display. On 17 July 1688, she watched a 'Pyrotechnic Opera', which featured thousands of rockets, machines that discharged water balloons and water rockets (a type of firework that burned on the water) over the Thames, with letters of fire spelling out 'Vivat Rex' (long live the king).[33] Pyramids were constructed, with a figure of Bacchus and another of a beautiful woman in an azure robe, holding a British oak and symbolising Mary Beatrice's fecundity. The spectacle ended with a gun salvo from the Tower.[34] Far from 'long live the king', however, the writing was on the wall for the end of James's reign.

Less than three weeks later, the bishops being held in the Tower – those who had petitioned the king asking for the Declaration of Indulgence to be made illegal – were acquitted, against James's wishes. He had lost control of the law courts and the religious establishment. To make matters even worse, Londoners lit bonfires, burning in the flames an effigy of the Pope, James Francis Edward's own godfather.

As the bonfires were laid, a man disguised as a common sailor left England for the United Provinces – more specifically, for the state of Orange. His name was Rear Admiral Arthur Herbert, a dashing officer with something of the frog in his demeanour, and he carried with him a document called the Invitation to William. It asked William of Orange, himself a claimant to the English throne and married to James's elder daughter Mary, to stage an invasion of England, promising that if he did, the seven signatories of the invitation would rise up and support him. They were later called the 'Immortal Seven' by Whig propaganda, and since history is written by the victors, the revolution they engineered, replacing James with his daughter and son-in-law, has forever after been known as 'Glorious'. It is often cited as the beginning of British democracy, the signatories taking a stand against James's tyranny. James had no love for the Commons, but nothing is ever simple, and plenty of anti-Catholic bigotry motivated the invitation too.

At the beginning of November 1688, William's fleet reached Dover, where they 'bespangled the whole Channel with beautiful ships, and colours flying'.[35] James's navy had already started deserting, and his army quickly followed suit. Hampered by nosebleeds and a pro-William uprising, James's cause was falling apart. On 2 December, John Evelyn wrote, 'all the eminent nobility and persons of quality throughout England declare for the Protestant religion and laws, and go to meet the Prince; who every day sets forth new declarations against the papists'. Catholics in office fled in fear of their lives, resigning their responsibilities. Evelyn observed with both brevity and accuracy, 'it looks like a Revolution'.[36]

Rumours abounded that a Catholic counter-invasion from France was in the works. Immediately London dissolved into rioting, its citizens looting the house of the Spanish ambassador and destroying the chapel. They may have had another agenda: the ambassador was known for not paying his debts on time.[37] Remarkably, Catherine's residence and chapel escaped unscathed. Her relative popularity, however, did not stop her fear. Terrified that this was the beginning of another, even more violent Popish Plot, and without Charles to protect her this time, she anxiously watched events unfold from Somerset

House, situated on the Strand and uncomfortably close to the heart of Protestant London. Catherine's most senior officer, her trusted and well-connected chamberlain Louis de Duras, the Earl of Feversham, eventually arrived to help ensure her safety.

Feversham – though a Protestant – was loyal to both Catherine and the Duke of York, and was described by Bishop Burnet as 'an honest, brave, and good natured man, but weak to a degree not easily to be conceived'.[38] Catherine relied on him to manage her business affairs, and their closeness led to rumours of an affair that almost certainly never happened. He would sometimes be known as the 'king-dowager'. Puffy-featured in older age, with a cleft chin and impressively arching dark brows, he commanded James's forces against the Monmouth rebellion and against William's invasion, but disbanded the troops after James decided it was not worth fighting 'a foreign army and a poisoned nation'.[39]

James fled London for Kent, sending Mary and their children to France. When William marched through London, it was extraordinary to see the populace acclaim him and his invading troops, the shouts of welcome and 'hurrah' overwhelming the sound of marching feet.[40]

What did this change of monarchy mean for Catherine? While friendly with James and Mary Beatrice, and entangled with their reign as she promoted Catholicism and supported their son's claim to legitimacy, she had for some time not felt entirely easy. Although James had acted with great respect, she felt he had always put his own interests first, without considering how that affected her position, writing that he was 'always inclin'd towards' his 'own Advantage, which be that of diminishing ours'.[41] Perhaps she resented being trotted out at public events as a prop to his faltering power. He had ignored her petition to spare Monmouth, and had not acted to disentangle her monetary problems, even while Mary Beatrice supported her claims. When she had been used as a tool, why should she feel particularly loyal to James or his regime?

Although Catherine was shocked by the suddenness of the revolution, and afraid initially of mob violence, she accommodated herself in public to the new regime. In private, she harboured mixed feelings, grateful to William for his courtesy towards her, but with lingering loyalty to James. She had always endeavoured to get on well with James's daughter, the hot-tempered, passionate Mary, consoling the teenager when she was sent to Orange as a young bride in 1677 and welcoming her back to England as queen just as warm-heartedly. She would of course have been disappointed that pro-Catholic measures never came into force, but Catherine was a student of realpolitik, and did not openly complain about the situation, keeping her own chapel a refuge for English Catholics just as she had always done. She also exchanged cordial, remarkably normal visits with the new king and queen, hosting them at Somerset House.

As a mark of her friendship with both parties, Catherine's most senior officer, Feversham, was employed as an intermediary. While carrying a letter from James to William in the autumn of 1688, William had him arrested in an attempt to pressure his father-in-law into leaving the country. He could not arrest and kill James, as this would have made him look rather bad.

When William came to call on Catherine at Somerset House on 30 December, a mark of the friendly feeling between them, he found her uncharacteristically doing nothing. If there was one activity that sustained her, it was playing cards, but no card table was set up before her, no hand laid face-down on the table mid-play as she greeted her nephew-in-law. William asked why she did not play, to which Catherine responded that she had no heart for cards since Feversham had been absent. William, formal and ever serious in manner, answered that 'he would no longer interrupt Her Majesty's diversions'.[42] Feversham was freed, returning to his post as Catherine's chamberlain.*

Catherine and James had met for the last time on English shores on 18 December. Poignantly, James recalled his father's words in similar circumstances: 'there is little difference between the prisons and the graves of princes'.[43] James and Mary Beatrice, however, enjoyed a very comfortable exile in France, where James was accounted very boring, while the beautiful Mary Beatrice was pitied and petted. Ironically enough, their flight to France was used as an excuse by many of James's subjects to excuse themselves from allegiance; he had chosen France, and French national interests, over England.

On 11 April 1689, William was crowned William III, sharing power with his wife and co-ruler, Queen Mary II. On the same day, the couple were offered the Scottish crown too.

Catherine watched events with great interest from Somerset House, reporting William's politeness towards her to her brother Pedro, who was alarmed enough by the strange events in England to warn her of the potential for double-dealing: 'notwithstanding that the Prince of Orange acts decorously towards your Majesty, with that respect which he owes your family, it

---

* Feversham was left in charge of her business in England when she finally departed for Portugal. Catherine continued to look out for his interests, even from abroad, securing a position for him as master of St Katherine's Hospital, worth at least £700 a year (around £120,000 today).

appears to me that the period of fine weather passes rapidly to storm, and therefore those people who in this world act a double part are precise in observing this maxim'. Pedro too was an apt student of realpolitik, well aware of the serpent's gaze behind the smiling face. He implored his sister to return to Portugal, promising to help wind up her financial affairs from there, and signing himself 'The Brother who much loves your Majesty'.[44]

Mary was as zealously Church of England as Catherine was Catholic, and anti-Catholic sentiment continued in England, but William does not seem to have had a negative agenda towards Catherine. Public prayers continued to include her, just as they had done in the reign of James and Mary Beatrice, and nothing was done to upset her status as the third-highest-ranking person in the kingdom. This was remarkably generous considering that her residence of Somerset House had become a nest of plotters, while Catherine looked on benignly. So conveniently located on the Thames, it was the one of the few places Catholics could legitimately meet, and was the focus for the faction agitating for James's return to the throne – otherwise known as the Jacobites.

Catherine and her former disputant, the Earl of Clarendon, were friends once more, pushed together by their lingering loyalty to James (despite the fact that Clarendon was also Queen Mary's uncle, and his younger brother one of the signatories of the Invitation to William). In the spring of 1690, there were several meetings that were almost certainly Jacobite plotting sessions at Somerset House, and Catherine rather ironically intervened to protect Clarendon from the potential legal fallout.

One of her officers, Richard Graham, Lord Preston, was another frequent visitor and definite Jacobite, regarded by some as the shadow Secretary of State. He fomented trouble in the north of England and Scotland and received substantial payments from Louis XIV in exchange for his seditious activities. The novelist and sometime spy Daniel Defoe was full of grudging admiration for his talents, writing that 'it must be own'd he is a great *Master of address*, and his words are so charming, his motions so graceful, that a fitter person cou'd hardly be found out, or even made on purpose to bewitch Men from their duty and Alegience'.[45] Despite these qualities, Graham was undone when he attempted to carry secret correspondence to James in France, disguising himself as a smuggler on a small fishing boat and sailing down the Thames just as the new year of 1691 dawned. He and his friends were actually settling down to a celebratory meal of roast beef and mince pies when their vessel was boarded and the incriminating parcel of letters discovered. Although it had been weighted with lead so it would sink quickly should such a thing happen, Graham did not act quickly enough to throw it overboard, and he was arrested and condemned to death, only pardoned when he made a full confession that implicated all his fellow Jacobite conspirators, including Clarendon. Born under a lucky star, Clarendon was only briefly imprisoned in the Tower, before being released on bail. Considering this was his second offence, this light sentence may have been thanks to Catherine's influence.

The fact that Jacobites like Clarendon and Graham met frequently at Catherine's residence suggests that she broadly supported James's claim to the throne. However, she did not join their plots openly, managing to keep her head above water when Graham made his comprehensive confession. But she was aware of 'the great risk which I run', an allusive statement that might refer to her Catholicism as well as her knowledge of the plotting around her.[46]

William and Mary were relatively tolerant and continued to treat Catherine graciously despite her close relationship with known Jacobites. However, William requested that she remove herself to a slightly less public location. Having a hotbed of Jacobite plotting on the Strand was embarrassing, and the Graham incident had taken things too far. Catherine explained William's request to Pedro: 'he wished me to leave this, my own house, for this summer, and that I might choose some other house of his, or that of any private person, as long as it was at least ten or twelve miles from London, and also that I should not take this ill, as it was for the public good, and also that it was not because of me, myself, but because of the meetings which were held in my Palace, and that it was not seemly to make a very strict search in my presence, and that there were a great many reports abroad, although he believed no ill of me'.

Her response to William's lengthy explanation was perhaps a little delusional, considering the plotting that had become associated with Somerset House: 'I was much surprised at this message, since I was abiding quietly in my house without giving any occasion for it, nor was there anything from which occasion could be taken.' She complained that 'It was hard upon grounds so weak, and above all so uncertain, I should have to quit the only house which I have in England, and which my dower secures to me.' She either did not see her actions as traitorous, or wanted to continue playing a very dangerous game. She went on, 'he deprived me of my house without giving me another, and that, for a woman who found herself alone, having lost her husband, and whose brother was so far away, to be suspected of acting against the government without other cause than the whims of any one who chose to invent them, was very sad, and there was very little security in a nation where such a thing can be'.[47] Catherine was right: the situation was unfair, and she was at the whims of rumour-mongers, although the fact that she consorted closely with Jacobites was entirely her own fault.

Her relationship with her niece, Mary, had been testy for some time, and came to a head with a situation that was taken very seriously at the time, although it seems laughably unimportant now. When James attempted to take back Ireland, landing with a French army in 1689, William left to fight against his father-in-law. Mary, devoted to her husband and very keen on remaining Queen of England herself, ordered a prayer to be said in all churches to further William's success. The chaplain of the Savoy Chapel – used by Catherine's Protestant servants as it was attached to Somerset House – did not read the prayer. Mary, furious, arrested him and questioned him about this insubordination. Apparently Feversham had ordered the prayer not to be said. Mary told the Privy Council that 'she thought no more measures ought to be kept with the Queen-Dowager after this, if it were her order, which no doubt it was'.[48] Feversham took all the blame upon himself, so we will never know whether Catherine was deliberately flouting Mary's authority. But we do know that, behaving as a lofty Princess of Portugal, she refused to apologise for or even take any notice of the affair, an action that had Mary gnashing her teeth.

On 26 March 1689, the Commons tried to limit the number of Catherine's Catholic servants to 'Nine *Portugall* Men Servants, and Nine *English* Women Servants'.[49] It was part of a broader series of reforms that exiled Catholics from big cities. The Lords once more protected Catherine, as they had done in the days of the Popish Plot, and overturned the Bill. But as Catherine herself said, 'to be a Catholic is the difficulty'.[50] In July, there was another minor scandal, in which one of Catherine's maids-of-honour was charged with smuggling a child to France, away from its Protestant father, to be brought up a Catholic. Catherine was mentioned by association in the investigation, and, although she was not herself implicated or charged, the law once more was straying uncomfortably close to her affairs and her inner circle.[51]

She began to spend her time further from the centre, probably at her house in Islington, which she described as 'a very small house, hardly sufficient for a workman'. She was uncomfortable in England generally, writing to Pedro, 'I will say that I cannot remain quiet nor comfortable in a nation adverse to religion.' She turned her focus to the pet project begun under James: returning to her beloved Portugal. For some time she had been writing ardently to Pedro, begging him to facilitate her journey home, but now she redoubled her efforts, pleading 'to be united with You, Your Wife, & daughter, & at the same time to see my Home land on whose behalf I have been Exil'd from it for six-and-twenty years always longing to be there with you'.[52] She did not, it seems, feel that she had assimilated into English culture, instead considering herself to be in a state of exile. She suggested living far from Pedro's court when she returned so as 'not to embarrass you with my presence' and so that 'there can be no Jealous apprehension that my affection can be in any way of Influence with you'.[53] The letter shows that she was politically astute enough to be aware of the complicated dynamics a new player at court could bring to the political game, offering to remove herself from potential speculation.

However, from Pedro's perspective, now that William had shown himself courteous and unlikely to remove Catherine from power, she was more useful in England than she could be in Portugal, close to the king and queen while simultaneously providing safe harbour for Catholics and Jacobites. Although Catherine had left central London, her chapel continued to be one of the very few Catholic meeting places. For the same reasons, the French ambassador – under instruction from his master Louis XIV – was also vehemently opposed to her leaving England.

This was entirely against Catherine's inclination, having so long wished to return to her beloved homeland. She had now lingered in England for four extraordinarily tumultuous years after Charles's death. Europe was now a dangerous place, with France, the Holy Roman Empire, England, Spain and Portugal among those locked into the Nine Years' War, which had essentially been set off by Louis XIV's territorial ambitions. How was Catherine to make the journey to Portugal, even if Pedro pulled his finger out and actually arranged it? She wrote to him, 'how to make the journey at the present time, when all the world is on fire with war, is what I consider at every post. I hope with trembling, persuading myself that you will find some means, of which I may be ignorant, to devise some expedient for carrying it out.'[54] Even letters were blocked and had difficulty getting through. Catherine tried fruit ships, land routes and sending her own special messengers.

On Sundays and holy days, she travelled to her chapel in Somerset House to hear Mass, 'and that is all that for six months past there has been here by way of religion, so that the poor Catholics are very much oppressed'. She wrote sadly to Pedro, 'you may well judge what pain this must give me', having tried all her reign and in James's time to promote and protect Catholic worship in England. At this time, she was 'always under medicine, and trying new experiments', on one notable occasion living only on milk for fifteen days, which unsurprisingly 'weakened my stomach'.[55]

By August 1689, she had moved to an apothecary's house, which had a pleasant garden with trees where she could take her daily exercise, but not nearly enough space for her entourage. She described it as 'a small cottage, with two others, one on the right hand and the other on the left, which could be more properly called closets than houses'. Her servants had even worse berths, sleeping in 'cupboards and alcoves'.[56]

In desperation, she spoke to William about providing her with a ship. He gave a non-committal answer, which Catherine bitterly described as 'compliments which will not carry me to Portugal'. She asserted, 'if it had been in my power I would risk crossing the Pyrenees in the depth of winter, or embarking in ships full of spotted and malignant fevers, even were they certain to fight the enemy's fleet did they meet with it'. These highly charged passages are some of the most emotive and eloquent of her letter-writing career, a far cry from the formal congratulatory missives she had penned for the most part as queen consort. She said that 'if it had depended on me to place myself on a plank, and launch it into the sea, if I had persuaded myself that it would come to Lisbon, I would adventure everything'.[57]

She had ceased mincing words or falling in with the pretence that Pedro actually wanted to see her, despairing that she was the only one actively trying to get her to Portugal. She became increasingly frantic and despairing, planning to go off to 'some part of England where God only knows what can happen to me'. Her only idea was to find somewhere near the sea, where there might be some opportunity to get on a ship. She was deeply grieved to hear the news of her god-daughter Isabel Luísa's illness and eventual death, declaiming, 'there is no Princess like her to-day in all the world. I have not had a moment's peace since this news, hoping and longing for another and better message to contradict this evil one.'[58]

At the end of 1689, her hopes were revived when Maria Sophia, Pedro's queen, gave birth to a baby boy – later the fabulously extravagant João V, known as the Portuguese Sun King. Catherine wrote to her brother, 'May all the joys which I desire for you come to you and your crown.'[59]

In the end, it was deemed best that she leave England, despite Louis XIV engineering what diplomatic wrangling he could in order to force her to stay; he continued to believe that she might help James's cause by remaining there, though Jacobite plotting continued, often closely associated with her friends and allies. Pedro had finally agreed that it was safest for her to return to Portugal, and William enthusiastically assented. She sailed in March 1692 via France and James's court in exile, and would never to return to England.

This was just in time. In 1696 came yet another Jacobite plot, this time to assassinate William and his armed escort as he returned from hunting in the countryside south of London. The plotters were informed upon and arrested before the attempt took place, but one of the would-be assassins, Charles Cranburne, gained great notoriety for his final words on the scaffold: 'Kneeling down he pray'd for King *James*, Queen *Mary* his Consort, *Katharine* the Queen Dowager, his Royal Highness the Prince of *Wales*.'[60]

Catherine had spent thirty years in England, a time of revolutions, plots and almost-assassinations. She had survived them all to come home not in disgrace and bundled into a convent, but in triumph as queen dowager. She planned a new era of peaceful seclusion in her native land. But as we will see, fate – and the Portuguese people – had other plans.

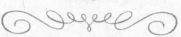

Return and Regency

IN A FLURRY of outriders, servants, carriages and dusty horses, Catherine arrived back in Portugal to a warm welcome around 15 January 1693. Her brother and all the court, fabulously dressed, met her on the road, a display to signal her status and to underline that Pedro intended to treat his sister with respect and acclamation now that she was home, whatever delays there had been about actually getting her there (it had been at least seven years since her first request to leave England). The forty-five-year-old king promptly plucked her from her coach, having no problem lifting down her slim figure, and she rode the rest of the way with him. It must have been odd for the middle-aged siblings to see one another, having last met when Catherine was twenty-four and Pedro an overexcited teenager on board the *Royal Charles* as she left for England.

The siblings had aged, certainly, but also changed. Pedro had deposed their brother and been married twice, while Catherine had lived through the death of her husband, rioting and constant plots to remove her from the throne. Attired in the newest French style, she looked very different to the shy young woman with the enormous farthingale and the side fringe who had left Lisbon. Pedro, while physically active, was rounded by the hint of a double chin. Still favouring traditional black, he made a concession to fashion by wearing an enormous curled wig, luxuriant locks falling in sausage curls that must have taken his hairdresser hours to achieve.

Accompanied by the court, Catherine and Pedro arrived together at the summer palace of Alcantara, just outside Lisbon, high on the east side of the Alcantara valley, then rolling farmland with tributary streams running into the Tagus rather than the post-industrial landscape of today. Even on the hottest day, a fresh breeze would blow from the sea in the evening. Pedro's wife, the popular, elegant Queen Maria Sophia, was there to welcome her sister-in-law, and Catherine stayed with the royal couple for a few weeks to recover from the bumpy, draughty journey through mountain passes and over boggy terrain.[1] Meanwhile, Lisbon celebrated her arrival: her marriage to Charles and the sacrifice she had made for her country were remembered and respected here at least.

After pining for her homeland so passionately, she was a little disappointed with what she found there, a perhaps inevitable reaction whenever dreams are confronted by reality. The English envoy and later ambassador John Methuen wrote that 'She seems to be somewhat shocked with the greate formality & stiffness here',[2] in contrast to the relative informality of English manners, particularly among the elite. It was normal in Portugal for servants to serve their masters and mistresses on bended knee, and the aristocracy demanded a greater show of deference from people they considered their inferiors. As one Portuguese writer commented, 'The Nobility think themselves Gods, and require a sort of Adoration . . . If this be so with the

Subjects, what is then the Prince, who is head of so many petty Gods?'[3]

Catherine was certain that the manners she observed were due to a transformation in Portuguese behaviour and the formal customs had not been the case when she was last here. Methuen wrote that she 'believes that Portugall is now extreamely different from what she lefte it whereas I fancy the only change is in her majestys thoughts having been soe long used to customes soe different'. After finally achieving the object of her desire, 'the Queen soe much desiring wee should thinke things quite changed here makes me believe she doth not approve of them as they are'.[4] Both English and Portuguese people tried to persuade her that she herself had changed after living in England for so long, but Catherine would have none of it, insisting that 'the manners and customs are totally different from what they were in her fathers time'.[5] She set about trying to alter things by example. Other than on days of ceremony, she attempted to convince her brother and sister-in-law that they did not need such formality around them, and in fact appeared more regal without it.[6] She was mostly met with a sort of benign puzzlement.

Another custom she had become used to in England was the style of conversation among women. Methuen reported that 'the company she sees at home being generally only the Portugall ladyes whose conversation or chatt is soe very trifling & different from what the Queen hath been used to in England that she cannot forbear exposing them to us'. Her brother asked what women talked about in England, and on Catherine's answering that they spoke of news, the king was 'scandalised at so undecent a liberty'.[7]

Presumably Portuguese women were expected to make

polite small talk about social affairs, fashion and the weather. It is entertaining to read how horrified Pedro was by the idea of women discussing such shocking topics as politics, especially considering that his own mother, Luisa, was a skilled and at times ruthless political manoeuvrer, only surpassed by his first wife, Marie Françoise. In fairness, the English at the time were particularly obsessed by the news, their common greeting often not 'How do you do?' but 'What's the news?'

Catherine had become – in relative terms – a feminist, since the problems she had with the more formal, traditional court she now found herself part of were almost entirely to do with norms of female/male behaviour. She disapproved of men's jealousy over their wives, echoing English accounts that compared the relative freedom of English women to Portuguese; her bilingual former page described Portuguese male jealousy as 'an Epidemical Distemper'.[8]

Another of her complaints was the 'strange retirement the ladyes are obliged to suffer'. This refers to the practice of women choosing to take the veil and become nuns. Not only did they vow to espouse Christ, but they were guarded with metal grates and firearms to stop them from leaving the convent. This was blamed on Queen Maria Sophia's English escort, the Duke of Grafton (Charles and Castlemaine's excessively handsome illegitimate second son, born a year after Charles and Catherine's marriage), and some of his companions, who had apparently tempted the nuns out of their convents to cheat on Christ when they had been in Portugal dropping Maria Sophia off for her marriage to Pedro.[9]

Although shocked by some of the differences between Portugal and England, Catherine was pleased to finally be settled in her homeland. She loved the novelty the country brought her, discovering its customs as though for the first time. In some ways, it *was* the first time. Her early years had been enormously sheltered, ruled by her mother and her own position as a young, unmarried woman. She now had (a limited amount of) money and the freedom of being both a queen dowager and a widow.

Now that she was finally home, she often thought fondly of England and her friends there. At her own little court in Alcantara, 'She affects in most things the continuance of all the English customs', insisting of course that they were actually long-abandoned Portuguese customs. This unbending attitude, very different from her willingness to adapt when she had journeyed to England, caused no little friction in Portugal. While Catherine was able to do largely as she liked, her English servants continuing with their own customs was not tolerated, and they were frequently got rid of by Pedro or the court.[10]

Catherine was not particularly interested in maintaining a correspondence with the friends she had left behind, and gave as an excuse the fact that she hadn't hired a secretary to write for her. Methuen's frustration – ever alive to her political importance – is palpable in his letters back home. He tried to hint to her that even three lines in her own hand would be better than nothing at all, and that 'she was wanting on her part in not keeping any sort of correspondence that the excuse of not having her secretary here was insufficient'. However, Catherine had never been a great letter-writer, and it was an uphill battle trying to get her to put pen to paper, one that Methuen was not very successful in. Instead, he manufactured compliments from her to his own correspondents (mainly the influential politician George Savile, Marquis of Halifax), assuring them of her good wishes and exchanging news about her day-to-day life. She herself 'never has had any other answer than that of general compliment', forcing the ambassador to get creative.[11] In a way, Methuen became her secretary, at least for her English correspondence.

Although for the most part Portuguese manners remained more traditional than Catherine's acquired informality, in terms of changing elite fashion she quickly found an ally in Queen Maria Sophia. Having been born near Düsseldorf (today in Germany), Maria Sophia already did not conform to traditional Portuguese fashions. An English chaplain described her appearance: 'The Princess was of a middle Stature, exceeding Fair, and a graceful Person. I do not know whether they that are Judges in these Matters, will allow her to have been a Perfect Beauty; but no doubt, all strangers will agree, that she appeared with great advantage among her Ladies, one cause of this, perhaps may be, her neglect of those Arts which they have recourse to set themselves off, for the *Portuguese* Women of all Ranks, do so discolour their Faces with Red Paint, that it renders them a very disagreeable Spectacle in the Eyes of Strangers.'[12]

Together Catherine and Maria Sophia petitioned Pedro to change the rules for dress, and to allow French fashions into Portugal. Catherine had been wearing the looser-fitting French-style gowns now for three decades, and it must have been extremely strange and uncomfortable to return to the restrictive portingales of her youth, with their enormous and unwieldy skirts. Interestingly, we know about this snippet of fashion history from James II. When in exile, he came to join Mary Beatrice after dinner one evening and announced: 'There are troubles at present in Portugal, because the King chooses that the Queen-

Dowager of England shall dress herself in Portuguese garb, which has much grieved her.'[13]

Much to Pedro's distaste, the two women's efforts were eventually successful, and tailors were sent for from France to remake the fashion of the Portuguese court. However, many ladies continued to wear veils and the enormous *guardinfante*, visitors squeezing through the door into Catherine's apartments with difficulty.[14] Catherine's fashion of wearing shorter skirts was decidedly eschewed: petticoats were made extra long to cover the feet, and some women were so cautious about showing a flash of foot or – God forbid – ankle that their footmen carried a cloth to cover their movement in and out of coaches as they travelled between residences.[15]

After recovering from her journey at the palace, Catherine lived in an ostensibly semi-retired location in the farmland west of Lisbon, fulfilling her promise to Pedro not to detract from his own court or cause political turmoil. However, in practice she entertained widely, accepting visits from foreign ministers and remaining on intimate terms with Methuen. She also returned Maria Sophia and Pedro's visits and was attended by vast swathes of the nobility on every feast day, as well as welcoming them whenever they felt like calling. Aside from these entertainments, her day-to-day life was much taken up with prayer and trying to settle her precarious finances, a common theme of her life following Charles's death. She was waiting both for her estates to be tied up and her plate to arrive. Methuen wrote that she was concerned for her attendants' welfare, being 'very uneasy & apprehensive that her family may suffer'.[16] By her 'family', she meant her servants, reflecting the seventeenth-century attitude towards the household.

When she was not entertaining some noble or dictating an important letter about money, Catherine would indulge in one of her favourite occupations. This was not dancing, singing or carousing, but visiting a convent to worship with the nuns.[17] Methuen watched her unusual hobby with growing apprehension, thinking she might be tempted to take the veil herself: 'Since I fear she would not be pleased in such a life & it were almost impossible for her afterwards to change.'[18] She was notable for her piety even in an extremely devout country, so much so that she 'sometimes frights one by her great devotions which engages her to goe abroad at unseasonable hours'.[19] Piety was now, as ever, 'the most distinguishing part of her Character'.[20] Indeed, she chose her house because it had easy access to a nunnery she liked to visit, even though there were nicer places on offer.[21] However, Catherine had never thought herself suited for an entirely religious life, pious as she might be, and was not about to embark on one now.

The other hobby that occupied much of her time was being ill. It is not that she was never genuinely ill, but she also liked to amuse herself with a variety of illnesses, and to undergo interesting courses of treatment to correct them. When it was pointed out to her that she might enjoy this a little too much, she blamed her physicians, while they claimed they were unable to divert her attention from excessive medical treatment.[22] She certainly tried some interesting medicines, finding great benefit in May and June 1692 from drinking asses' milk. Apparently it had a purging effect, which people in the early-modern era were very fond of in their medicinal treatments: they liked to see physical evidence of bad humours departing their bodies. It's not so different from our modern fondness for 'detoxing'.

Methuen reported back to England very assiduously on the state of Catherine's health, entering into medical debates on issues such as bathing at night with every appearance of intense interest. He several times reported on her 'loosness', referring to the looseness of her bowels, which he attributed to the dangerous practice of eating fruit and then drinking water straight after.[23] It is the kind of information an ambassador would probably not share today. When Catherine was ill in March 1693, Methuen hastened to her side to advise her to eschew meat and subsist on a diet of water gruel, horrified that her physicians allowed and even encouraged eating meat while ill.[24] He noted she was slow to recover, which 'is to be ascribed in great part to the Queens eating flesh three times a day contrary to all reason . . . & then supped on a large dish of Strawberys without any wine or other thing to correct the crudity of the fruit'.[25] She was pale from the four heavy bleedings her physicians tried as a remedy to correct the illness, which seems to have originally stemmed from an ulcer in her leg. Catherine declared that she had been more ill in Portugal than she had over the last seven years in England, although while in England she had claimed that all she needed to be well was to be in her homeland again.

However, her health was vital to Methuen's success as an ambassador. He relied on her close connection to the Portuguese royal family. Despite his occasional frustration with her lack of interest in sending letters, he did try to untangle her money difficulties, observing that 'not paying the Queens mony out of the Treasury will make the payment of her family impossible during the war & therefore it were very happy if some way could be found to gain the point which makes me thinke of the necessity the Queen is under of entertaining always a good correspondence with the King & Queen'.[26] Even in her ostensibly out-of-the-way location, Catherine served as an important diplomatic bridge between England and Portugal. She introduced Methuen to her brother Pedro, and although the two men then went on to forge their own relationship, Methuen was always mindful of Catherine's influence.

If she was unable to entertain Pedro and Maria Sophia at her house, this would cost England an important informal channel to the monarchs' ears, and Methuen was anxious not to lose this advantage through Catherine not having enough money, or – even worse – by her deciding to hole herself up in a convent.[27] To ensure that England and Portugal remained in close alliance, he tried his best to preserve Catherine's good opinion of England, amplifying the complimentary expressions he received from Whitehall. As her English servants were sent home by an exasperated Pedro, Methuen worried that Catherine's 'family' would become entirely Portuguese and the English influence wane.[28] He did his best to fan her fond memories of England and her friends there, but watched the French ambassador's frequent visits anxiously. The Frenchman would kiss Catherine's hands in a great show of deference, attempting to pull her into the Francophile sphere of the Portuguese court. Methuen's letters are full of fear over French policy.

This was, after all, during the most intense period of the Nine Years' War, a conflict bizarrely brought about by Louis XIV wanting to better defend France. Unfortunately, his idea of defence was annexing parts of Germany and aggressively controlling Italy so as to create a 'buffer zone' for France. He had already tried to acquire the Netherlands, and a key reason for William III to take the English throne was so that he could stop England, under his Francophile father-in-law James II, from siding with France. Things were going badly for the 'Grand Alliance' – the English, the Holy Roman Empire, the Dutch and their allies – at this point in the war, and Methuen's hand-wringing as Pedro repeatedly called him in to explain matters is palpable. In mid-November 1693, Methuen wrote, 'My access to the King although it serves my negociation yet for some months past hath been very uneasy being every day called on to answer for all the ill conduct & all the ill success of the Allyes in every part this hath kept me upon the wrack . . . Your Lordship observed very well that my condition here were to be envied being in soe fine a country & soe quiet as not to hear of war but in garetts very well in this Court extreamely favoured by the Queen & with the honour of your Lordships correspondence.'[29]

Unfortunately, Methuen could not be happy despite being in Catherine's favour: 'alas my thoughts are more engaged than if I were at home I thinke all day & dreame & start in my sleep at night'. It was a difficult time, and he constantly feared that the Portuguese would break their English alliance and go all in with the French. Catherine was a vital connection to try and prevent this, as she distinctly favoured the English. Fortunately for England and the Grand Alliance, French finances were already starting to fail, and the war began to turn, ending in diplomacy. One of the outcomes was William III being formally recognised by Louis as King of England. In reality, the European powers were just gearing up for another war, one in which Catherine would play a central part.

ॐ

For the time being, things continued much as they had since Catherine's arrival in Portugal three years earlier, with the daily round of convent-visiting and entertaining, and the occasional illness when life got boring. She celebrated her birthday annually with a grand celebration, just as she had in England, the nobles of Portugal trooping out en masse to mark the day. Methuen wrote that she 'endured all the fatigue from morning to night of the greatest court that ever was seen in Portugall'.[30]

However, she was still in rather embarrassing financial straits. Every time an English ship was sighted, she hoped it would be her plate arriving, and frequently feared that the ship might go down before it could get to her, leaving her financially stranded. Finally, on 20 December 1693, her plate did eventually arrive, placing her in a more secure financial position and safeguarding the payment of her 'family'.[31]

Also in December, Catherine sent poor Methuen into a tailspin of alarm by planning to move to the Vila Viçosa, the mansion far in the south where she was born and lived until the Braganzas had become monarchs. So far from Lisbon, she would be in 'a manner out of the world', he wrote, 'The greatest hope is that the Pallace there is very much out of repair soe as scarce to be capable of being repaired without falling down.'[32] He tried his hardest to dissuade her from the scheme, knowing that Catherine moving there would also remove one of his key chess pieces as ambassador. She threatened this up until March 1694, but eventually gave up the idea and stayed for the time being at Alcantara.

Catherine was a sociable soul and enjoyed living within the fringes of court life near Lisbon. She got bored and either ill or depressed (or both) quickly, and as a result did not stay in one place long, flitting between one noble's house and another's. A little like Goldilocks, wherever there was a *quinta* (country villa) with attractive gardens, the house was not big enough to house her 'family', and wherever the house was big enough, it was not attractive or green enough.[33]

In the end, she decided to sacrifice the beneficial air of the countryside to move closer to the hum of Lisbon, buying land in Bemposta and building her own residence, the Paço da Bemposta or Bemposta Palace, sometimes also known as the Queen's Palace; the street it was on is today called the Paço da Rainha (Queen's Palace). The condition of buying the land was that if buried treasure was discovered, it would belong to the seller's family rather than Catherine. Apparently, back in the mists of time, the family had buried treasure and inscribed the site on a ring, which was then lost. The treasure has still not been found, and perhaps awaits discovery by some future generation.[34]

For the project, Catherine hired the talented master stone-mason and architect João Antunes, who had spent a long career rising through the competitive ranks to become the royal architect. As she had in England, she was patronising the new baroque style – Antunes had pioneered sumptuous interiors and a new attitude towards space and angles with his use of polygonal plans. He combined classic blue and white *azulejos* with the broken pediments and trumpeting cherubs of the baroque.*

After living so long in London, attending dances and races and playing cards at some rather raucous parties, Catherine

---

* Unfortunately, thanks to the 1755 earthquake and subsequent reconstruction, all that is left of the palace today is two square doorways with plain brown doors, easily walked past and unnoticed, where the lion of England and the unicorn of Scotland look at one another over Catherine's coat of arms, between a very baroque broken pediment.

clearly enjoyed the hum of the city, but chose to be slightly removed from the heart of Lisbon. The close-set streets were impossible to navigate in a carriage; litters born by mules were used instead. One traveller described the rather unsavoury effect of such close-packed housing: 'The Houses are generally high and the Streets so narrow that the Sun comes little into them, to dry up the wet and filth that run from their Kitchins, which are all above Stairs: However their Houses are cool tho' the Streets are very nasty.'[35] Luckily, Catherine's father, João IV, had brought in a system of fines for failing to bury dead animals – an ox or sheep cost 200 reis, while a dog or cat cost a mere 50 reis.[36] These measures made the streets a little more savoury to walk down.

Ironically, although Antunes was the royal architect, Pedro was much more conservative than his sister when it came to art and architecture. This reflects their personalities; he was more conservative in fashion, manners and politics.[37]

Perhaps in part due to her lavish spending on a new palace, Catherine was still plagued by financial troubles, having to borrow money and occasionally having a rather uncomfortable time of it. When she moved into the Paço da Bemposta in 1702, she wrote to Pedro that 'It is very retired here, almost a desert, which is not disagreeable to me.' She was lucky enough to 'have the very great comfort of a monastery of Dominicans' to keep her entertained.[38] But she was perfectly content to live as she did, an observer writing in 1700 that 'tho' her Majesty be her self the same, her outward Circumstances are somewhat alter'd, since her leaving England; her Court is lessen'd almost to a private family'. He continued, 'there is no Noise, nor Ostentation of Grandeur about her House, but all things are quiet and still, except it be on days of Ceremony, when Persons of Quality will be coming to express the great Veneration they have for her; then, indeed, her Court is as great, and full, as the Nobility of the Country can make it'.[39] She still enjoyed the occasional noisy party.

While the palace was still being built, Catherine's retirement was to change. In 1699, her sister-in-law, the popular Queen, Maria Sophia, died, possibly from a bacterial infection. The two women had had much in common, from their piety to their love of French fashion, and Catherine was 'inconsolable'. Pedro 'never went to bed during the time of her Sickness, but lay on a Piece of Cork in the same Chamber', and 'while the Corps was carried away, expressed his Passion in such a manner, as is not to be described, it being so violent'. Both he and his sons had done penance on their bare feet, praying that Maria Sophia would survive, but to no avail.[40] The court and the people mourned her sincerely, but for Catherine there was little time to grieve. There was work to be done.

It was traditional in Portugal for children's education to be overseen by a female family member. Maria Sophia's six children now became Catherine's responsibility, as the closest female relative. João, the heir to the throne, was only nine at the time of his mother's death. Catherine was already fond of him, often sending her love to her nephew by letter when they were apart. But now she was his main female role model and responsible for his education – somewhat ironic considering how little actual education she herself had received at the hands of her capricious mother.

João would become known as the Portuguese Sun King, famous for his extravagant building projects, diplomatic embassies and many public mistresses, following in Charles II's mould rather than that of his more discreet father. He enjoyed a reign that would have had Charles gnashing his teeth in envy, never calling the Cortes or parliament and always flush with gold thanks to a Brazilian gold rush that coincided with his rule. Catherine would have been very shocked that one of his longer-term paramours was a nun, not removed from the convent but rather promoted to abbess when she became the king's mistress. Perhaps this was why among his other titles of 'Magnificent' and 'Magnanimous' was included 'The Visitor of Convents'.

But all this was in the future. For now, Catherine had a crucial role acting as a mother figure and supervising the education of her nieces and nephews, which would continue until her death. Like his aunt, João would prove to be profoundly religious and also profoundly autocratic. He would be a lover of art and music, and Catherine may have imbued him with her own passion for the arts. One of his principal concerns throughout his life was to patronise, promote and fund religion. For his efforts the Pope awarded him the title Fidelissimo (most faithful), of which Catherine would have been incredibly proud.

In November 1700, Charles II of Spain died without issue. His death had been long anticipated by the vulture-like European powers. Titled 'the Bewitched', he was sickly from the day of his birth and cursed after centuries of inbreeding with multiple health problems. He is most famous for his 'Hapsburg jaw', a prominent underbite that made chewing difficult. Despite being one of the most privileged children in the world at the time, he was also malnourished and had childhood rickets, combined with a possible hormone deficiency. He was thirty-five when he died, and was almost certainly impotent by this time; his autopsy showed only one remaining testicle, and that one was wasting away. The autopsy also revealed that he had a 'brain the size of a peppercorn'.[41]

Normally, when there is no offspring, the throne would go to the next heir. The problem was that Charles's sisters had made fabulous dynastic matches: the elder had married the pomp-loving Louis XIV and the younger had married socially awkward Holy Roman Emperor Leopold I, making both of their descendants claimants to the Hapsburg dominions. The two powers each put pressure on Charles to nominate their candidate as his heir, and during his lifetime the sickly king wrote wills back and forth, favouring one or another. His last will named Philip of Anjou as heir to the Hapsburg dominions, specifying that they not be broken up. The problem was that Philip was Louis XIV's grandson, firmly in the French axis of power. The Holy Roman Empire, England and the Dutch preferred their candidate, Emperor Leopold's younger son the Archduke Charles, believing (rightly) that Philip of Anjou on the Hapsburg throne would give France too much power over world affairs. So began the Wars of the Spanish Succession, only four years after the Nine Years' War and involving almost all of the same players. To a great extent, it was a repetition of the same conflict, and one that would play out again and again through the eighteenth century.

Portugal was in a difficult position, preferring not to get involved in a risky and potentially expensive war that would do little but disrupt trade. However, sharing a land border and so close to Spain by sea, they could hardly avoid being drawn into it in some capacity. All Pedro could hope for was to avoid total commitment one way or the other, and for trade to continue with Portugal's most important colony, Brazil. On 18 June 1701, he signed a treaty with France, promising to close Portuguese ports to France's enemies. This was everything Methuen had feared, the result both of France's proximity and of Louis XIV's long policy of French intermarriage and courting Portugal.

However, it was an uneasy alliance. Louis XIV believed that Pedro was a weak king since he had not seized on the chaos following Charles's death to annexe parts of Spain, and while secretly approving Portugal's War of Independence, France had been notably absent. The *povo*, the backbone of the Portuguese army, were not, as a result, particularly pro-French.

Moreover, French diplomats had become complacent. Their ambassador in Lisbon, de Rouillé, while an able, well-informed man, adhered to a point of protocol that seriously hampered his ability to do anything. The French insisted that an ambassador not call on anyone who had not called on them first, while Portuguese protocol insisted that the ambassador make the first move. Thus there was gridlock, with de Rouillé only able to see the Duke of Cadaval, who had visited him first. Cadaval was admittedly influential, but he was far from being the king. De Rouillé also made a tactical error in assuming that Catherine was pro-French, possibly because of her outspoken Catholicism and the fact that her ally James II had until his death in 1701 been a ward of France. On his death, Catherine had shown every appearance of sympathy and ordered Somerset House – still her official residence in England – to be hung with black for a year. However, now that she had left England, Catherine thought fondly of it with all the warmth of nostalgia, and had no particular love for James over William.

On 8 March 1702, the dour William died following complications after a fall while riding. Since his horse had thrown him after it stumbled on a mole hole, Jacobites toasted 'the little gentleman in the black velvet waistcoat' for the mole's part in his death.[42] Keeping up the role of diplomat she had played throughout her life, Catherine sent a letter of condolence to the new queen, Anne, James II's younger daughter, writing of 'the particular love which I have for the person of Your Majesty'. We have no reason not to believe her sincere when she wrote, 'It was with great pain that I received the notice your Majesty sent me of the King, whose person and virtues I always greatly esteemed.' She even appeared to approve of Anne's being the next in line to the throne, although she could hardly express otherwise: 'It gave me consolation to know that Your Majesty is established in the government of that Kingdom in which for so many years I knew the greatest happiness.'[43] Catherine's letter is of a piece with her generally fond sentiment for England while in Portugal – it seems she was destined for a life of eternal *saudade* wherever she was. She had been kind to both sisters, Mary and Anne, when she herself reigned as queen, and it is an elegant and affectionate piece of diplomatic correspondence, which is just as it should be, since she had had forty years to perfect her style.

William's death did little to change England's role in the war, and Catherine was still prayed for in the liturgy of the Church of England, as queen dowager and one of the principal living personages in the land, even though she was not technically *in* the land any more.

John Methuen had left his capable son Paul in charge of diplomacy with Portugal while he went to work as speaker in the Irish House of Lords, but after William's death he was sent back to Lisbon, thanks to his close friendship with Pedro and Catherine. His instructions were urgent: having lost Tangier and become embroiled in war with France, England needed a port in the Mediterranean. Methuen was to bring Portugal back into the Anglosphere, rather than remaining in the Francosphere. If he could not persuade Pedro to join the Grand Alliance, he was instructed to ask that English ships be allowed into Portugal's ports at the very least.

Methuen had arrived back at exactly the right time. Despite Louis XIV's promise to send a fleet to protect Portugal in their agreement of alliance, the French king had not followed through. Instead a fleet of Grand Alliance ships had sailed perilously close to the mainland, a serious threat to Portuguese security as well as trade. Playing into Methuen's hands was the French ambassador's continuing stiff insistence on protocol and inability to negotiate with anyone, alongside the *povo*'s decidedly anti-French sentiments. This helped Methuen gain influential allies at court, including Padre Sebastião Magalhaes, the king's confessor, who was afraid that a mob would rise to riot against a French alliance.[44]

While France was stymied, Catherine, Magalhaes and other influential members of the court were disposed to think well of Methuen. Tipping the scales even further in his favour, in 1702 the Grand Alliance's candidate for the Spanish throne, Archduke Charles of Austria, was making a visit of great pomp to Lisbon (the pomp all paid for by the Alliance, presumably in the hope that Portugal would agree to switch sides on seeing such magnificence). He was only nineteen, rather idealistic and wide-eyed, and accompanied by his tutor, Anton Florian, later Prince of Liechtenstein. Portraits show a long, oval face, a sloping nose, rosy cheeks, and a propensity to dress in armour, showcasing his abilities as a martial leader defending his right to the Spanish succession.

Realising her influence for good or ill, the young arch-duke, perhaps advised by Florian, was extremely anxious to see Catherine. This caused something of a furore in her semi-retirement in her palace at Bemposta. It would not do for an international visitor to see one of the grandees of Europe living so modestly. All was hustle and bustle as courtiers and servants had to quickly be borrowed from Pedro's retinue, the palace arranged, and protocol managed. To Charles's repeated requests to see her, Catherine calmly replied that 'she awaited with equal desire his coming, and that she left the appointment of a day and hour to him'.[45] While she appeared serene, in the background servants and courtiers scrambled to put on a good show.

Catherine was in bed at the time of Charles's visit, and may actually have been ill, although, like the boy who cried wolf, it is always rather hard to tell whether she was really sick or just enjoying a good bout of doctoring and asses'-milk cures. Either way, it was a visit of great ceremony, Charles arriving with his head uncovered, possibly as a mark of respect but more likely because any headgear placed over his enormous chestnut wig would have been extremely unstable and likely to fall off. A chair of stately black velvet had been placed for him near Catherine's bedside, and they exchanged a formal string of cour-tesies. The archduke made an embarrassing gaffe, leaving the room before his chair had been removed, clearly not aware of the extraordinary nuance of Portuguese etiquette. Otherwise the visit was very successful.

Even while suffering from illness, Catherine had an impressive majesty of manner, perhaps inherited from her mother and honed during her time as Queen of England. Despite her palace being a distinctly less grand setting than the courts and palaces in which she spent most of her life, 'she convinces the World, that the Formalities of Pomp and State are not inseparable from Majesty; and that true Greatness, instead of being set off by such Helps, appears to the best Advantage without them'.[46] Except, of course, for the awkward moments when a foreign dignitary arrived and insisted on seeing her.

Lisbon was in a spirit of festivity and goodwill, crowding to glimpse the young archduke. He was a favourite with the people, who had no love for the French. On his visit, he was to be recognised by Pedro as Charles III, King of Spain. This was as good as a declaration that the country had switched sides. Methuen just had to swoop in and take the credit, seizing this propitious moment to propose a treaty without being able to check whether his superiors approved of the terms. He was racked with anxiety, writing home with every ship that sailed London-wards. The treaty was quickly passed by the English Parliament, but thanks to bad weather it took three months for word to reach an uneasy Methuen, in a tremor over whether he had overstepped his role.[47]

It was signed on 16 May 1703 not by Pedro but by Catherine. She had been increasingly playing a role not just diplomatically but in government. Her brother's health was failing, and João was only fourteen. The Quadruple Treaty of Offensive Alliance, as it was known, meant that she had for the second time in her life brought Portugal and England into an allied war. Portugal had officially ended its allegiance to France in the War of Spanish Succession, and was now part of the Grand Alliance.

This made it much easier for the Alliance to launch an invasion into Spain – the contested territory – which they attempted in 1704. Archduke Charles was brought back to Portugal by the English to attempt to install him on the Spanish throne. At the same time, Pedro – increasingly afflicted with illness, which took the form of being very tired – nominated Catherine as his regent. In 1704, she took control of the government and directed the war. She reigned capably and successfully, and led Portugal to victory on the battlefield just as her mother had done.*

However, she would only reign for a year as regent. Despite her favourite hobby being to call on doctors to discuss some unusual illness, her end came quickly and simply. She died quite suddenly and unexpectedly on 31 December 1705, of the 'colic'. This was not so much a disease as a description of her main symptom, severe abdominal pain, which in the seventeenth century could have been anything from food poisoning to a tumour. She was attended at Bemposta by her physicians, at least one of whom was English.

One of the few accounts we have of her death is a flattering one, a surprising circumstance considering it was written by an arch-supporter of Titus Oates. The historian John Oldmixon records that he spoke to one of her physicians, who had been there for her last moments. According to this physician, she sat up in bed and called softly to him to come closer, saying 'that she had never been a Promoter of the French Interest; on the Contrary, that it was one of her greatest Griefs, at her going

---

* The war was eventually concluded in April 1713, mainly at a loss on France's part, although the drawn-out conflict had weakened all the participants and the French candidate – Philip of Anjou – became King of Spain. In the peace treaty, France ceded Portugal previously contested control of South American territories. The Archduke Charles was apparently so disappointed at not being proclaimed King of Spain that he adopted Hapsburg dress, wearing 'a black doublet and hose, black shoes and scarlet stockings'.

out of the World, to think that when she was gone, the French
Faction, in her Brother's Court, might do the Confederates ill
Offices, for it was she that had kept him firm to them'.[48]

The source is doubtful, since Oldmixon was not exactly
known for his factual accuracy as a historian, and somewhat
tellingly he reported Catherine saying she never tried to 'bring
in Popery' to England while she reigned as queen, which is not
true, self-professed zealot that she was. However, the idea that
she was promoting an English alliance and took a relatively
anti-French stance in Portugal does fit with her fond letters back
to England, her support of Methuen, and her nostalgic way of
viewing the country almost as soon as she had left it.

In her will, she asked to be buried next to her beloved brother
Teodósio, and this wish was granted, but not before all due ceremony was carried out for the highest-ranking woman in the
land. The streets outside her palace at Bemposta were crowded
with clergy, who accompanied her funeral procession to the
monastery at Belem where her brother was buried. Her nephews
João, Francisco and Antonio sprinkled holy water on her body
before the procession began. As was the custom, her shroud was
pulled down to show her face to the public one last time, as she
was carried in a litter from her home. All public businesses were
shut for eight days, while the court went into official mourning
for a year. The *povo* wept in the streets.

Her will was read aloud the night she died. It began in characteristic fashion: 'First, I recommend my soul to God the Lord
who created it, trusting in His infinite mercy and goodness that
He will pardon all my Faults and Sins, and carry me to the enjoy-
ment of His happiness, where I may praise him to all Eternity.'[49]
She left ten thousand cruzados for an extravagant ten thousand

Masses to be said for her soul, alongside multiple bequests to her favourite religious houses and funds for virgins who wished to become nuns.

Other notable bequests included money for freeing debtors and slaves, 'on condition nevertheless what if there shall be amongst the said slaves and Little Boys or Girls they shall be the first which shall be redeemed'. She remembered her servants by name in her will, for the most part paying them a year's salary plus any other bequests, and made a touching request on their behalf to Pedro: 'By reason of the Love and Civility which these and other of my men and women servants have served me there is due to them all the demonstration of esteem and thanks which I could not be wanting to them in, and that there only remains for me to desire the King my Brother and Lord favourably to consider and support them with such particular attention as I have always had for those who I have had an affection for.'[50] During all her money troubles, she had often been worried about her 'family', and had always shown great loyalty to friends and relations.

Catherine was remembered fondly in her adopted country of England, but this was nothing compared with the mourning in her home country, both as reigning regent and – according to many of her contemporaries – as the saviour of Portuguese independence. She was celebrated in paintings, statuary and the requisite bad poetry that had followed her actions like an unwanted guest throughout her life. Her virtuous life, her sighs and her religious convictions were expounded upon at length.

Pedro de Azevedo Tojal composed a particularly tortuous epic poem called *Carlos Reduzido, Inglaterra Illustrada*, published in 1716. Interestingly, he wrote it for Portugal's Sun King João V, claiming that he had been labouring on it continually for twelve years – a dubious achievement since the poem is not of great artistic merit, although it is certainly very long – and declaring that he had been fuelled by the 'Catholic zeal, and the fervent spirit' of the king's aunt, the dedication suggesting that Catherine remained an important spiritual guide and memory throughout João's reign.[51] The poem gets closer to Catherine's real Catholic agenda while Queen of England than Oldmixon did. De Azevedo Tojal spends a great deal of descriptive energy on the subject; 'given over to a mad barbarism', in England 'holocausts give way to the black abyss'.[52] He puts Charles II's conversion down to Catherine, and imagines them celebrating the sacraments together in heaven, alongside lots of scenes of Catherine looking resplendent in a crystalline sphere, raising her hands and tearful eyes to celestial figures. Who knows, perhaps she and Charles are enjoying a Catholic Mass as I write.

Charles II being presented with the first pineapple grown in England by his gardener John Rose. One of many Restoration fashions in food, including ice cream.

NIEUW AMSTERDAM OFTE NUE NIEUW JORX OPT TEYLANT MAN

A shockingly pastoral New Amsterdam (now New York), painted in 1665, the year it was taken by the English.

Queens Room in Merton College, Oxford, where Catherine fled to escape the plague.

Sir Frescheville Holles, 1641–72, and Sir Robert Holmes, 1622–92, by Peter Lely
(c. 1672). Jointly credited with starting the Third Anglo-Dutch War, Holles' posture
hides his missing left arm.

The *Royal Katherine*, built in 1664 and named in Catherine's honour.

Huge plumes of smoke rise as fire consumes the city in the Great Fire of London, 1666. The blaze could be seen over 50 miles away in Oxford.

Sir Christopher Wren's design for the dome of the new St Paul's Cathedral, following the Great Fire. His plan to remake the rest of the City of London was mostly impossible, since the land was owned by private citizens not willing to exchange it for grand boulevards.

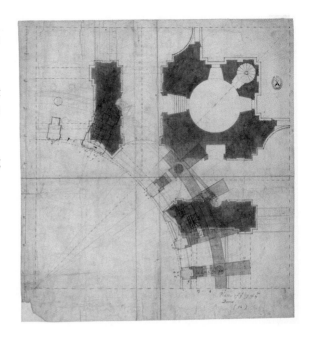

Bathing at the King's and Queen's Baths in Bath, a surprisingly public experience.

(*above*) Catherine's favourite god-daughter, Isabel Luísa.

(*left*) Marie Françoise of Savoy, Queen of Portugal by two different husbands.

Anthony Ashley-Cooper, Earl of Shaftesbury, popular politician and Catherine's inveterate enemy.

Louise de Kérouaille, Duchess of Portsmouth and Catherine's close friend, despite some friction in their relationship.

Sir Edmund Berry Godfrey, whose death precipitated one of the most difficult episodes of Catherine's reign.

Titus Oates, whose false accusations almost brought an end to Catherine's reign.

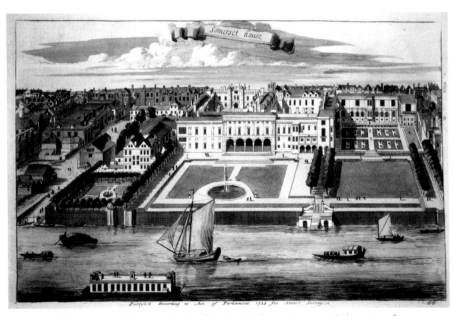

Somerset House, Catherine's principal residence and the site of much imagined and actual Catholic plotting.

William III (of Orange), Catherine's nephew-by-marriage. They had a somewhat tumultuous relationship, but always expressed great respect towards each other.

The same cannot be said of Queen Mary, who was frequently exasperated by her aunt's lack of respect and harbouring of Catholic conspirators.

Queen Maria Sophia of Neuburg, Pedro's second wife and queen consort of Portugal. A practical, pious woman with whom Catherine had much in common.

John Methuen, Catherine's close ally once she returned to Portugal and the ambassador there for England.

(*above*) João V of Portugal, known as the Portuguese Sun King. Catherine's nephew would share her piety but none of her minimalism.

(*left*) Queen Anne, Catherine's niece. Despite their religious differences, Catherine was always very kind to both nieces, and expressed pleasure when Anne succeeded her brother-in-law as Queen of England.

Catherine's coat of arms on what remains of her palace at Bemposta (extensively reconstructed after the 1755 earthquake).

Epilogue

IN 1998, PROTEST erupted in Queens, New York, over a statue of Catherine that – had it been put in place overlooking the East River – would have been the second-tallest statue in the city after Lady Liberty. Highlighted with gold leaf and stained glass, she cost about $2 million to sculpt, and was paid for by a series of fundraisers, including one notable event where white stallions were in attendance.

Residents of Queens and further afield felt that Catherine was guilty by association, having been a royal and therefore benefiting from the slave trade. Her Portuguese family certainly did so, as did her husband, Charles II, helping to set up the Royal African Company in 1660. However, somewhat surprisingly, considering contemporary attitudes and the fact that many men and women of the Restoration court had slaves, there is no evidence of Catherine personally owning any or being involved in the slave trade. As we have seen, in her will she gave money for them to be freed, and seems to have been particularly concerned over child slavery, asking for the children to be freed first.

In retrospect, erecting the statue was an odd choice for a nation that prides itself on throwing off kings and queens.

Queens as a district owes nothing to Catherine but its name, whereas she profoundly shaped Portugal's history, as well as that of the United Kingdom. In her lifetime, she really only cared about Portugal.

She was certainly a woman of her time, and perhaps we are lucky that few of her letters survived, since she most likely held views that would be objectionable today. Mostly, in the fragments that remain, we read that she was concerned with her own suffering, with a love of Portugal, and with great loyalty and kindness to those close to her.

For better or worse, Catherine's life had a profound impact on history. In 1662, when he finally – after much arguing – agreed to hand over Bombay to the English, the viceroy António de Melo e Castro prophesied that it would be the beginning of the end of Portugal in India, and in some ways he was right.[1] Bombay would become a staging post for British trade, troops and people entering India, and the country would remain dominant on the subcontinent until the twentieth century, when the last British troops to leave India would depart from Bombay in February 1948.

The alliance with England that Catherine helped to forge would prove important many times throughout the nations' joint history. In 1762, Spain tried to invade Portugal again. Pombal, the great statesman of his day, invoked the alliance, and an English – or rather by this time British – force was duly sent. Early the following century, Napoleon I planned to dismember Portugal, and invaded the country three times, but was thwarted by Anglo-Portuguese troops. In 1815, Britain cancelled a debt in exchange for Portugal's help in diminishing and eventually ending the slave trade. It also propped up the Portuguese monarchy, however unpopular with the people. Although officially neutral in World War I, Portugal supported the British alliance, fighting in Africa and on the Western Front.

The treaty also played a stealthy but significant part in World War II, when Portugal was officially neutral once again but quietly supported Britain and her allies. As soon as war broke out, the authoritarian head of state, António de Oliveira Salazar, announced that the Anglo-Portuguese alliance remained intact. Official neutrality lasted until Britain invoked the alliance so it could use the Azores, a group of strategic Atlantic islands in the possession of Portugal. Churchill announced: 'I take this opportunity of placing on record the appreciation by His Majesty's Government . . . of the attitude of the Portuguese Government, whose loyalty to their British Ally never wavered in the darkest hours of the war.'[2]

He actually invoked the original 1373 treaty between Edward III and Eleanor, Queen of Portugal, which promised that the two countries would 'be friends to friends and enemies to enemies, and shall assist, maintain and uphold each other mutually, by sea and by land, against all men that may live or die'.[3] However, this was ratified and furthered in Catherine's 1703 treaty, which Churchill also credited. Having a stop-off in the Atlantic was an important part of protecting convoys against U-boats, allowing supplies and troops to travel from the US to Europe and ultimately enabling D-Day.

Catherine was also a taste-maker, helping to introduce the baroque to England, popularising tea drinking and changing English music. In her own time, she started a vogue for short skirts, and was ever-dutiful as a queen, maintaining diplomatic relations with half of Europe.

When reading about her life, the mob prejudice from which she suffered, the constant embarrassments and threats to her position, it is difficult not to at least admire the fact that at all times she remained dignified. She won the grudging respect of those who were her religious and political opposites. She was depressed one moment, then laughing over the turn of a card the next. She refused to be dismissed, or to remain down, like a weed that keeps on growing. In the great tradition of Portuguese monarchs and their descriptors, she should perhaps be called Catherine the Tenacious.

Endnotes

Prologue

1 Wynne.
2 Campbell Davidson, p.viii.
3 There have been two books on Charles II's mistresses in the last decade: *The King's Bed*, Don Jordan and Michael Walsh (2015) and *Mistresses*, Linda Porter (2020). Porter's book includes two chapters on Catherine of Braganza and acknowledges her significance, as does *Later Stuart Queens, 1660–1735*, ed. Eilish Gregory and Michael Questier (2024).
4 'Catherine of Braganza', Wikipedia, 23 Jan 2023, https://en.wikipedia.org/wiki/Catherine_of_Braganza
5 Kishlansky, p.236.
6 Lancelot Reynolds, p.5.

1   Assassination, Education and an Accidental War

1 Vallance, p.33.
2 Editors of the Encyclopaedia Britannica.
3 Newitt, pp.32–3.
4 Harold Johnson, pp.156–7.
5 Moréri, sig. Nn1r.
6 Costa e Sousa, pp.27–30.
7 Vertot, p.45.
8 Cited in Viera Nery, pp.66–7.
9 De Sousa, p.213.

10   Flecknoe, pp.50–52.
11   John Dryden, *Mac Flecknoe*, https://www.poetryfoundation.org/poems/44181/mac-flecknoe.
12   Vertot, p.35.
13   Lanier, p.13; Anna Reynolds, p.162.
14   Richard Flecknoe, in Macaulay, p.82.
15   Vallance, p.29.
16   Ibid., pp.25–6.
17   Ibid., p.33.
18   Ibid., p.34.
19   Elliott, pp.193–4.
20   Vallance, p.35; Raposo, p.86.
21   Raposo, p.91.
22   De Faria y Sousa, pp.135–6.
23   Vallance, p.28.
24   Ibid., pp.38–9.
25   Vallance, p.41.
26   De Faria y Sousa, p.389.
27   Vallance, p.42.
28   Ibid., p.43.
29   Ibid.

2   *A Play for the Throne*

1   Disney, p.209.
2   Raposo, p.143.
3   R. B., p.205.
4   Disney, p.203.
5   Vertot, p.44.
6   Ibid., p.45.
7   Raposo, p.149.
8   Disney, p.219.
9   Vertot, pp.33–4.
10   Ibid., p.26.
11   Disney, p.220.
12   Raposo, p.156.
13   Ibid.
14   Ibid.

15 Campbell Davidson, p.6.
16 De Faria y Sousa, p.395.
17 R. B., p.212; Vertot, p.25.
18 De Faria y Sousa, p.209.
19 Da Silva, vol. 4, pp.157–71.
20 Ibid., p.215.
21 Carte, p.153.
22 Disney, p.223.
23 Newitt, pp.43–5.
24 Richard Flecknoe, in Macaulay, p.82.
25 *Retrato de D. Catarina de Bragança, infanta*, José de Avelar Rebelo
    (*c.*1653), Museu de Évora (Inv. ME 1443). Also see: *O infante
    D. Teodósio*, Arquivo Nacional Torre do Tombo; *Retrato de D. Joana
    de Bragança*, attributed to Manuel Franco, Museu de Évora (Inv.
    ME 1537).
26 Tron and Lippomani, p.121.
27 Jerosch Herold.
28 Edward Hyde, p.490.
29 DGLAB/TT, *Colecção de São Vicente*, Livro 20, fl.312.
30 Vallance, p.29.
31 Ibid., pp.228, 229.
32 Van Kessel, p.573.
33 De Faria y Sousa, pp.404–5.
34 Disney, p.224.
35 Shaw, p.26.
36 Ibid., pp.27–8.
37 Ibid., pp.11–13.
38 Ibid., pp.13–14.
39 Newitt, p.84.
40 Kitson, p.43.
41 Warburton, p.298.
42 Kitson, p.32.
43 Ibid., p.46.
44 Flecknoe, p.82.
45 De Sousa, p.274.
46 Ibid., pp.266–7.
47 Warburton, p.301.
48 Ibid., pp.303–4.

49 Kitson, p.34.
50 Macaulay, p.50.
51 Ibid., p.47.
52 Warburton, p.302.
53 Ibid., p.50.
54 Ibid., pp.50–51.
55 Macaulay, p.52.
56 Warburton, p.305.
57 Ibid., p.306.
58 Ibid., pp.309–10.
59 Ibid., p.313.
60 Macaulay, p.54.
61 De Menezes, vol. 2, p.418; Flecknoe, p.82.

3   *The Bridegroom Hunt*

1   Vallance, p.144.
2   Edward Hyde, p.171.
3   Disney, p.228.
4   De Lacerda, p.9.
5   Colbatch, p.44.
6   Ibid., p.3.
7   Vallance, p.160.
8   Ibid., p.161.
9   Archives Conde da Ponte 1, f.296 (760–760v), Melo to Luisa, London, 20/30 March 1660, cited in Shaw, p.79.
10 Vallance, pp.161–2.
11 James Stuart, *Memoirs*, vol. 2, p.291; Pepys, 11 Feb 1660.
12 Pepys, 16 March, 7 Feb, 11 Feb 1660.
13 Ibid., 1 May, 25 May 1660.
14 Treaty printed in de Abreu y Bertodano, p.305.
15 Shaw, p.82.
16 Schedel de Castello Branco, p.363.
17 Ibid., p.373.
18 Ibid., p.362.
19 *A. P. C.* 1, f.322v (841), Melo to Luisa, London, 13 July 1660 N.S.
20 Schedel de Castello Branco, pp.369–70.

21   Ibid., p.357.
22   Strickland, p.183.
23   Edward Hyde, vol. 2, p.148.
24   Ibid., p.149.
25   Ibid.
26   Ibid., p.152.
27   Ibid., p.153.
28   Ibid., pp.153–4.
29   Ibid., p.154.
30   Ibid., p.161.
31   Ibid., p.162.
32   Ibid., pp.162–3.
33   Hamilton, p.195.
34   Edward Hyde, vol. 1, p.165.
35   Ibid., p.167.
36   Ibid., p.168.
37   Ibid.
38   Ibid., p.171.
39   Ibid., p.176.
40   Ibid., p.182.
41   Lingard, p.71.
42   Edward Hyde, p.169.
43   MS translation by John Adamson, cited in Strickland p.282.
44   Shaw, p.90.
45   Edward Hyde, vol. 1, p.177.
46   Newitt, p.87.
47   State Papers 89/4, f.189, Maynard to Nicholas, Lisbon, 3/13 Nov 1660.
48   Schedel de Castello Branco, p.404.
49   *Carta de Martim Correia da Silva para D. Pedro Fernandes Monteiro*, Biblioteca da Ajuda, MS 51-IX-1, 24 de Agosto de 1661, fl.206–7.
50   *Carta de Martim Correia da Silva para Sua Magestade dando notícias das luminárias*, Biblioteca da Ajuda, MS 51-IX-1, fl. 205v.
51   London, 2 July 1661. Trans. Sir Robert Kerr Porter. Cited in Strickland, pp.284–5.
52   Wunder, p.126.
53   Carte Papers, MS 73, Bodleian Library, fls. 598 and 608.

54 Fisher, pp.230–1.
55 Pepys, 8 Feb 1661.
56 Vitkus, p.80.
57 Davis, p.87.
58 Newitt, p.131.
59 Montagu, pp.99–100.
60 Ibid., p.100.
61 Ibid., p.101.
62 Ibid., p.102.
63 Layton, p.81.
64 Lincoln, p.418.
65 Pepys, 28 Sept 1663.
66 Elbl, p. 7.
67 Infante D. Luís to Lourenço Pires de Távora, 26 Jan 1550, in Pires de Távora, p.58.
68 De Almada, p.43.
69 Stein, p.989.
70 Anon, *A Discourse Touching Tangier*.
71 From Elbl, p.10. CO 279/3 fols 193–194 July 1664.
72 Montagu, p.121.
73 Shaw, p.92.
74 'Peterborough's Reports to the Lords of the Council and Others', 12 Feb 1662, in Routh, p.15.
75 Routh, p.124.
76 Ibid., p.125.
77 Ibid., p.126.
78 Ibid.
79 Ibid., p.127.
80 Edward Hyde, vol. 1, p.177.
81 Montagu, p.132.
82 Luisa to Catherine, No. 2 (24 April 1662), cited in Vallance, Appendix.

4   *Marriage and the Mistress*

1 Almeida Troni, p.136.
2 Montagu, p.134.
3 Ibid.

4 Fraser, *King Charles II*, p.266.
5 Waller, p.112.
6 Fraser, *King Charles II*, p.189.
7 Lansdowne MS 1236, f.124.
8 Saunders, p.155.
9 Lansdowne MS 1236, f.124.
10 Cited in Buckley, p.214.
11 *Boddington Commonplace Book*, vol. 1, MS 10823, London Metropolitan Archives, pp.38–9.
12 Tuke, p.6.
13 Ibid.
14 Anon, *Policy, No Policy*, p.1.
15 Fraser, *King Charles II*, p.237.
16 Anna Reynolds, pp.92–5.
17 Powys, pp.2–11.
18 Charles Stuart, 'Portsmouth 23 May 1662', in Stuart and Henriette-Anne, p.43.
19 Montagu, p.140.
20 Schellinks, p.90.
21 Montagu, p.140.
22 Annesley, sig. A3r.
23 Whitford, sig. Ir.
24 Crouch, *Mercurius Democritus*, p.499; Crouch, *Flowers strowed by the muses*, p.31.
25 Anon, *The Cavaliers Comfort*.
26 Pepys, 7 Sept 1662.
27 Wilmot, 'Signior Dildo', 1673.
28 Pepys, 21 May 1662.
29 Ibid.
30 Stuart and Henriette-Anne, p.47.
31 Ibid., p.49.
32 Pepys, 26 July 1662.
33 Edward Hyde, vol. 1, p.334.
34 Ibid., p.341.
35 Ibid., p.566.
36 Rau, p.569.
37 Edward Hyde, vol. 1, p.325.
38 Disney, p.228.

39   Appleby, p.331; Childs, pp.135–6.
40   Thomas Carte, *Original Letters*, vol. 2, pp.328–9, cited in Miller, p.28; Edward Hyde, vol. 2, p.18.
41   Anon, *Mercurius Publicus*.
42   Hardacre, p.120.
43   Little.
44   Appleby, pp.331–2.
45   Calendar of State Papers, Domestic Series, 1663–4 , pp.315, 553.
46   Hutton, p.188.
47   Metzger.
48   Stuart and Henriette-Anne, p.314.
49   Pepys, 8 Feb 1664.
50   Birken.
51   Pepys, 20 Oct 1663.
52   For a more detailed description of this 'cure', see Markham, p.66.

5   *Fashion and Frivolity*

1   Hamilton, p.143.
2   Keay, p.116.
3   Ibid., pp.117–18.
4   Lindenov, p.35.
5   Keay, p.119; Calendar of State Papers, Domestic Series, 1673–5, p.43.
6   Magalotti, p.31.
7   De Monconys, p.19.
8   Keay, pp.143, 50.
9   BL, Stowe MS 562, fol. 3r.
10   Magalotti, p.378.
11   Misson, p.313.
12   Ashmole, p.612.
13   Ibid., p.611.
14   Dwyer Amussen, p.83.
15   Evelyn, vol. 2, p.290.
16   Chevalier, pp.289–90.
17   Magalotti, pp. 377–8; Fiennes, p.155.
18   Peter Paul Rubens, *Hercules Slaying Envy*, ceiling of the Banqueting

House, Whitehall, c.1632–4, oil on canvas; *Minerva Spearing Ignorance*, ceiling of the Banqueting House, Whitehall, c.1632–4, oil on canvas.

19   Peter Paul Rubens, *The Apotheosis of James I*, ceiling of the Banqueting House, Whitehall, c.1632–4, oil on canvas.

20   Schellinks, p.91.

21   *Historical Manuscripts Commission. Third Report*, 'The Manuscripts of his Grace the Duke of Devonshire at Hardwicke Hall, Co. Derby', p.92.

22   Playford, p.9; Pepys, 31 Dec 1662.

23   De Monconys, p.24.

24   Ibid.

25   Ibid.

26   Ibid., p.148.

27   Ibid., pp.143–7.

28   Hamilton, pp.150–51.

29   Pepys, 17 Feb 1663.

30   Hamilton, p.246.

31   Ibid.

32   Ibid.

33   Herrick, p.28.

34   Mace, p.232.

35   Cited in Mackay, p.111.

36   Hamilton, p.135.

37   Gibson.

38   Dethloff.

39   Jacob Huysmans, *Catherine of Braganza*, oil on canvas, c.1664–70, Royal Collection Trust.

40   Van Eikema Hommes, pp.109–66, 110.

41   Corp, p.62.

42   Vertue, p.124.

43   'Baroque, adj. and n.', *OED Online*, Oxford University Press, Dec 2020 [accessed 26 Feb 2021], www.oed.com/view/Entry/15685.

44   Jacob Huysmans, *Queen Catherine as a Shepherdess*, oil on canvas, 1638–1705, Royal Collection Trust.

45   Wood, p.509.

46   Wilmot, p.23.

47 Pepys, 26 Aug 1664.
48 J. W. Johnson.
49 Hayward, p.251.
50 BL Egerton MS 1534, fol. 126r.
51 De Monconys, p.21.
52 Cardoso Pinto, p.76.
53 Leech, p.584.
54 Evelyn, 9 June 1662; Pepys, 21 Sept 1663.
55 Pepys, 30 Oct 1662.
56 Mabbett, p.239.
57 Pepys, 22 March 1668.
58 Ibid., 28 Sept 1668.
59 Ibid., 7 June 1663.
60 Ibid.,13 July 1663.
61 Magalotti, p.31.
62 Prat, sig. A2r.
63 Lewknor, p.2.
64 Hamilton, p.305.
65 Pepys, 13 July 1663.
66 Hamilton, p.135.
67 Ibid.
68 'Smallpox, n.', *OED Online*, Oxford University Press, Dec 2020 [accessed 25 Jan 2021], www.oed.com/view/Entry/182423.
69 Charles Stuart and Henriette-Anne, p.154.
70 Wilmot.
71 Ibid.
72 Pepys, 15 Nov 1666.
73 Ibid., 8 Oct 1666.
74 Sketch in Lord Sandwich's journal, cited in de Beer, p.108.
75 Pepys, 17 Oct 1666.
76 De Beer, p.110.
77 Evelyn, 30 Oct 1666.
78 Anna Reynolds, p.15.
79 Henshaw, p.40.
80 Campbell Davidson, p.235.

6   *Plague, Fire and New York City*

1   Kessler and Rachlis, p.233.
2   Ibid., p.254.
3   Ibid., p.253.
4   Ibid., p.260.
5   Ibid., p.256.
6   Ibid., p.262.
7   Ibid., p.266.
8   Ibid.
9   Burnet, vol. 1, p.278.
10 Pepys, 27 Dec 1668.
11 Ibid., 28 June 1662.
12 Calendar of State Papers Domestic Series, 1664–5, p.30.
13 Brunsman.
14 Calendar of State Papers, Domestic Series, 1664–5, pp.92, 100.
15 Montagu.
16 Burnet, vol. 1, p.128.
17 Lansdowne Letters 1236, 'De Lione's Despatches', in Campbell Davidson, p.212.
18 Pepys, 17 Jan 1668.
19 Sarah Churchill, p.73.
20 Pepys, 26 Oct 1664.
21 Fox, p.95.
22 Anon, *Joyfull News for England.*
23 Pepys, 1 Sept 1661.
24 Ibid.
25 Ibid., 17 Dec 1664.
26 UCL MS Add. 3996, fol. 12 93v.
27 Gadbury, p.54.
28 Wood, pp.53–4.
29 Ibid., p.54.
30 Danforth, pp.14, 17; Gadbury, p.48.
31 Pepys, 30 April 1665.
32 Ibid., 7 June 1665.
33 Leasor, p.40.
34 Ibid., p.49.
35 Pepys, 27 July 1665.

36   Hamilton, p.311.
37   Leasor, p.89.
38   Wood, p.59.
39   Ibid.
40   Ibid., pp.46, 70.
41   Ibid., p.61.
42   Pepys, 9 Jan 1665/6.
43   Wood, p.49.
44   Leasor, pp.64–5.
45   Allin.
46   Ibid., p.46.
47   Ibid., p.73.
48   Pepys, 25 Aug 1665.
49   Leasor, p.46.
50   Pepys, 16 Oct 1665.
51   Wood, p.68.
52   Ibid., p.67.
53   Leasor, p.175.
54   Manuel Dias, p.519.
55   Ibid.
56   Pepys, 1 April 1666.
57   Wood, p.68.
58   Tinniswood, p.2.
59   Ibid., p.5.
60   Ibid., p.7.
61   Evelyn, 4 Sept, 3 Sept 1666.
62   Pepys, 2 Sept 1666.
63   Evelyn, 4 Sept, 3 Sept 1666.
64   Wood, p.85.
65   Tinniswood, p.54.
66   Ibid., p.30.
67   Ibid., p.31.
68   Ibid., p.36.
69   Ibid., p.56.
70   Wood, p.86.
71   Evelyn, 13 Sept 1666.
72   Rogers, p.53.
73   Bennet, p.172.

74 Rawlinson MS A 195, ff.129, 107.
75 Pepys, 10 June 1667.
76 Ibid.
77 Temple, vol. 2, p.40; Andrew Marvell, 'The Loyal Scot', Sloane MS 6555, f.18.
78 Pepys, 12 June 1667.
79 Ibid., 13 June 1667.
80 Evelyn, 28 June 1667.
81 Rau, p.568.
82 Madge, pp.31–2.

7 *Divorce*

1 Pierrepont, pp.2, 6.
2 Edward Hyde, vol. 2, p.978.
3 https://www.historyofparliamentonline.org/volume/1660-1690/member/manners-john-1638-1711.
4 Fraser, *The Weaker Vessel*.
5 Wolseley, p.1.
6 John Wolffe, 'Cooper, Anthony Ashley, seventh earl of Shaftesbury (1801–1885)', *Oxford Dictionary of National Biography*.
7 North, p.60.
8 Dryden, *Absalom and Achitophel*.
9 Anon, 'Queries', p.296.
10 Anon, 'To her Ma[]tie upon her dancing, Ano 1670'.
11 Stuart and Henriette-Anne.
12 Haley, p.276.
13 Oman, p.3.
14 Ibid., pp.3–4.
15 Ibid., p.5.
16 Ibid., p.4.
17 Ibid., p.28.
18 Ibid., p.31.
19 Ibid., p.40.
20 Ibid., p.37.
21 Ibid.
22 C. T.
23 Disney, pp.231–2.

24 Colbatch, p.44.
25 Blouin, pp.43, 45.
26 Pepys, 17 Oct 1661.
27 Vertot, p.154.
28 Colbatch, p.70.
29 Ibid., p.83.
30 Blouin, p.56.
31 Ibid., pp.201–2.
32 Colbatch, p.95.
33 Rau, p.566.
34 BL Egerton MS 534, Letter 2.
35 BL Egerton MS 534, Letter 29.
36 Bennet, vol. 2, p.211.
37 Jackson.
38 Jordan and Walsh, p.201.
39 Evelyn, 4 Nov 1670.
40 Wynne.
41 Stuart and Henriette-Anne, p.332.
42 Evelyn, 9/10 Oct 1671.
43 Ibid.
44 Colbert de Croissy, cited in Campbell Davidson, p.275.
45 Christie, p.xliii n.
46 Calendar of State Papers Venice, p.183.
47 https://www.britishmuseum.org/collection/object/
    P_1881-0611-85.
48 Hutton, p.335.
49 Calendar of State Papers Venice, p.305.
50 Fraser, *King Charles II*, pp.376–7.
51 Calendar of State Papers Venice, p.305.
52 Wynne.
53 Ibid.
54 Dryden, *All for love, or, The world well lost a tragedy*, p.31.
55 Ibid., pp.35–6.

8 *Plots True and False*

1 North, p.199.
2 Wynne.

3   Ibid.
4   Marvell.
5   L'Estrange, p.227.
6   Anon, *The Burning of the Whore of Babylon*.
7   Anon, *A Hue and Cry*.
8   Elliot, pp.1–2.
9   Warner, vol I, p.415, in Birrell.
10 *Cobbett's Complete Collection of State Trials*, vol. 10, p.110.
11 Oates, *A true narrative of the horrid plot*, sig. B1v.
12 Ibid., sig. Br.
13 Kenyon, p.16.
14 Ibid., p.64.
15 Oates, *A true narrative of the horrid plot*, sig. A2v.
16 Ormonde MSS, new ser., 4.207.
17 L'Estrange, p.2.
18 Kenyon, p.88.
19 Ibid., p.90.
20 Ibid.; Ormonde MSS, new ser., 4.467, 470, 473.
21 Evelyn, 18 Jul 1679.
22 Kenyon, p.92.
23 Ibid., p.96.
24 Ibid., p.98.
25 Ibid., p.110.
26 Ibid., p.111.
27 Ibid.
28 Ibid., p.112.
29 Ibid., p.97; Add. 32059, ff.47–8 (North Papers).
30 Charles Stuart, p.304.
31 Kenyon, p.214.
32 Charles Stuart, p.303.
33 Ibid.
34 Rau, p.566.
35 Oates, *A sermon preached at an Anabaptist meeting*.
36 Kenyon, p.99.
37 Alan Marshall, 'Oates, Titus (1649–1705), informer', *Oxford Dictionary of National Biography*.
38 Rau, p.564.
39 Kenyon, p.102.

40 Ibid., p.109.
41 Rau, p.564.
42 Ibid., p.566.
43 Francis Parry, letter to Coventry, 22 Jan 1679, Francis Parry letter-book, BL Add MSS 35, 100, fol. 17.
44 Ibid.
45 Rau, p.565.
46 Ibid.
47 Ibid., p.566.
48 Ibid.
49 Ibid., p.564.
50 Kenyon, p.153.
51 Rau, p.565.
52 Kenyon, p.136.
53 Ormonde MSS, new ser., 4.526.
54 North, p.206.
55 *Cobbett's Complete Collection of State Trials*, vol. 7, pp.79–142.
56 North, p.568.
57 Sidney, p.86.
58 Rau, p.567.
59 Kenyon, p.175.
60 Evelyn, 18 Jul 1679.
61 Hutton, p.378.
62 Warner, vol. I, pp.306–7, in Birrell; Kenyon, p.178.
63 DeF. Lord, vol. ii, pp.290–1; Kenyon, p.177.
64 James Stuart, *Memoirs*, vol. 1, p.561.
65 Anon, *The righteous evidence witnessing the truth*, p.1.
66 Christie, p.378; cf. p.380.
67 Anon, *The Tragick-comedy of Titus Oates*.

9 *The Queen Dowager*

1 Evelyn, 4 Feb 1685.
2 Ibid.
3 Hudleston.
4 Ibid.
5 Oman, p.82.
6 Manuel Dias, p.518.

7   Ibid., p.520.
8   Ibid., p.84.
9   Ibid., p.517.
10   Cited by Pincus, p.104.
11   Ibid.
12   Historical Manuscripts Commission, *The Manuscripts of the House of Lords*, vol. 2, pp.393–4.
13   Oman, p.91.
14   Ibid.
15   Evelyn, 15 Jul 1685.
16   Dorset Record Office, DL/LR/A3/1, 20; BL Add. MS 41804, fol. 168.
17   Sowerby, p.42.
18   Oman.
19   Campbell Davidson.
20   Ibid.
21   Burnet, vol. 1, p.473.
22   Ibid.
23   Ibid., p.27.
24   Henry Hyde, p.28.
25   Ibid, p.26.
26   Ibid.
27   Anon, *At the Council-chamber in Whitehall*, p.1.
28   Oman, p.109.
29   Campbell Davidson.
30   Henry Hyde, p.20.
31   Anon, *At the Council-chamber in Whitehall*, pp.1–3.
32   Ibid., p.2.
33   Bate, pp.88–9.
34   Beckman.
35   Whittel, p.31.
36   Evelyn, 2 Dec 1688.
37   Morrice, p.383.
38   Burnet, vol. 3, p.50.
39   Ibid.
40   Quoted by Charles-Édouard Levillian, 'London Besieged? The City's Vulnerability during the Glorious Revolution', in McElligott, p.101.

41 Rau, p.571.
42 Campbell Davidson, p.424.
43 James Stuart, *His Majesty's Letter to the Lords and Others of His Privy Council.*
44 Campbell Davidson.
45 Defoe, pp.9–10.
46 Campbell Davidson, p.427.
47 Ibid.
48 Ibid., pp.454–5.
49 Ibid.
50 Journals of the House of Commons, 26 March 1689, p.66; Campbell Davidson, p.453.
51 Journals of the House of Commons, 5 July 1689, pp.205–8.
52 Rau, p.568.
53 Ibid., p.571.
54 Campbell Davidson, p.431.
55 Ibid.
56 Ibid.
57 Ibid.
58 Ibid.
59 Ibid.
60 Anon, *A True account of the dying behaviour of Ambrose Rookwood, Charles Cranburne and Major Lowick.*

10 *Return and Regency*

1   John Methuen, 24 Jan 1692, BL Add MS 75364.
2   Ibid., 25 Feb 1693.
3   Emanuel de Feria, cited in Stevens, p.89.
4   Methuen, 25 Feb 1693.
5   Ibid., 2 May 1693.
6   Colbatch, p.126.
7   Methuen, 2 May 1693.
8   Stevens, p.87.
9   Ibid.
10 Ibid.
11 Methuen, 11 July 1693.
12 Colbatch, p.109.

13 Campbell Davidson, p.478.
14 Bromley, p.5.
15 Ibid.
16 Methuen, 25 Feb 1693.
17 Ibid., 2 May 1693.
18 Ibid., 12/22 Aug 1693.
19 Ibid.
20 Colbatch, p.125.
21 Methuen, 2 May 1693.
22 Ibid., 25 July 1693.
23 Ibid., 5 Sept 1693.
24 Ibid., 11/21 March 1693/4.
25 Ibid., 5 May 1694.
26 Ibid.
27 Ibid., 30 May 1693.
28 Ibid., 12 Sept 1693.
29 Ibid., 10/20 Nov 1693.
30 Ibid.
31 Ibid., 26 Dec 1693.
32 Ibid.
33 Ibid., 14/4 October 1693.
34 Rosenthal (1937), p.16.
35 Rosenthal (1938), p.69.
36 Ibid.
37 Leonor Farrão, 'Anthunes, João', in Grove Art, Oxford University Press, 2003, https://doi-org.lonlib.idm.oclc.org/10.1093/gao/9781884446054.article.T003329.
38 BL Egerton MS 534, letter 82.
39 Colbatch, p.126.
40 Ibid., pp.123–4.
41 García-Escudero López, et al.
42 Van der Kiste, p.255.
43 Stowe, 17020, f.20. Cited in Campbell Davidson, p.484.
44 BM Add. MSS 29590, fo. 28. Cited in Francis, p.109.
45 Memoirs of the Duke de Cardavall, cited in Campbell Davidson, p.483.
46 Colbatch, p.126.
47 Cited in Francis, p.121.

48 Oldmixon, p.618.
49 Campbell Davidson, p.493.
50 Ibid., p.498.
51 de Azevedo Tojal, p.2.
52 Ibid., p.6.

Epilogue

1 Gerson da Cunha, p.258.
2 Winston Churchill.
3 Ibid.

Bibliography

Primary Sources

MANUSCRIPTS

British Library, London
Egerton
Lansdowne
North Papers
Sloane
Stowe

OTHER COLLECTIONS

Carte Papers, Bodleian
DGLAB/TT, Colecção de São Vicente
MS 10823, London Metropolitan Archives
MS Add. 3996, UCL
MS don b8, 206–7, Bodleian
MS 51-IX-1, Biblioteca da Ajuda
Ormonde, National Archives London
Rawlinson, Bodleian

PRINTED TEXTS

Allin, John, 'I. – Notices of the Last Great Plague, 1665–6; from the Letters of John Allin to Philip Fryth and Samuel Jeake. In a Letter to Sir Henry Ellis', ed. W. Cooper, *Archaelogica*, 37.1, pp.1–22.

Annesley, James, *Domiduca Oxoniensis* (Oxford, 1662).

Anon, 'Queries' (1679), in *Poems on Affairs of State: Augustan Satirical Verse, 1660–1714*, vol. 2 (New Haven: Yale University Press, 1965) ed. Elias F. Mengel.

Anon, *A Discourse Touching Tangier* (London, 1680).

Anon, *A True account of the dying behaviour of Ambrose Rookwood, Charles Cranburne and Major Lowick who were executed at Tyburn for high treson on Wednesday, April 29: with Mr. Cranburn's speech at the place of execution* (London, 1696).

Anon, *At the Council-chamber in Whitehall, Monday the 22th. of October, 1688* (London, 1688).

Anon, *Joyfull News for England, or, a Congratulatory Verse upon our late happy Success in Firing 150 Dutch Ships in their own Harbours* (London, 1666).

Anon, *Mercurius Publicus* (2–9 July 1663).

Anon, *Policy, No Policy: or, the Devil Himself Confuted* (1660).

Anon, *The Burning of the Whore of Babylon, as it was Acted, with Great Applause, in the Poultrey* (1673).

Anon, *A Hue and Cry* (London, 1678).

Anon, *The Cavaliers Comfort* (London, 1664–5).

Anon, *The righteous evidence witnessing the truth being an account of the sickness and deathbed expressions of Mr William Bedlow* (1680).

Anon, *The Tragick-comedy of Titus Oates, who sometime went under the notion of the Salamanca Doctor* (London, 1685).

Ashmole, Elias, *The Institution, Laws & Ceremonies of the Most Noble Order of the Garter* (London, 1672).

Bate, John, *The mysteries of nature and art in four several parts* (London, 1654).

Beckman, Martin, *A Description of the Royal Fireworks* (London, 1688).

Bennet, Henry, *The Right Honourable the Earl of Arlington's Letters to Sir William Temple, July 1665–September 1670*, ed. Thomas Bebington (London, 1701).

Blouin, Michel, *The Portugal history, or, A relation of the troubles that happened in the court of Portugal in the years 1667 and 1668 in which is to*

be seen that great transaction of the renunciation of the crown by Alphonso the
Sixth, the dissolution of his marriage with the Princess Maria Francès Isabella
of Savoy: the marriage of the same princess to the Prince Don Pedro, regent
of the realm of Portugal, and the reasons alleged at Rome for the dispensation
thereof, trans. anon (London, 1677).

Bromley, William, *Several years travels through Portugal, Spain, Italy, Prussia,*
Sweden, Denmark and the United Provinces (London, 1702).

Burnet, Gilbert, *Bishop Burnet's History of His Own Time* (London:
A. Millar, 1753).

C. T., *Narrative of the visit of his majesty King Charles the Second to Norwich,*
ed. D. Turner (1846).

Calendar of State Papers Venice, ed. R. Brown, H. F. Brown &
A. B. Hinds (London, 1864–1947).

Calendar of State Papers, Domestic Series, 1663–4 (London, 1861).

Calendar of State Papers, Domestic Series, 1664–5 (1863).

Calendar of State Papers, Domestic Series, 1673–5 (London, 1904).

Carte, Thomas, *The History of the Revolutions of Portugal, from the*
foundation of that kingdom to the year MDCLXVII. With the letters of
Sir Robert Southwell during his embassy there to the Duke of Ormond
(London, 1740).

Chevalier, John, *Journal de Jean Chevalier,* ed. J. A. Messervy (St Helier:
Société Jersiaise, 1906).

Churchill, Sarah, *Memoirs of Sarah Duchess of Marlborough, and the court of Queen*
Anne, vol. 1, ed. Katherine Thomson (London: Henry Colburn, 1839).

Churchill, Winston, *Agreement with Portugal,* Historic Hansard,
https://api.parliament.uk/historic-hansard/commons/1943/oct/12/
agreement-with-portugal

Cobbett's Complete Collection of State Trials, vol. 7 (London: Hansard, 1810);
vol. 10 (London: Hansard, 1811).

Colbatch, John, *An Account of the Court of Portugal under the Reign of the*
Present King Dom Pedro II. With some discourses on the interests of Portugal,
with regard to other sovereigns; containing a relation of the most considerable
transactions that have passed of late between the court, and those of Rome,
Spain, France, Vienna, England etc. (London, 1700).

Crouch, John, *Mercurius Democritus, or, A true and perfect nocturnall*
(London, 1653).

——*Flowers strowed by the muses, against the coming of the most illustrious*
Infanta of Portugal, Catharina, Queen of England (London, 1662).

Danforth, Samuel, *An Astronomical Description of the Late Comet or Blazing Star* (Cambridge, Massachusetts, 1665).

de Abreu y Bertodano, Felix Jose Antonio, *Colleccion de los tratados de Paz* . . . (1750).

de Lacerda, Fernando Correa, *Catastrophe de Portugal na deposição d'El Rei D. Affonso o Sexto, & subrogação do Princepe D. Pedro o Unico* (Lisbon: Maguel Manescal, 1669).

de Monconys, Balthasar, *Journal des Voyages de Monsieur de Monconys*, vol. 2 (Lyon, 1666).

deF. Lord, George (ed.), *Poems on Affairs of State: Augustan Satirical Verse, 1660–1714* (New Haven: Yale University Press, 1963).

Defoe, Daniel, *An account of the late horrid conspiracy to depose Their present Majesties, K. William and Q. Mary, to bring in the French and the late King James, and ruine the city of London* (London, 1691).

Dryden, John, *Absalom and Achitophel* (London: 1681).

——*All for love, or, The world well lost a tragedy* (London, 1692).

Elliot, Adam, *A modest vindication of Titus Oates, the Salamanca doctr from perjury* (London, 1682).

Evelyn, John, *The Diary of John Evelyn*, ed. Austin Dobson (Cambridge: Cambridge University Press, 2015).

Fiennes, Celia, *The Illustrated Journeys of Celia Fiennes*, ed. Christopher Morris (London: MacDonald, 1982).

Flecknoe, Richard, *A relation of ten years in Europe, Asia, Affrique, and America* (London, 1656).

Gadbury, John, *De Cometis* (London, 1664).

Hamilton, Anthony, *Memoirs of Count Grammont*, trans. Horace Walpole (Philadelphia: Gebbie, 1888).

Henshaw, 'Mr Henshaw to Sir Robert Paston', in *Select Papers Chiefly Relating to English Antiquities*, ed. John Ives (London, 1773).

Herrick, Robert, *The Poetical Works of Robert Herrick*, ed. L. C. Martin (Oxford: Oxford University Press, 1956).

Historical Manuscripts Commission, *The Manuscripts of the House of Lords* (London: Eyre and Spottiswoode, 1894).

Historical Manuscripts Commission. *Third Report* (London, 1872).

Hudleston, J., *A Brief account of particulars occurring at the happy death of our late Sovereign Lord King Charles the 2nd*, 2nd series, vol. 4, ed. Henry Ellis (London, 1827).

Hyde, Edward, *The Life of Edward Earl of Clarendon* (Oxford: Clarendon Printing House, 1759).

Hyde, Henry, *The State Letters of Henry Earl of Clarendon Lord Lieutenant of Ireland During the Reign of K. James the Second: and His Lordship's Diary for the Years 1687, 1688, 1689, and 1690*, vol. 2 (Oxford: Clarendon Press, 1763).

Journals of the House of Commons, vol. 10, 1688–1693 (London: His Majesty's Stationery Office, 1802).

Kemp, W., *A brief treatise of the nature, causes, signes, preservation from, and cure of the pestilence collected by W. Kemp* (London, 1665).

Lanier, François, *Informes de Francisco Lanier sobre Francisco de Lucena e a corte de João IV* (Coimbra, 1931).

L'Estrange, Roger, *A brief history of the times* (London, 1687).

Lewknor, John, *Metellus his dialogues the first part* (London, 1693).

Lindenov, Christopher, *The First Triple Alliance: The letters of Christopher Lindenov, Danish Envoy to London 1668–1672*, trans. Waldemar Westergaard (New Haven: Yale University Press, 1947).

Mace, Thomas, *Musick's Monument* (London, 1676).

Magalotti, Lorenzo, *Travels of Cosimo the third, Grand Duke of Tuscany, through England during the reign of King Charles the Second (1669)* (London: J. Mawman, 1821).

Manuel Dias, 'King Charles II and Queen Catherine Two Letters', trans. Virginia Rau.

Markham, Gervase, *Countrey contentments, or The English huswife* (London, 1623).

Marvell, Andrew, *The History of Insipids* (London: 1674).

Misson, *M. Misson's memoirs and observations in his travels over England. With some account of Scotland and Ireland*, trans. Mr Ozell (London, 1719).

Montagu, Edward, *The Journal of Edward Montagu First Earl of Sandwich*, ed. Roger Charles Anderson (London: The Navy Records Society, 1929).

Moréri, Louis, *The great historical, geographical and poetical dictionary being a curious miscellany of sacred and prophane history* (London, 1694).

Morrice, *Entring Book*, vol. 4 (December 1688).

North, Roger, *Examen* (London: 1740).

Oates, Titus, *A sermon preached at an Anabaptist meeting in Wapping on Sunday the 9th February by the Rev T. O.* (London, 1669).

————A true narrative of the horrid plot and conspiracy of the popish party against the life of His Sacred Majesty, the government and the Protestant religion: with a list of such noblemen, gentlemen and others as were the conspirators, and the head-officers both civil and military that were to effect it (London, 1679).

Oldmixon, John, The history of England (London, 1730).

Pierrepont, Henry, The Lord Marquesse of Dorchesters letter to the Lord Roos with the Lord Roos's answer thereunto (London, 1660).

Pires de Távora, Álvaro, História dos varoens illustres do appellido Távora continuada em Os Senhores da Caza e Morgado da Caparica com a rellaçam de todos os successos publicos deste Reyno e suas conquistas desde o tempo do Senhor Rey D. Ioam Terceiro a esta parte (Paris: Rui Lourenço de Távora, 1648).

Playford, Henry, The Second part of The dancing master (London, 1698).

Prat, Ellis, A short treatise of metal & mineral waters (London, 1684).

R. B., Extraordinary adventures and discoveries of several famous men with the strange events and signal mutations and changes in the fortunes of many illustrious places and persons in all ages (London, 1683).

Reynolds, Lancelot, A panegyrick on Her Most Excellent Majestie, Katharine, Queen of England, Scotland, France, and Ireland (London, 1661).

Saunders, Richard, Saunders physiognomie, and chiromancie, metoposcopie the symmetrical proportions and signal moles of the body, 2nd edn (London, 1671).

Schellinks, William, Journal of William Schellinks' Travels in England, trans. and ed. Maurice Exwood and H. L. Lehmann (London: Offices of the Royal Historical Society, 1993).

Sidney, Henry, Diary of the times of Charles II, by the Honourable Henry Sidney, afterwards Earl of Romney; including his correspondence with the Countess of Sunderland and other distinguished persons at the English Court; to which are added letters illustrative of the times of James II and William III, vol. 1, ed. R. W. Blencowe (London, 1843).

Stevens, John, The ancient and present state of Portugal (London, 1705).

Stuart, Charles, and Henriette-Anne de Orléans, Charles II and Madame, ed. Cyril Hughes Hartmann (London: William Heinemann, 1934).

Stuart, Charles, The Letters, Speeches and Declarations of King Charles II, ed. Sir Arthur Bryant (London: Cassell, 1935; repr. 1968).

Stuart, James, His Majesty's Letter to the Lords and Others of His Privy Council (London, 1689).

Temple, William, *The Works of Sir William Temple* (London, 1720).

Tuke, Samuel, *A Character of Charles the Second* (London, 1660).

Vertot, Abbé de, *The History of the Revolutions in Portugal in the year, 1640* (London, 1700).

Vertue, George, *Note books*, vol. 2 (London: The Walpole Society, 1929).

Waller, Edmund, *Poems, & c.* (London, 1694).

Whitford, David, *Domiduca Oxoniensis* (Oxford, 1662).

Whittel, Martin, *An Exact Diary of the Late Expedition of His Illustrious Highness, the Prince of Orange, now King of Great Britain, from his Palace at The Hague, to his landing at Torbay , and from thence to his Arrival at Whitehall &c.* (London, 1689).

Wilmot, John, *The Complete Poems of John Wilmot Earl of Rochester*, ed. David M. Vieth (New Haven, Connecticut: Yale University Press, 1962).

Wolseley, Charles, *The case of divorce and re-marriage thereupon discussed by a reverend prelate of the Church of England and a private gentleman. Occasioned by the late act of Parliament for the divorce of the Lord Rosse* (London, 1673).

Wood, Anthony, *The Life and Times of Anthony Wood, antiquary, of Oxford, 1632–1695, described by Himself*, ed. Andrew Clark, vol. 2: 1664–81 (Oxford: Clarendon Press, 1892).

Secondary Sources

Almeida Troni, Joana, *Catarina de Bragança (1638–1705)* (Lisbon: Edições Colibri, 2008).

Appleby, David J., 'Veteran Politics in Restoration England, 1660–1670', *The Seventeenth Century*, 28.3 (2013), pp.323–42.

Birken, William, 'Prujean, Sir Francis (bap. 1597, d. 1666), physician', *Oxford Dictionary of National Biography*, https://www.oxforddnb.com/view/10.1093/ref:odnb/9780198614128.001.0001/odnb-9780198614128-e-22848

Birrell, T. A. (ed.), *The History of English Persecution of Catholics and the Presbyterian Plot*, trans. J. Bligh (London: Catholic Record Society, 1953).

Brunsman, Denver Alexander, *The Evil Necessity: British Naval Impressment in the Eighteenth-Century Atlantic World* (Charlottesville, Virginia: University of Virginia Press, 2013).

Buckley, Veronica, *Madame de Maintenon: The Secret Life of Louis XIV* (London: Bloomsbury, 2008; repr. 2009).

Campbell Davidson, Lillias, *Catherine of Bragança, Infanta of Portugal, & Queen Consort of England* (London: J. Murray, 1908).

Cardoso Pinto, Augusto, 'The Processional Cross at the Chapel of Catherine of Braganza', *The Burlington Magazine*, 99.648 (March 1957), pp.76–8.

Childs, John, 'The English Brigade in Portugal, 1662–8', *Journal of the Society for Army Historical Research* 53 (1975), pp.135–47.

Christie, W. D., *A life of Anthony Ashley Cooper, first earl of Shaftesbury*, vol. 2 (1871).

Corp, Edward, 'Catherine of Braganza and cultural politics', in *Queenship and Britain, 1660–1837: Royal Patronage, Court, Culture, and Dynastic Politics*, ed. Clarissa Campbell Orr (Manchester: Manchester University Press, 2002), pp.53–73.

Costa e Sousa, Luis, *Alcácer Quibir 1578: visão ou delirio de um rei?* (Lisbon: Tribuna da História, 2009).

da Silva, L. A. R., *História de Portugal nos séculos XVII e XVIII*, 2nd edn, vol. 4 (Lisbon: Livros Horizonte, 1971–2).

Davis, Robert C., 'Counting European Slaves on the Barbary Coast', *Past & Present* 172 (Aug 2001), pp.87–124.

de Almada, José, *A Aliança Inglesa*, vol. 1 (Lisbon: Imprensa Nacional de Lisboa, 1946).

de Azevedo Tojal, Pedro, *Carlos Reduzido, Inglaterra Illustrada* (Lisbon, 1716).

de Beer, Edmond S., 'King Charles II's Own Fashion: An Episode in Anglo-French Relations, 1666–1670', *Journal of the Warbury Institute*, 2.2 (Oct 1938), pp.105–15.

de Faria y Sousa, Emanuel, *The history of Portugal from the first ages of the world, to the late great revolution, under King John IV*, trans. John Stevens (London, 1698).

de Menezes, Luiz, *História de Portugal restaurado*, ed. António Doria, vol. 2 (Porto: Livraria Cililização, 1945).

de Sousa, António Caetano, *Provas da história genealógica*, vol. IV, new edn; revised by M. Lopes de Almeida and César Pegado, *História Genealógica da Casa Real Portuguesa* (Coimbra: Atlântia-Livaria Editoria, 1950).

Dethloff, Diana, 'Lely, Sir Peter (1618–1680), portrait painter and art collector', *Oxford Dictionary of National Biography*, 21 May 2009,

https://www.oxforddnb.com/view/10.1093/ref:odnb/
9780198614128.001.0001/odnb-9780198614128-e-16419

Disney, A. R., *A History of Portugal and the Portuguese Empire* (Cambridge: Cambridge University Press, 2012).

Dwyer Amussen, Susan, *Caribbean Exchanges: Slavery and the Transformation of English Society, 1640–1700* (Chapel Hill: University of North Carolina Press, 2007).

Editors of the Encyclopaedia Britannica, 'Battle of the Three Kings', *Encyclopaedia Britannica* (July 2020), https://www.britannica.com/event/Battle-of-the-Three-Kings

Elbl, Martin Malcolm, *Portuguese Tangier (1471–1662): Colonial Fabric as Cross-Cultural Skeleton* (Peterborough, Ontario: Baywolf Press, 2013).

Elliott, J. H., *The Revolt of the Catalans: A Study in the Decline of Spain 1598–1640* (Cambridge: Cambridge University Press, 1963; paperback edn, 1984).

Fisher, Godfrey, *Barbary Legend: War, Trade, and Piracy in North Africa, 1415–1830* (Oxford, 1957).

Fox, Frank L., *The Four Days' Battle of 1666* (Barnsley: Seaforth Publishing, 2009).

Francis, A. D., 'John Methuen and the Anglo-Portuguese Treaties of 1703', *The Historical Journal*, 3.2 (1960).

Fraser, Antonia, *King Charles II* (London: Phoenix, 2002).

——*The Weaker Vessel* (London: William Heinemann, 1984).

García-Escudero López, Ángel; Arruza Echevarría, A.; Padilla Nieva, Jaime; Ramon Puig Giró, 'Charles II; from spell to genitourinary pathology', *History of Urology*, 62.3 (2009).

Gerson da Cunha, J., *The Origin of Bombay, Journal of the Bombay Branch of the Royal Asiatic Society*, Extra Number (Bombay, 1900).

Gibson, K., 'Best belov'd of kings': the iconography of Charles II, 1997, PhD dissertation.

Haley, K. H. D., *The First Earl of Shaftesbury* (Oxford: Clarendon Press, 1968).

Hardacre, P. H., 'The English Contingent in Portugal, 1662–1668', *Journal of the Society for Army Historical Research*, 38.155 (1960), pp.112–25.

Hayward, Maria, '"The best of Queens, the most obedient wife": Fashioning a Place for Catherine of Braganza as Consort to Charles II', in *Sartorial Politics in Early Modern Europe*, ed. Erin Griffey (Amsterdam: Amsterdam University Press, 2019), pp.227–52.

Hutton, Ronald, *Charles II: King of England, Scotland and Ireland* (Oxford: Clarendon Press, 1989).

Jackson, Clare, *Devil-Land: England Under Siege, 1588–1688* (London: Allen Lane, 2021).

Jerosch Herold, Bernardo, 'The Diary of the Swiss Leonhard Thurneysser and Black Africans in Renaissance Lisbon', *Renaissance Studies*, 32.2, pp.463–88.

Johnson, Harold, *Camponeses e Colonizadores: Estudos de História Luso-Basileira* (Lisbon: Editorial Estampa, 2002).

Johnson, J. W., 'Did Lord Rochester Write "Sodom?"', *The Papers of the Bibliographical Society of America*, 81.2 (1987), pp.119–53.

Jordan, Don, and Michael Walsh, *The King's Bed: Sex, Power and the Court of Charles II* (London: Abacus, 2016).

Keay, Anna, The Ceremonies of Charles II's Court, 2004, PhD dissertation.

Kenyon, John, *The Popish Plot* (London: Heinmann, 1972).

Kessler, Henry H., and Eugene Rachlis, *Peter Stuyvesant and His New York* (NY: Random House, 1959).

Kishlansky, Mark, *A Monarchy Transformed: Britain 1603–1714* (London: Penguin Press, 1996).

Kitson, Frank, *Prince Rupert: Portrait of a Soldier* (London: Constable, 1994).

Layton, Simon, 'The "Moghul's Admiral": Angrian "Piracy" and the Rise of British Bombay', *Journal of Early Modern History*, 17 (2013).

Leasor, James, *The Plague and the Fire* (NY: McGraw Hill, 1961).

Leech, Peter, 'Musicians in the Catholic Chapel of Catherine of Braganza, 1662–92', *Early Music*, 29.4 (2001), pp.570–87.

Lincoln, Margarette, 'Samuel Pepys and Tangier, 1662–1684', *Huntington Library Quarterly*, 77.4 (2014).

Lingard, John, *The History of England*, vol. IX, 5th edn (London: Charles Dolman, 1849).

Little, Patrick, 'O'Brien, Murrough, first earl of Inchiquin', *Oxford Dictionary of National Biography*, Oxford University Press, 2004, https://www.oxforddnb.com/view/10.1093/ref:odnb/9780198614128.001.0001/odnb-9780198614128-e-20463

Mabbett, Margaret, 'Italian Musicians in Restoration England (1660–90)', *Music & Letters*, 67.3 (1986), pp.237–47.

Macaulay, Rose, *They Went to Portugal* (London: Jonathan Cape, 1946).

Mackay, Janet, *Catherine of Braganza* (London: J. Long, 1937).

Madge, Tim, *Royal Yachts of the World* (East Molesey: Thomas Reed, 1997).

McElligott, Jason, *Fear, Exclusion and Revolution: Roger Morrice and Britain in the 1680s* (Aldershot, 2006).

Metzger, Edward Charles, 'Montagu, Ralph first duke of Montagu (bap. 1638, d. 1709) politician and diplomat', *Oxford Dictionary of National Biography*, https://www.oxforddnb.com/view/10.1093/ref:odnb/9780198614128.001.0001/odnb-9780198614128-e-19030

Miller, John, *Charles II* (London: Weidenfeld & Nicholson, 1991).

Newitt, Malyn, *The Braganzas: The Rise and Fall of the Ruling Dynasties of Portugal and Brazil, 1640–1910* (London: Reaktion Books, 2019).

Oman, Carolina, *Mary of Modena* (Bungay, Suffolk: Hodder and Stoughton, 1962).

Pepys, Samuel, *The Diary of Samuel Pepys*, ed. R. C. Latham and W. Matthews (London: HarperCollins, 1971).

Pincus, Steve, *1688: The First Modern Revolution* (New Haven: Yale University Press, 2009).

Porter, Linda, *Mistresses: Sex and Scandal at the Court of Charles II* (London: Picador, 2020).

Powys, Marian, 'The Lace of King Charles II', *The Needle and Bobbin Club Bulletin*, 12.2 (1928), pp.2–11.

Raposo, José Hipólito, *Dona Luísa de Gusmão, duquesa e rainha (1613–1666)* (Lisbon: Empresa Nacional de Publicidade, 1947).

Rau, Virginia, 'Letters from Catherine of Bragança, queen-consort of Charles II to her brother, Dom Pedro II, king of Portugal (1679–1691)', *The Historical Association: Lisbon branch. Annual Report and Review* 9 (1945): 559–72.

Reynolds, Anna, *The Art of Tudor and Stuart Fashion* (London: Royal Collection Trust, 2013).

Rogers, Philip G., *The Dutch in the Medway* (London: Seaforth Publishing, 1970).

Rosenthal, E., 'Notes on Catherine of Bragança, Queen Consort of King Charles II of England', *The Historical Association: Lisbon branch. Annual Report and Review*, 1 (1937), pp.14–17.

——'Notes on Catherine of Bragança, Queen Consort of King Charles II of England and Her Life in Portugal', *The Historical*

Association: Lisbon branch. Annual Report and Review, 2 (1938), pp.568–75.

Routh, E. M. G., *Tangier: England's Lost Atlantic Outpost, 1661–1684* (London: John Murray, 1912).

Schedel de Castello Branco, Teresa, *Vida do Marquês de Sande* (Lisbon: Libreria Ferin, 1971).

Shaw, L. M. E., *Trade, Inquisition and the English Nation in Portugal, 1650–1690* (Manchester: Carcanet, 1989).

Sowerby, Scott, *Making Toleration: The Repealers and the Glorious Revolution* (Cambridge, MA: Harvard University Press, 2013).

Stein, Tristan, 'Tangier in the Restoration Empire', *The Historical Journal*, 54.4 (2011), pp.985–1011.

Strickland, Agnes, *Queens of England*, vol. 2 (London: Longmans, Green, Reader, & Dyer, 1873).

Stuart, James, *Memoirs of James II*, vol. 2 (Colchester, 1821).

Tinniswood, Adrian, *The Great Fire of London* (London: Penguin Random House, 2016).

Tron, Vincenzo, and Girolamo Lippomani, *Viagem a Portugal dos Cavalleiros Tron e Lippomani* (1580), cited in A. Herculano, *Opúsculos*, vol. VI (Lisbon: Viúva Bertrand, 1884).

Vallance, Monique, *A rainha restauradora: Luisa de Gusmão* (Lisbon: Círculo de Leitores, 2012).

Van der Kiste, John, *William and Mary: Heroes of the Glorious Revolution* (Stroud: The History Press, 2003).

van Eikema Hommes, M. H., *Discoloration in Renaissance and Baroque Oil Paintings. Instructions for Painters, theoretical Concepts, and Scientific Data* (2002).

van Kessel, Elsje, 'The making of a hybrid body: Corpus Christi in Lisbon, 1582', *Renaissance Studies*, 34.4 (2019), pp.572–92.

Viera Nery, Rui, The music manuscripts in the Library of King D. João IV of Portugal (1604–1656): A study of Iberian music repertoire in the sixteenth and seventeenth centuries, 1990, PhD dissertation, University of Texas at Austin.

Vitkus, Daniel J., ed., *Piracy, Slavery, Redemption: Barbary Captivity Narratives from Early Modern England* (New York: Columbia University Press, 2001).

Warburton, Eliot, *Memoirs of Prince Rupert, and the Cavaliers*, vol. 3 (London: Richard Bentley, 1849).

Wunder, Amanda, 'Innovation and Tradition at the Court of Philip IV of Spain (1621–1665): The Invention of the *Golilla* and the *Guardainfante*', in *Fashioning the Early Modern: Dress, Textiles and Innovation in Europe, 1500–1800*, ed. Evelyn Welch (Oxford: Oxford University Press, 2017), pp.111–34.

Wynne, S. M., 'Catherine of Braganza', *Oxford Dictionary of National Biography*, 23 Sept 2004, https://www-oxforddnb-com.lonlib.idm.oclc.org/view/10.1093/ref:odnb/9780198614128.001.0001/odnb-9780198614128-e-4894

Acknowledgements

I WOULD LIKE TO thank the fantastic team at Atlantic for getting this book out into the world. Thanks especially to James Nightingale for his insightful editing. All mistakes are of course mine.

Thanks also to my ever-knowledgeable and supportive agent, Charlotte Seymour, as well as her team at Johnson & Alcock.

I would also like to thank the Society of Authors for much-appreciated funding in the research stages of this book.

And finally, thank you to my parents, friends and family for all their support. Special appreciation goes to my husband, Uther, for reading everything and hearing about it all. Pity him for the next book.

Illustrations

Portrait of Mary of Modena by Willem Wissing, c. 1685 (*Wikimedia Commons/ArcoCc*)
Portrait of John Wilmot, 2nd Earl of Rochester by Jacob Huysmans, c. 1665 (*Heritage Image Partnership Ltd/Alamy*)
Queen Catherine of Braganza as Saint Catherine of Alexandria by Jacob Huysmans (*Zuri Swimmer/Alamy*)

Charles II of England being given the first pineapple grown in England by his royal gardener, John Rose, by Hendrick Danckerts, 1675 (*incamerastock/Alamy*)
A view of New York by Johannes Vingboons, 1664 (*Wikimedia Commons/ Patrickneil*)
The Queens Room in Merton College, Oxford (© *John Cairns Photography. All Rights Reserved*)
Sir Frescheville Holles 1641–72 and Sir Robert Holmes 1622–92 by Peter Lely, c. 1672 (*Art Collection 2/Alamy*)
A portrait of the Royal Katherine by H. Vale, c. 1664 (*The History Collection/Alamy*)
The Great Fire of London 1666 (woodcut) (later colouration) by English School (17th century) (*Bridgeman Images/Museum of London*)
Plan of the south-east quarter of the crossing at church-floor level, 1675, nearly as built (*St Paul's Cathedral/Google Arts Project*)
The King's bath and the Queen's bath in Bath, England (*bathnewseum*)
Portrait of Maria Francesca Elisabeth of Savoy Nemours, c. 1666 (*Castello di Racconigi/Catalogo generale dei Beni Culturali/CC-BY 4.0*)
Isabel, Princesa da Beira (*The History Collection/Alamy*)
Anthony Ashley-Cooper, 1st Earl of Shaftesbury by John Greenhill, c. 1672 (*The History Collection/Alamy*)
Louise de Kérouaille, Duchess of Portsmouth, Studio of Peter Lely (*Historic Images/Alamy*)
Sir Edmund Godfrey, chalk drawing by an unknown artist, c. 1678 (*Britannica/National Portrait Gallery*)
Titus Oates (1649–1723) by Godfrey Kneller, n.d. (*The History Collection/ Alamy*)
Somerset House and River Thames, London by Jan Kip, 1772 (*Chronicle/ Alamy*)

William III (1650–1702) when Prince of Orange by Willem Wissing, 1685 (*Logic Images/Alamy*)

Queen Mary II in Blue by Peter Lely, c. 1677 (*Wikimedia Commons/Alonso de Mendoza*)

Rt Hon John Methuen as Lord Chancellor of Ireland by Adrien Carpentiers, c. 17th century (*Art Collection 2/Alamy*)

Portrait of Maria Sofia of the Palatinate by Antonio Oliveira de Louredo, c. 1690 (*Wikimedia Commons/RickMorais*)

Queen Anne by Michael Dahl, 1705 (*Wikimedia Commons/Dcoetzee*)

Portrait of King John V of Portugal alluding to the Battle of Cape Matapan by Georgio Domenico Duprà, 1719 (*Museu de São Roque/Google Arts Project*)

East wing of the Palácio da Bemposta (*Wikimedia Commons/Lijealso/ Cristiano Tomás/CC-BY-SA 3.0*)

Index

Tangier, 5, 27, 55, 62, 69–71, 169, 195, 270
tea drinking, 78–9, 4, 279
Teodósio II, Duke of Braganza (grandfather), 11–13, 15
Teodósio of Braganza (brother), 18, 27, 35, 38, 44, 274
Test Act (1673), 172–3, 186
Thirty Years War (1618–48), 21–2, 27, 36
Tonge, Israel, 196–7, 200
Tower of London, 91, 227
Treaty of the Pyrenees, 48
Trelawney, Jonathan, 200
Trevor, John, 184
Tripoli, 66
Tromp, Cornelis, 138
Tunbridge Wells, 120–23
Tunis, 66
typhus, 94–5

United Provinces of the Netherlands, 34, 51, 62, 129, 132–4, 137

Vane, Charles, 41
de Vasconcelos, Miguel 26
Vila Viçosa, Portugal, 12, 17, 29, 262
Villiers, George, 2nd Duke of Buckingham, 100, 126, 182, 184

Villiers, Mary, Duchess of Buckingham, 126, 136
Vlie, Netherlands, 138–9, 150

Wakeman, George, 200–201, 212–15
Waller, Edmund, 79
Walter, Lucy, 93
Warmestre, Miss, 108–9
Wars of the Spanish Succession (1701–14), 267–72
Wells, Winifred, 108–9
Whitehall Palace, 102, 104–5, 119, 139, 153, 219–21, 224
William III, King of England, Scotland and Ireland, 232, 236–41, 243–4, 248, 260–61, 269
William of Orange *see* William II
Wilmot, Elizabeth, Countess of Rochester, 114
Wilmot, John, Earl of Rochester, 1, 114, 115–16, 123
de Witt, Johan, 133
Wood, Anthony, 140, 143–5, 147, 155, 225
wool industry (England) 124–5
World War I (1914–18), ,279
World War II, (1939–45) 279
Wren, Christopher, 2, 155–6
Wyatt, Thomas, 148

A Note About the Author

SOPHIE SHORLAND HAS a PhD in Early Modern English literature and is a former Research Fellow at the University of Warwick. She was a semi-finalist in the BBC's New Generation Thinkers competition and the proposal for *The Lost Queen* was shortlisted for the Tony Lothian Prize.